BEHOLD A PALE HORSE

BEHOLD A PALE HORSE

*A Novel of Homosexuals
in the Nazi Holocaust*

Lannon D. Reed

Gay Sunshine Press
San Francisco

AUTHOR'S NOTE

Although this book is fiction, actual incidents have provided the basis for the story, its framework having been extrapolated from historical fact. The personalities who exist within the pages of this book are composites of individuals who dominated or submitted, survived or perished, fought or surrendered, loved or hated, lived or died, in a time when reason and sanity seemed to have left the realm of man's endeavors, taking, as it were, an extended sabbatical.

First Edition 1985
BEHOLD A PALE HORSE is copyright © 1985 by Lannon D. Reed

Cover design by Timothy Lewis.

ISBN 0-917342-09-7

Gay Sunshine Press
P.O. Box 40397
San Francisco, CA 94140

And I looked, and beheld a pale horse:
and his name that sat on him was Death,
and Hell followed with him. And Power
was given unto them over the fourth part
of the earth, to kill with the sword, and
with hunger, and with death, and with the
beasts of the earth.

APOCALYPSE 6 : 8

1

F RANZ RICHTER LOOKED BOREDLY out the window: his elbows resting on the window ledge, his hands cupping his fair-complexioned face, fingers extending upward toward his thick wavy blond hair. His cupped hands braced against each other at the wrists thrust his pouting lips out even farther. His youthful facial features were contorted into a ridiculous mask. Franz was mad at the entire world. At fifteen, he could not remember an anger equal to the one now tearing at his insides. He wanted to stomp, scream, throw a tantrum. But, why bother? He was alone. A tantrum without an audience was just a waste of time.

His pale green eyes stared out the third story window. The old German castle-like house felt like a prison. He looked down at the same old landscape he had seen for nearly four days. In front of the house was Lichtentaler Avenue, the most elegant street in Baden-Baden. Along the street's route ran the Oos, a beautiful little river that added to the lushness of the area. Its banks were made even more colorful by the well-tended gardens and lawns of the great houses of the wealthy. He gazed at the various shades of green interspersed with the rainbow hues of the many flowers. It was not a picture of spring beauty to Franz but rather a foreign landscape. It might as well have been the Sahara desert. He longed to go home.

Home was Berlin: wonderful, exciting, lively Berlin—a worldly city, full of marvelous things and interesting people. He thought of the apartment in the Adlon Hotel on Unter den Linden, the most exclusive hotel on the most famous of streets. Franz and his mother had lived there all of his life. It made this house on Lichtentaler seem like a hovel. His mind was filled with the wonders of Berlin: the Imperial Palace, the University, the Winter Garden Theater, the Forum Fredericianum with its Royal Opera House and all his other favorite places. Who could possibly care for Baden-Baden's River Oos or Lichtentaler Avenue after having seen Berlin's Spree River or the beauty of the Tiergarten or the Charlottenburg gardens?

Franz watched the local children walking along Lichtentaler on their way home from school. Over the massive hedges of azaleas that formed the borders of the lawn and gardens for the house in which he and his mother were staying, he could see groups of two or three walking together, books in tow, laughing and talking, enjoying themselves on this spring day. The air was laden with the sweet fragrances of roses, wisterias, azaleas and rhododendrons having an almost narcotic effect. He pulled the window completely closed. The people who owned the house were away for the season and Franz and his mother were practically alone there.

Watching the children with their books, he suddenly struck the window ledge with his fist. He missed school. And, even worse, he missed his voice and dance lessons. He struck the ledge again, hurting his fist much more than the ledge. He groaned from the pain and the thought that his mother had made him come with her to Baden-Baden while she took the baths during the day and played the Casino at nights. Unforgiveable, he thought, selfish and unforgiveable.

Franz noticed the large wisteria vines that wound their way up the side of the house next door. Long racemes of blues, whites, purples and deep reds hung delicately from the travelling tentacles. The beauty and apparently fragile delicacy of the blossoms reminded him of his mother. She was strong and determined, well equipped to cope with anything with which the world of Berlin society confronted her. When she wanted, she could give the illusion of delicate innocence, a piece of gossamer easily frayed or damaged by her surroundings. She usually had her way, sometimes using her strength and determination, other times resorting to innocent vulnerability.

Franz's opinion of his mother was fairly accurate. Erica Tatina von Stauffenberg, the daughter of Count Georg von Stauffenberg, had decided she would marry Wieland Richter the first time she saw him. Richter's lack of money and social standing had been of no concern to her. Despite the Count's violent objections to her marrying beneath her dignity or class, she married Wieland and made her father accept the match. When Franz was born, Tatina chose the name for her new son. Wieland had fallen completely under her spell from the moment of their marriage vows. Her husband died six months after Franz's birth, and many gossiped that Tatina had stifled him psychologically, even though the official cause of death had been pneumonia.

Erica Tatina von Stauffenberg Richter, she still kept her maiden name, tacking the Richter on the end, was not left without means.

The Count, her father, always provided for her every need and, when he died only a few months after Tatina's husband, she was the only heir to an enormous estate. Since she preferred living at the Adlon in the excitement of Berlin, she immediately sold the estate, thus providing herself with much wealth. She spent her time with the grand society of Berlin, usually at a gala social event or in preparation for an upcoming party.

Franz existed on the periphery of her life. She seldom saw him in the mornings. Rising around noon was her custom, and on those occasions when she did see him after school or his voice or dance lessons, she was in heavy preparation for that night's social event.

Tatina went to Baden-Baden at least twice a year to bathe in the hottest sodium-chloride springs in Europe, and to gamble in the magnificent Casino. The city of Baden-Baden, near the French border, was a long train ride from Berlin, nearly six hundred kilometers. Tatina—everyone who knew her well, even Franz, called her that, not Erica—loved the trips to Baden-Baden. To her, it was like going to another world, an enchanted place, prompting her to often refer to it as "her fairytale village". When she went, she often left Franz in Berlin. In fact, he had only been with her twice before and then he was a baby. But this year was different. Tatina had decided to go early, before the regular season. Finding no one else free to go with her, she took Franz out of school for a few days.

She casually told Franz of her plans only two days before they were to go.

"We leave on the morning train day after tomorrow, Monday. Please do have all you need packed and be ready to leave about eight. Good night, Dear."

And that was what had brought Franz, despite his protests, to Baden-Baden, to the window of the big house on Lichtentaler Avenue where he watched Baden-Baden's young walking home from school. Enough of this wasted time, he thought. I should be practicing those new dance steps or doing the voice exercises, or both. Leaving the beautiful spring day to the young of Baden-Baden, he started to rise and return to his practice. Half standing, half sitting, hands on the window ledge balancing him as he rose, he froze. In that strange position, his attention had been captured by two school boys who had just come into view. There was nothing particularly unusual about them. Both were about the same age as Franz. But the taller of the two boys was different. Franz watched him intently as they passed along the sidewalk in front of the house. The tall boy was strikingly good looking, he thought, even handsome. His straight black hair, his muscular build, dark eyes—everything about him was demanding of attention.

Franz opened the window to see if he could hear them talking. He heard them but not enough to make out what they were saying. All the way past the house, as long as he could see them, Franz watched, never taking his eyes off the tall one. God, he thought, maybe Baden-Baden isn't such a horrible place after all.

They were gone now, out of the range of Franz's vision. He sat back down and thought about the tall, dark haired boy for a long while.

The two teenage boys walking along Lichtentaler in the midst of that panorama of spring colors were oblivious to all of it. Busy with adolescence, they had little time to notice either the beauty of their surroundings or the other boy watching them so closely from the window of the house they had just passed.

"Isn't she pretty, Van? I think she's the prettiest girl in school, don't you?"

"Ah, yes," Van replied to Ernst Hoffman. "She is not only the prettiest but also the nicest girl around."

Watching Sheila approach them in her usual zestful, happy way, the way she seemed to do everything, Ernst began to see her as a boy sees a girl. The three of them had played together for as long as they could remember. Child's play and friendship were being replaced by thoughts, dreams and fantasies of a more mature nature. Somewhere within Ernst there was a true romantic emerging, seeking to takeover the plump, pimple-faced lad and turn him into the most dashing of lovers.

Ernst stood on his tiptoes, cupped his mouth to Van's ear with his hand and whispered, "I'm going to ask her to go to the school party with me. Do you think she'll go?"

Van had to bend down a bit to hear Ernst's whispering. He brushed his long black hair from his deep-set dark eyes and, watching Sheila as she drew nearer them, laughingly replied: "I don't know if she will go with you or not, Ernst. You are such a blockhead that, if she does go with you, it will only prove that she doesn't have good sense!"

Sheila skipped toward the two whispering boys, her blonde hair bouncing up and down on her back with each skip. Smiling broadly, she waved to them both. Van and Ernst, she thought. How different they are and yet how much I like them both, especially Van. He has become so handsome lately. He reminds me of some dark, secret lover that would slip into a girl's room at night and take her away with him.

When she reached Van and Ernst, the three continued their walk down Lichtentaler, all talking at the same time. Van was teasing Ernst because he had taken Sheila's books and was now struggling along with a double load of books. Sheila enjoyed Ernst's attention but wished it had been Van that had asked to carry her books.

Van talked happily with the two of them, but his thoughts were not altogether on the conversation. He was very conscious of the changes in Ernst and Sheila. Ernst had a new interest in Sheila; she was a girl. Sheila seemed to have a new feeling toward Van. He reasoned that it must be because he was a boy. And strangest of all, he did not share their new awareness. What was wrong, he wondered. Why was it that Sheila was still just a friend, much the same as Ernst. He thought of the ever present ugliness he kept hidden within but immediately pushed it from his mind.

Along tranquil Lichtentaler Avenue, the little group followed its accustomed path home from school, three friends enjoying and sometimes sharing the warmth and exhilaration of youth's expected but unpredictable changes that would eventually thrust them into adulthood. There was nothing particularly unusual about these three being together. Nothing to warrant a second look or start the clacking tongues of the town gossips. True, Van and Ernst were Jewish and Sheila was not. Or, one could say that Sheila was a Christian and Van and Ernst were not. But in the Baden-Baden of the early 1920's few would have noticed this fact.

Baden-Baden was, and had been for nearly two thousand years, a resort city primarily concerned with the good health and pleasure of its large number of tourists. Consideration of Jewish matters was not a priority, and the discussion of the Jewish Problem or Jewish Question that was raging in many parts of Germany was almost unknown here. Baden-Baden was, after all, a place to escape the everyday dullness of life and renew the body while partaking of its pleasures. It was a resort city of some forty to fifty thousand people, a shimmering jewel nestled within the Black Forest. Each year during the season, the city swelled to many times its normal population when visitors came for the baths and the Casino. Even at the age of fourteen, Van felt that he could stay in Baden-Baden and still learn much by watching the tourists that came there from all over the world.

They walked on down Lichtentaler. As they passed his own house,

Ernst did not seem to notice or alter his pace at all. Laden with Sheila's books, he had no intention of leaving her until he had carried them safely all the way to her destination.

"Sheila," Ernst began, almost in a whisper, head averted and eyes downcast, "will you . . . uh, would you . . . uh, can you . . . uh."

"Ernst, I can hardly hear you," Sheila implored. "What are you saying? Sounds like you are practicing your verbs."

Blood rushed to poor Ernst's face, making it resemble a chubby, pimpled, scarlet mask. He felt he could walk under the row of border flowers along the lawn they were passing, hide among the small red blooms and never be seen again. With much clearing of the throat, Ernst managed to blurt out his question.

"Will you go to the Pring Sarty with me?"

"Pring Sarty?" Van hooted, breaking into loud laughter.

"What is a 'Pring Sarty'?" Sheila managed to gasp between her fits of doubling-over laughter.

Suddenly Ernst realized what he had said and he too joined in the laughter. When the laughter began to subside, Van was picking up the books he had dropped and Ernst, relieved of his embarrasment by the good laugh, spoke more calmly and confidently.

"Sheila, I meant Spring Party. Will you go with me?"

She looked immediately at Van and Van quickly looked at the most distant mountains as though he were seeing them for the first time. He knew, or thought he knew, why Sheila was looking at him and he did not want to face that look and her implied plea for help. He could not help her, not this time. He felt numb and a little sick.

"Oh Ernst, Sheila moaned, "I don't know yet. I haven't even asked Mother and Daddy if I can go. They will probably let me go because it is a school party and all that, but they probably won't let me go with a boy. They both think I am still too young to date."

She felt miserable. Lying was not her nature. Her parents did feel that she was too young to date, but they would not object to her going with Ernst or Van. That was the lie. She had been taught never to tell a lie, not even a small one.

"Lies are the termites in the house of life," she could hear her father saying.

"Well, Sheila, if they decide to let you go, and with a date, will you go with me?" Ernst asked.

"I will think about it and let you know, Ernst."

They were standing in front of Sheila's house by then. Ernst returned her books to her, gouged Van in the ribs causing him to drop his books again, and then started running back down Lichtentaler toward his own house.

"I'll get you for that, Fatty!" Van yelled at him.

"Poor Ernst," Van said to Sheila, picking up his books and joining her. She had placed her books on the grass and was sitting on them.

"He has always wanted to go with you," he said. He had plopped himself down on the grass near Sheila. "Why don't you go with him?"

"I don't know, Van. Ernst is a good friend, but I never wanted to date him." She paused and then went ahead with her question. "Why don't you ever ask me to go anywhere with you?"

Her pointed question was so unexpected that it surprised Van. They had all been friends for years, always playing together, going places as a threesome and getting into trouble together. It had never occurred to Van to date Sheila, or any other girl, for that matter. How could he answer her question without divulging his inner turmoil? For the first time in his life, Van felt uncomfortable with Sheila.

"Sheila, I never really thought about asking you out, like a date. You are more a sister to me than anything. You and Ernst are my truest friends, and we are with each other all the time. I just thought you would prefer to date someone you weren't with so often."

"So, I'm like your sister. I don't know if that is good or bad."

The subject had to be changed. The conversation was becoming too difficult for Van to manage. "Sheila, I meant it to be good when I said you were my sister. You will always be my sister. I think we like each other too much to date. Does that make sense to you?"

"In a strange way, yes, it makes a little sense. Maybe you are right. We are the best of friends, always have been. We could ruin that if we dated," Sheila said sadly.

He had to change the subject. He was afraid his secret monster would escape and Sheila would see it in all its sinfulness.

"Sheila, why do you wear that cross around your neck?"

"Because I am a Christian. You know that. Why don't you ever wear one, Van?"

"Now you are being silly. You know we are Jews, not Christians. If I put one of those crosses on, my parents would both die of heart failure."

"Since you brought the subject up, I have wondered what it means to be a Jew. Why don't you wear one of those Stars that you have around your house and on your church?"

"Boys don't wear those things like girls do. And it's not a church.

It's a synagogue."

"All right, don't get mad. You didn't answer my question about what it is to be a Jew."

From a dilemma to a mystification, Van thought. He did not like the conversation about boys dating girls, and he certainly did not like this question about being a Jew. Both subjects were puzzles to him and he could not explain either one. Sheila and Van were on the edge of the adult world and already the adult questions were ruining everything.

"Sheila, I don't know exactly what being Jewish means. I know we don't have Christmas, we don't have crosses to wear, we don't have Easter and we don't go to church on Sunday like you do."

"Those are things that being Jewish doesn't have. I want to know what it does have and what it all means," she said, refusing to let the subject die.

Van could not answer for a few minutes. Trying to remember something he had learned in bar mitzvah classes, he stalled for time. Finally, the only thing he could think of to say was, "Jews have many trials and tribulations."

"What?"

"Oh, Sheila! I don't know. I'll ask Mama and then I'll tell you what she says."

"I hope so!" she said.

She got up from her seat on the books and started to pick them up. Van handed the books up to her and looked into her eyes as he did. He thought he saw a strange sadness, or maybe it was loneliness. It was a look one might have when the loss of something dear has been discovered. When Sheila noticed him looking so intently at her, she tried to feign anger at him for not being able to answer her question about being Jewish.

When she was about half way up the front walk of her house, she turned and said, "Find out what it means to be a Jew and let me know. I might want to become one."

2

S HE BUSIED HERSELF arranging flowers from her garden in a large vase. They lay on the kitchen counter, a rainbow of colors for the alabaster vase which she would place in the sitting room. Her scissors worked deftly in her plump hands, cutting the stems varying lengths to create the proper round bouquet effect she wanted. A strand of her long black hair had mysteriously loosened itself and hung along her right cheek. With her thumb and index finger still tightly wedged in the round handles of the scissors, she lightly grasped the wandering strand of hair and delicately intertwined it back into its proper place, scissors pointing upward as she worked with her hair. Her fingers were so chubby that once the scissors were in place, she seldom removed them until she was finished using them.

The maid was sitting at the small table in the corner of the kitchen. She was reading the list of items for the night meal and considering how much work each would require. Sipping her cup of hot tea, she asked, "Isn't it about time for Van to be coming in from school?"

"Yes, Hilda, he should be here any moment now," Mama Bertholds replied, her scissored hand returning to the flowers. Glancing around the large kitchen with its tall cabinets and expansive counter working areas, she was so thankful for Hilda. This room was built for a tall person with long arms, she mused. If I did not have Hilda, nothing would ever get done in this kitchen. I am just too short and my arms would never reach to the back of these counters. I'd also need step ladders all over the place for all these tall cabinets and cupboards.

"Mama, I'm home," Van shouted as he came in through the back and entered the kitchen through the back hallway.

"Yes, Van, and it's late already. What took you so long? Now you will be late getting to Papa's cafe and you know how he needs you."

"We were talking, Sheila, Ernst and me, and I just forgot the time."

"Hurry to Papa's. Straight away with you now."

Van brushed his mother's cheek with a hasty kiss, waved to Hilda and ran up the winding stairs to his room. He dropped his books and changed his clothes. Back down the stairs and out the front door he ran.

Van's father owned a cafe on the Augustaplatz, in the center of the city, where most of the city's activity began or ended. The cafe was on the west side of the plaza, directly across from the largest bus-service connection. Papa Bertholds always allowed his son to spend hours in the cafe. The cafe had been in Papa's family for generations. It was his domain and he ruled it with jovial and loving care; there he was president, kaiser and even rabbi. Someday it would be Van's and, principally for that reason, Papa encouraged him to spend so much time there. As Van grew older, he cleaned tables, washed dishes and did anything else his father told him to do. What started as fun soon became a job and Papa expected Van to work as often as he could. Van did not mind the work. Papa's cafe offered a daily chance to see many people who lived in Baden-Baden and, best of all, he could watch the visitors from distant places; watch and marvel, watch and learn.

Mama watched Van rushing down the street to get to Papa's without being any later. Such a fine son, she thought, truly the joy of our lives. But where did he ever come by those features? It certainly wasn't from his Papa or me. We are both short and dumpy and lean to the fat side. Lean to the fat, Mama thought, chuckling to herself. Listen to me. I'm beginning to sound like one of those travelling jesters or Gypsies that come through Baden-Baden and perform for pennies from the crowd. Oh well, we fat ones are known for our humor and wit.

Papa and Mama Bertholds were both zaftig—short, plump and jovial—and also much fairer of complexion than Van. He was tall with well-defined muscles and hair so black it sometimes appeared to be deep blue. His features were sharp with a squared jaw, and his dark eyes, well set in deep-shaded eye sockets, sometimes gave the illusion that he was wearing the shadows of midnight.

"He was left on our doorstep by some Gypsies," Papa would say jokingly when Van began to grow into a tall reverse image of his parents.

Papa's father had bequeathed him the cafe on the Augustaplatz where he had worked since early childhood. The business was family and Van in his turn was to have it. Everyone in Baden-Baden expected Van to take the cafe when Papa retired. Everyone, that is, except Van.

When Jeremiah Bertholds married Minnie Steinfeldt, his new wife brought much inherited wealth with her. The large house on Lichtentaler had been built by Grandfather Steinfeldt, the banker. The grandeur and elegance of the Steinfeldt domain had been tempered and much improved by its new owner and his wife.

Papa and Mama Bertholds were heavy contributors to the synagogue, attending regularly and always ready to help anyone in need. The family religion was taken for granted by Papa. He took care of the cafe while Mama kept the family faith in much the same way one keeps a treasured heirloom. It was there, not thought of much by Papa but being cared for and loved by Mama, always holding it ready for the times he or anyone else had need for it. Van had been exposed to his faith and heritage but the exposure had not been complete. Learning by rote what was required, he drifted through the bar mitzvah classes, fooling Rabbi Eschel and perhaps, Van thought, even God.

After Van was completely out of Mama's view, she left the kitchen and took the vase of flowers into the sitting room, placing them carefully in the center of a small table. She seated herself in her favorite chair and began rummaging through her sewing basket for just the right needle and thread for her mending. It was not really necessary for her to do the mending, but she enjoyed the peace and contentment of sewing in the bright, cheerful sitting room. The room was shaped like a slice of pie with the crust end entirely filled with windows which flanked a pair of French doors that led to the porch outside. The sitting room was the family's favorite. When he was younger, Van had called it the smile room, and now the entire household called it that. Sunlight streamed through the windows and french doors, enriching the shades of bright yellows which covered the room's walls, creating an almost dazzling spectacle of warm, rich color which filled the room like an aura might surround a saint.

A little music would be nice, Mama thought. She switched on the radio next to her chair. While it warmed, Mama softly hummed a snip of a hymn from last Sabbath's service. She loved Sabbath services and seldom missed one. Mama's thoughts were full of the service last Friday and the opening Psalm flowed through her mind to the tune she was humming.

"O come, let us sing unto the Lord, let us joyfully acclaim the Rock of our salvation. Let us approach Him."

"Meanwhile," the radio interrupted Mama's thoughts, "the new leader of the National Socialist German Workers' Party, Adolf Hitler, has publicly called for national revenge against the Jews in Germany who conspired and cooperated with the enemy for the defeat of Germany in the recent war. According to Hilter, these conspirators and vermin should be removed from . . ."

Mama switched the radio off.

"Not true! Lies!" she spoke aloud to no one but herself. "Scum! The whole lot of those National Socialists are scum and garbage. Thank God the German people have enough sense to ignore their malicious lies."

Her confidence in the collective sanity of the German people calmed and reassured her, but she could no longer concentrate on her sewing. She laid it aside and walked through the double doors onto the porch surrounded by her gardens and gazed at the sweeping view of the city.

Tulips, irises, daffodils and many varieties of budding trees filled the gardens and flowed down the gently sloping landscape to the lushly green-clad banks of the friendly, meandering little river. Looking across this brilliant splash of color to the rooftops of Baden-Baden, sprinkled like salt and pepper among the trees, and still farther to the pine-covered mountains that framed the entire view, Mama reflected on the horrid news from the radio and the beauty of the land before her and decided that God was firmly in control and no small band of illiterate madmen would ever change it.

Papa Bertholds gazed out of the cafe's largest window once again. It was not like Van to be late, and Papa always needed to worry about something.

"Van late again, Bertholds?" old Kern, the pawnbroker, asked.

"Yes, but he'll be here any minute. Van's a good worker, always here when he should be, but he's growing fast. He's probably out chasing the girls. He'll be here soon. If he isn't, we'll know he caught one."

"Yes, or maybe one caught him," Kern replied, laughing at his intended humor.

Papa smiled with Kern and thought about his growing son. He was already taller than his parents. Papa was proud of his fine son. "Smart in the books and good in the looks," he would say to anyone who would listen. Van had grown tall and had become so strong due partly to his interest in school sports, an interest that Papa could not understand. Nonetheless, he was secretly pleased that Van did not look like some of the other Jewish boys, milksops who cowered before any and all Aryans.

Papa cleaned some of the tables so Van would not have to do the work. Business was slow this fine spring day and Papa knew most people were outside, not interested in sitting in a stuffy old cafe. Years of restaurant work had taught Papa to feel the volume of each day's business before he even unlocked the cafe's door. Tourists taking the baths or letting the Casino take them had not arrived in large numbers yet. It was still early in the season for the real rush of the tourist trade with their "out-of-town money" as Papa liked to call it. Kern was his only customer when Van came rushing in.

"Hello, Papa, Mr. Kern. I'm sorry I'm late, Papa," Van said, trying to catch his breath.

"Don't worry about it, Van. Business is not here today. It'll be here in a week or so. For now, all we have are these locals, like old Kern there. Most of them don't have any money and those that do are planning to carry it with them to that cemetery out at the edge of town. I'd rather have out-of-town money anyway."

Papa went back behind the counter and, with nothing to do, folded his arms on his rather large stomach. Van began to busy himself with rearranging all of the tables and chairs in the cafe. After each set had been moved about gingerly, he found himself also with nothing to do.

"I'll be going now, Bertholds," Kern said. "Someone may want to pawn something of great value. Hell, they never want to pawn anything that isn't of great value, to hear them tell it."

Papa and Van were alone in the cafe. The other employees had left after lunch, to return just before the dinner hour.

"How was school today? Did you manage to fight all the girls off long enough to learn anything?"

Van, blushing, walked to the front of the cafe and looked out the large window at the people waiting for one of the many buses or street cars.

"Yes, Papa, I fought them off gallantly and kept my head buried in books all day. But I don't recall learning anything."

Papa's smile vanished. Glancing at him, Van knew a lecture was coming.

"That is not good, Van. You must learn something each day. School is your job now. You learn about little things and big things. You learn about people in far lands, about the world and the great stars beyond the world. But most important, Van, you learn about numbers and math and bookkeeping and money. That is the most important lesson. You learn that now and when you have the cafe, that job will be much easier."

"Papa, I was only making a joke. I did learn today. I learn every day. I just tried to make a joke because I am tired. I must have spring fever."

"Spring fever or girl fever?"

Van did not answer. What could he say? He felt uneasy, like a fly with one foot caught in a spider's web. This conversation, like the one with Sheila, was bothering him. "Change the subject!" something within him screamed. Did Papa hear that, he wondered.

"Van, we are not going to have any more business today. It's a nice day, a day to be outside. Why don't you go on and chase those girls or whatever you feel like doing."

"Can I, Papa, really?"

"Yes, go on, Van. I'll see you later tonight at home. You get home before dark now, so Mama won't worry."

Van, removing his apron, rushed to the door.

"Bye, Papa. See you tonight."

He was half a block away when he suddenly stopped and ran back to the cafe.

"Papa, thanks."

Van crossed the Augustaplatz and wound his way through the ancient, crooked city streets. He passed the Thermal Spa District and walked along the banks of the River Oos. On the opposite side of the river, across from the Spa District, was the Kurhaus with its Casino, the Art Gallery, a theater and fine hotels. The strains of a Strauss waltz filled the air as the orchestra played the daily concert in front of the Kurhaus. Papa had been correct, thought Van. This day was made to be enjoyed outside, not from behind the windows of the cafe.

He followed the Oos upstream until he was out of the city and climbing up into the hills, deeper into the forest. Turning away from the river, he walked about two kilometers along a stream that had merged with the Oos. Now the late afternoon sun was almost completely obscured by the hills and a thick stand of trees.

Van knew exactly where he was going. He had not discovered this particular secluded spot by himself. Years ago, when Van was only seven or eight, Rudy Hoess had brought him to this place, his secret fishing hole. According to Rudy, no one in the world knew about this spot except him and he had named it "Rudy's Special Place". And, to

Van, if Rudy said that no one knew about this place, it had to be the absolute truth.

Van seated himself on the bank of the stream and leaned back against the trunk of a large pine tree. Splinters of sunlight pierced through the dense forest and even reached the ground in many spots. They would suddenly be cut off only to return almost immediately. Van imagined each sliver of sunlight as a flicker of God's sight that had penetrated the resisting forest. In a constant effort to shut out God's view of this place, the trees would rally and close the opening, but the eye of God would inevitably triumph and the rays of sun return, lighting the landscape and seeing all.

Van did not want to fish, just to relax and contemplate. He closed his eyes and thought about how lonely the fishing spot was without Rudy. His mind wandered back to all those times he and Rudy had fished, talked and enjoyed this hideaway. One particular early spring day burned in his memory. Van was ten or eleven, he could not remember exactly which, and Rudy fifteen or sixteen. They were fishing but not having much success that day. Spring's warmth and penetrating laziness had made Van sleepy. Rudy had caught him dozing two or three times.

"You don't seem to be able to keep your eyes open, Little Brother," Rudy had said when he noticed Van sleeping again. Rudy had begun calling Van "Little Brother" early in their friendship. He had first seen Van at Papa's cafe and immediately liked the young boy. Seeing him at the cafe almost daily, Rudy began teasing and joking and it was not long before a bond of friendship developed between them, Rudy becoming Van's hero and Van becoming Rudy's alter ego.

"I'm sleepy, Rudy. No fish are biting today anyway. Why don't they bite?"

"Maybe they are full and not hungry. Or maybe they are sleepy like you. Why don't you lie down here and nap a while?" indicating his lap, "I want to try my luck at fishing a little longer."

Van stretched out on the grassy stream bank and placed his head in Rudy's lap, leaving the fishing to his friend. Rudy continued to fish, oblivious to anything unusual about Van's behavior. Lying there, his head in Rudy's lap, he looked up at Rudy and, for the first time in his life, became afraid of his own feelings. He had realized long ago and accepted Rudy as his hero, his ideal; but at that instant he felt something more than hero-worship. A gnawing, bittersweet sensation spread over his being from some deep, dark place within him. His body actually tingled, the skin on his arms prickling with goose bumps, his temperature seeming to elevate many degrees. He felt he was going to be violently ill. These strange sensations slowly ebbed away leaving only his thumping heart in their wake. It was beating so hard and so loud that he just knew Rudy would hear and even feel it.

Van feigned sleep to conceal his struggle. What is this thing within me, he wondered, this unnamed craving that will not leave me, much less be still? Surely it's an evil thing placed in me by Satan himself. "Oh, God," Van silently prayed, his eyes closed so tightly that his face became a contortion of hard lines and scowls, "deliver me from this evil! Please take it away! Please, God!"

Small tears trickled down the hard lines of Van's face, falling silently and unnoticed, dropping on his shirt and fading into the threads of the fabric, leaving only a few damp spots as drops of moisture from the heavens might do. Into his troubled and confused thoughts came some words from one of Rabbi Eschel's recent sermons. "If a man also lie with mankind, as he lieth with a woman, both of them have committed an abomination: they shall surely be put to death; their blood shall be upon them."

Van bolted up from his position in Rudy's lap. Is this, he wondered, a man also lying with mankind? Have we just committed an abomination? He paled, his sudden pallor heightened by the darkness of his hair. Startled by Van's sudden movement, Rudy looked at him sitting there on the grass beside him, his skin the color of old milk, his eyes reflecting a genuine look of pure horror.

"What's wrong, Van? Are you sick?"

Van looked quickly at Rudy and tried to answer but nothing came from his mouth. It was raw and dry as sandpaper. He swallowed a few times.

"Van, you look terrible. Have you been crying? What is wrong with you?"

"I . . . I had an awful dream. It scared me. Oh, Rudy, it was terrible!"

"Is that all? I thought you were sick. Just a bad dream, eh? Well, dream's over. It's time we started home. Come on, let's go."

The thoughts of that day were always with Van, but, now, in Rudy's Special Place, where the incident actually happened, Van felt it more keenly. His secret torment was more demanding when he was there or when he was in Rudy's presence. It was a sinful thing that he must rid himself of soon or it would damn him to eternal hell. It must be ended, he reasoned, it must be over. But how? He didn't know.

Who could he ask for advice or help? Convinced his hidden feelings were from the Devil, he reasoned his only help was with God.

Van rose from the stream bank and started the dark walk home. The sun had gone, taking with it the rays of God's vision, leaving Van completely alone. He was frightened. Aloud, he began to pray as he hurriedly walked the forest trail.

"Dear God, please hear my sincere pleas. Deliver me from this evil within me the way you delivered us out of Egypt. I have no other place to go for help. If You don't help me, I am damned. Please, God, take this from me. Free me, God, please."

When Van left the dark of the forest, rejoining the path of the Oos, he could see the many lights of the city. It was fully night by now, and the lights sparkled all over the valley, easing Van's strange fears and, to a degree, comforting him. He did not feel so alone and helpless. Soon he would be home with Papa and Mama and he would be safe. He was walking very fast, already on the streets of Baden-Baden. Nearing the train station, he could see the Berlin train loading and preparing for its departure.

On the station platform, the porters struggled with the many pieces of luggage to be loaded on the train for Berlin. Tatina watched their every move. She counted the familiar luggage with her monogram.

"Fourteen. Yes, fourteen. Well, so far they haven't managed to lose or destroy any of my luggage. Such louts. They handle my things like they were loading garbage. Terrible! Simply terrible!"

Franz was not really listening to her. This was another of her rituals well known to him. He anxiously waited for her to complete her supervision of the baggage men so they could get out of this place. Elated with the prospect of waking up in Berlin, he could hardly wait to begin the trip.

"Well, I do believe they have finally managed to force every piece of my luggage into the baggage car without completely demolishing any of it. I believe we can get on the train now, Franz."

She walked gracefully along the platform until she arrived at their car. As she stepped up onto the boarding step, the conductor placed his hand under her mink-clad arm to assist her. She smiled condescendingly at him and looked behind her to see that Franz was there. He was not.

"Oh, bother!" she said.

"Pardon me," the conductor replied. "Is something wrong?"

"Yes. It's my son. Wherever has he gotten off to? Would you please get him for me. There he is, down there by the baggage car.

Just standing there! What *is* he doing? I thought he was anxious to leave this place."

Franz was standing perfectly still, more like a statue than a young boy. He had turned from the baggage car and started to follow Tatina when he saw Van walking briskly past the train station.

The tall one, he thought. What is he doing here at the train station? And why is he walking so fast? He looks frightened, as if he is being chased. I wonder what the trouble is.

"Young man! Young man!"

Franz was startled by the conductor and jumped when the man tapped him on the shoulder.

"Your mother is waiting and the train will be leaving soon. You better come along and board."

"Yes, thank you. I'm on my way," Franz replied.

He ran down the platform and joined Tatina who had an exasperated expression on her face.

"What were you doing?" she demanded.

"Nothing. I was just thinking about something and didn't realize you were already on the train."

"Well, come on now. We're on our way back to Berlin. I hope you're happy about that. I know how glad you are to be leaving Baden-Baden."

He peered off in the direction that Van had been going. In the distance, beneath one of the street lights, he could see Van for a brief moment and then he was gone into the darkness. He turned back and looked up at Tatina. She had followed Franz's searching gaze down the distant street and also had seen the tall, young boy as he disappeared into the darkness.

"Find something that interested you, my dear?" she asked, smiling broadly. "And all this time I thought you hated this place."

Tatina advanced up into the train car, her merry laughter filling the car and making Franz relax some. He laughed slightly and followed her into the car. After they were both seated, Franz looked out the train window but could see nothing.

"One that got away?" Tatina inquired, smiling teasingly.

Franz smiled at her and said nothing. It certainly is wonderful, he thought, to have Tatina for my mother. She knows about everything. He laid his head on her shoulder, turned his face toward her and snuggled in the mink. Tatina's perfume filled his nostrils. Life is wonderful, he thought as he sighed into the mink. And now we are on our way home where it is even more wonderful.

3

S HEILA COULD NOT RECALL ever having seen the school concert hall so radiantly alive. Only its raised stage and the slight hint of the usual musty odor that was always there reminded her that it was the school concert hall. It was truly magnificent, meticulously converted by the Spring Party Committee from a dull performing hall into a splendidly decorated celebration of spring. "The Flowers of Baden-Baden" was the theme that year and the committee had surpassed all expectations.

"Well, what do you think of it, Mother?" Sheila inquired as they came through the long archway from the main door of the building into the hall. Constructed for this one occasion, the archway was a skeleton of wood completely covered with red roses, so thick and abundant that not one splinter of the wooden skeleton could be seen. Massed in such numbers, the roses created the illusion of a tunnel constructed of plush red velvet leading from the door into the giant hall. When passing through the long archway, some older guests had difficulty breathing, so strong and sweet was the smell of roses.

"Sheila," her mother answered, "I've never seen anything so beautiful in my entire life. And to think you were on the committee that did this. Wherever did you get so many beautiful red roses?"

Even Sheila's father was impressed, and generally Mr. Gebhardt was unimpressed with anything other than business matters.

"I'll bet those roses cost a fortune. They had to. There are so many of them. I must admit, it is an outstanding sight."

Sheila nearly burst with pride. She and the committee had worked on this project for a year: raising the money, buying the materials and flowers, and finally, doing all the work.

Inside the hall, through the tunnel of roses, the scene was almost overwhelming. All of the seats had been moved out and none of the walls or the ceiling were visible. Bunting, balloons, ribbons and thousands of flowers were draped all around, forming a giant canopy peaking in the center of the great hall. The canopy encompassed the stage area and surrounded it with an array of tulips. Ensconced on the stage among all the tulips was the orchestra that performed the daily concerts in front of the Kurhaus.

The Gebhardts walked around the dance floor to the refreshment area. Although the dance floor slanted gently downward to the stage area, no one seemed to notice. Sheila walked up behind Van and Ernst.

"How did you two get in here? This is supposed to be an elegant affair."

Van and Ernst both turned and smiled broadly. Ernst turned crimson as usual.

"Oh, we were walking by the front door, on our way to the local garbage dump to scrounge a bit of supper, when this brawny man grabbed us by the necks and, telling us he needed some clean-up people, dragged us in here," Van replied. "And here we are. Ernst is searching for a mop and I am looking for some old rags. Oh, I see you have worn some."

Sheila laughed and struck at Van. Everyone joined the laughter and the conversation settled down to daily niceties.

"How are you?"

"Such a lovely dress."

"You are looking so well."

"How is your old Aunt Harriet?"

All the while this idle talk continued, the dance floor was alive with couples dancing to the orchestra, twisting and whirling around in great clouds of silks, laces, brocades and taffetas. The effect of it all was, at first, dizzying to Sheila. She looked from the dance floor activity to Van.

"Have you found the answer to my question, yet?" she whispered.

"What question?" he asked.

She looked at him with some irritation and replied, "What does it mean to be a Jew?"

He realized that he had completely forgotten all about it. His mind was too involved with his own question to seek an answer for hers.

"No, not yet," he whispered back to her.

Van was spared any more from Sheila on the subject as a large commotion erupted on the dance floor. A quadrille had been called for and the throng was gathering for it. Over two hundred people lined up in two separate lines facing one another. The music began and the flurry of activity prevented any further whispering between Van and Sheila. Instead, they joined the quadrille with the three groups of parents. After the quadrille, the three sets of parents, the Gebhardts, the Hoffmans and the Bertholds, moved to the side of the refreshment area and settled down to watch the young people dance. Van, Sheila and Ernst moved to a small vacant area surrounded by irises of deep, dark purple. The orchestra was playing a Richard Strauss waltz from *Der Rosenkavelier.*

"Strauss waltzes," Ernst remarked, "are not for listening; unlike Lanner's waltzes, they compel one to dance." Then he smiled bravely at Sheila and said, "Fair damsel, may I have this dance?" He took Sheila's extended hand and placed his other arm around her small waist. They moved into the throng of happy dancers.

Van watched them glide around the floor with the others. Sheila and Ernst were his focal point and all the other dancers were slightly out of focus, blurred into the background by his intense interest in his two dearest friends. He was surprised how well Ernst danced. How strange that Ernst did not look so fat when he was dancing.

Sheila was truly beautiful. Her long blonde hair had been done in great long rolls that cascaded down her shoulders and fell down her back almost to her waist. When she whirled with the music, her hair appeared to float in the same direction. Lights sparkled from her pale blue eyes, dazzling Ernst and all who glanced her direction. When she smiled, her small nose turned up a bit more than usual and her whole countenance radiated joy and youth and life.

Van's eyes followed Sheila and Ernst while they danced. He saw her beauty and wondered why he only saw it but did not feel it. He desperately wanted to feel that she was not only attractive but also desirable. He sensed his secret monster stirring. "Be still!" he silently screamed to it. "Go away from me, forever!" It stirred, moved outward and demanded attention; becoming full grown it grew even more until it consumed him. Demanding recognition, it growled and scratched at his insides. It fought for control and won.

Van thought of Rudy and wished that he were with him instead of here at the dance. Watching Sheila and Ernst with his eyes, he saw only Rudy with his mind.

Rudy adjusted the new black and red arm band on his left sleeve and tried to see his reflection in the hazy mirror. A long zig-zagging crack ran the length of the smoky mirror; the two pieces were held together by bits of old graying tape. Even the older pieces of tape had tape over them to stop their curling deterioration. Layers of different ages of tape, placed on the old mirror by its different users were like layers of geological deposits, each layer tinted a different color by time; each layer revealing a bit of history of the Hoess family's efforts to keep the mirror intact.

What Rudy Hoess saw were two halves of himself, divided haphazardly by the crack. The halves did not fit together properly and one half of Rudy's reflection was taller than the other, presenting an imperfect reflection of a man not properly put together.

Dimly reflected in the two halves of the mirror were the contents of Rudy's small room. The aged mirror's distortion could not worsen the true image of the room. Just large enough for a half bed, an ancient chest, one chair and a wash stand, the room was a most depressing place. The one window, not even large enough to get a man's head through, opened out on Safien-Allee, a narrow thoroughfare. Beyond the door that connected the room to the remainder of the house, he could hear his drunken father screaming at Helga, Rudy's mother.

"The son-of-a-bitch is your son, not mine! He was fathered by some scum you drug in from the alley just outside the door!"

"Joseph, must you yell? He can hear you. You're drunk again. Always drunk. And you a good Catholic."

"Shut up you old bitch! If I am such a god-damn good Catholic, why can't I get our son to make a priest of himself? That's all I ever wanted from this miserable life, a son in the priesthood. Is that too much to ask? Tell me, why won't he even think on it?"

"It's God's will, Joseph."

"Shit on God's will!" Rudy's father screamed, loudly falling over something. "Who the hell put the chair in the way there?"

Rudy was immune to the daily ritual coming from the next room. He had heard it so often he knew the words almost before they were uttered.

The reflection gazed back at Rudy. It wore a new brown shirt, military cut. On its left sleeve was the red arm band. Its circle of white was the only light-colored thing in the room. Within this white circle, the one small spot of light in the room, was the darkest object of all. Black as death it stood on its field of white, waiting for its day of triumph, Rudy thought, which he hoped was rapidly drawing near. Rudy looked at the reflected arm band and then at the real band on his left arm. The swastika burned in Rudy's mind. At last, he had found something to which he could belong and which could belong to him. No Mass, no prayer book, no confessional, no priesthood ever offered such. He had found a cause, a refuge, a religion, a god.

He looked admiringly at the uniformed figure in the mirror, making a few minor adjustments before turning to leave. He stopped before opening the door and, once again, looked back at the glass effigy. He smiled ever so slightly as he opened the door. The crack in the looking glass distorted the slight smile into a sneer, an ironic scowl, on the image's face.

"Look at him, Helga, wearing that stupid outfit. What is that piece of crap on your arm?"

"Nothing, Father, just part of the uniform we wear," Rudy replied, walking quickly to get out of the house and escape the usual scene.

"Rudy, don't stay out late. These spring nights still get cold and damp and you'll catch pneumonia," his mother pleaded.

His father would not stop his alcoholic raging. Stumbling toward Rudy, he screamed, "Uniform *who* wears? You belong to that damned group of rabble that think they are going to change the world?"

Rudy slammed the front door behind him. Nineteen years of his father had been time enough to hear everything the old man had to say, some of it many, many times. He was already late for the meeting and, as a new member, he did not want to be. He turned and ran down the rough cobblestone street, unique to the older part of the city, and wished he were leaving for the last time.

Rudolf Hoess, member of the National Socialist German Workers' Party. He liked the sound of it. This is my chance, he thought, my best chance to get away from miserable Baden-Baden and see some excitement in the world. There's nothing in this place but old, rich people trying to get well at the baths or win more money at the Casino. I hate everything and everyone here.

He reached Michaelsberg Park, the announced gathering place for the meeting that night, about thirty minutes late. Rudy had wondered why the meeting was in a park instead of the usual hall where they met. Approaching the crowd of men dressed in the same type uniform as his, he realized the reason.

Rudy drew near a group of around thirty or fifty men. He could not be certain of the number or their identities because of the darkness. However, he knew he was in the right place because of their uniforms and he eventually recognized a few individuals. Some had lighted torches while others carried signs and posters. It was evidently to be a parade or a demonstration. He tried to read the signs but all he could see were the black swastikas. Finally, he was able to decipher a few words. Momentarily lighted by the flickering flames of the various torches as they swayed to and fro, Rudy read the scrawled words: Jew-Pigs, Scum of the Earth, Christ-Killers and Germany-Forever, Jews-Never.

There could be no doubt in anyone's mind. The Spring Party had been a phenomenal success. The Bertholds family arrived home in a state of exhaustion and exhilaration, completely drained from the dancing and the sheer pleasure of the night. Papa, after seeing Mama and Van into the house, left to make a quick trip to the cafe. He had entrusted it for the night to some trusted employees with many years of service. But he still felt the necessity of checking on it before he retired.

Mama and Van went into the sitting room to relax and wait for Papa's return from the cafe. Mama sewed while Van thumbed through a magazine. The windows and the double doors leading to the outside were open. Night sounds from the gardens provided the background for the other noises in the room. The sound of Van's flipping magazine pages outnumbered the ticks of the grandfather's clock that measured the passing of time. Obviously, he was neither reading the magazine nor paying any attention to the pictures. He glanced at his gold watch, a bar mitzvah gift from Papa, and checked the clock, which he determined to be three minutes slow.

Mama watched Van between stitches. His thoughts are far away, she decided. He's probably thinking about the dance and Sheila.

"Van, dear, didn't you enjoy the party," she said, not as a question but a declaration.

He did not answer.

"Van, did you hear me?"

"No, Mama. What did you say?"

"I was just commenting on how wonderful the party was. Didn't you think so?"

"Yes, it was much better than I had expected it to be."

Mama smiled and continued, "Did you notice Mrs. Blum's dress? It must have been stored away since the last century. It was so out of date."

While Mama continued her review of the night's activities and everyone involved, Van remembered Sheila's question.

"Mama,"—he interrupted her between Mrs. Offmier's offensive bosoms and Mrs. Blick's extremely broad hips—"what does it mean to be Jewish?"

The clock ticked furiously. Van was certain that, in an effort to make up the lost three minutes, the clock was ticking much faster. The crickets and other night creatures speeded up their accompaniment. Mama's mouth was open but no sound came out.

Finally, Mama spoke, "What did you ask?"

"I asked you what it means to be a Jew."

Mama still did not understand the question. She could not believe he had actually asked what being Jewish meant. Putting her sewing down, she replied, "Van, you ask such a question? I don't understand. You attended bar mitzvah classes with Rabbi Eschel. Didn't you learn then?"

"Oh, Mama," Van said in exasperation, "I paid no attention to all that. I just memorized what I had to for bar mitzvah."

This revelation did not please Mama. She turned in her chair uncomfortably. Facing Van, she drew a deep breath and sighed loudly. Then she drew another deep breath, looked intensely at Van and spoke more seriously than Van could ever remember.

"We are Jews! We are God's Chosen People! You must realize this and live accordingly. God chose Moses and made a Covenant with him. The Covenant made us His Chosen People of all the people in the world. We are his special children. We must obey God's laws and keep our part of the Covenant. The punishment for breaking God's laws for a Jew is death. When God talked to Moses and gave him the Law, this punishment was made very clear."

God had talked with Moses, Van thought. He wondered if God had been whispering Van's secret to Mama. The thought made Van squirm with subconscious guilt.

Mama continued, unaware of Van's discomfort. "The Covenant between us and God also promises that He will take special care of us if we obey His Laws. You know that God's Laws are in each synagogue and they are called the Torah or scrolls. They are not there just for decoration. They are the basis of our Covenant with God.

"There are certain things, unclean things, that God forbids us to eat. The clean foods we call kosher. This is just one part of our agreement with God.

"Another part is racial purity. Now, don't be frightened by this term. All it means is that a Jewish boy must marry a Jewish girl to keep the Jewish blood pure. Since we are God's chosen, we can't marry those who are not chosen. It is against God's Law, and the punishment is death."

Visions of Rudy, Sheila and Ernst raced through Van's mind. Sheila was not a Jewish girl, he thought. And his evil within chorused, "And neither is Rudy." Van trembled in his chair; the unexpected voice of his secret had surprised him.

"Am I upsetting you with my explanation, Van?" Mama asked.

"No, Mama, I just felt a chill run through me."

Mama got up and closed the windows and doors. She even closed the hallway door. When she came back to her chair, she looked strangely pale and worried.

God *had* been talking to Mama, Van was sure of it. He still talks to people as he did in the Torah. He has told her the awful secret thing about me. She is going to tell me she knows.

"Van, there is something else I have been wanting to talk to you about."

Here it comes, Van said to himself.

"I know that you have been friends with Rudy Hoess for years. I think it all started at Papa's cafe. He has been good to you, taking you fishing and such. But, Van, he is not Jewish. Now, that is not always bad but, with Rudy, I think it *is* bad."

A flood of relief engulfed Van. God had not yet talked with Mama about the forbidden subject.

"If you get too close with someone like Rudolf Hoess, there are too many dangers. A lot of people who are not Jewish hate us because we are God's favorite people. They are either jealous of this fact or convinced we are crazy for believing such a thing. Also, there are those that blame all Jews for the crucifixion of Jesus. They hate us for that and seek revenge."

"But, Mama," Van interrupted, "we didn't do that. The Romans did that, not us. Why do they blame us?"

"Why? Why? Don't ask me to explain their actions. I am not really sure why they blame us for that. I believe it is a matter of our being a scapegoat. You know what scapegoat means?"

"Yes, it is a goat that has done no wrong but everyone blames it for anything that goes wrong."

"That is close enough. So we are the scapegoats for Jesus' death. Nearly two thousand years of this blame and other things have made being a Jew a hard job. You have to work at it.

"People like Rudolf Hoess will be friendly to your face one day and the next day they will be among your enemies, not for something you do but just because you are a Jew. His father is Catholic and has always wanted Rudolf to become a priest in that church. So Rudolf

Hoess receives a lot of pushing and shoving at home. Their home life is rather bad, I understand. He has been in a lot of trouble that you don't know about."

"What kind of trouble?" Van asked, his curiosity aroused.

"I don't see any reason to go into all that. Just take my word for it, stay away from him."

Mama picked up her sewing, signalling that the subject of Rudolf Hoess was closed. Van stared at the grandfather clock, considering what Mama had told him.

Being Jewish was more serious than he had thought. The truth was that he had seldom actually considered it at all. What was the trouble Rudy had been involved in? Did it have anything to do with Van's secret?

He thought about Sheila and her question. He could never explain all of what Mama had told him to Sheila. Even if he could explain it as well as Mama, Sheila would never understand. He would have to avoid her question as best as he could, he decided.

His overriding thought was his thankfulness and a great relief that God had not been talking to Mama. He then sent an urgent prayer to God asking Him to please keep His silence.

"What are you two doing in here with all the doors closed?" Papa asked, as he opened the hallway door and came into the room.

Mama explained to him that they were discussing Van's bar mitzvah classes. She also told Papa about her advice to Van to stay away from Rudy and asked if Papa agreed. Mama knew that Papa would, he always did on family matters.

Papa replied, a worried expression on his face, "What a coincidence that you would be discussing Rudy Hoess. There was a large gathering tonight on the Augustaplatz of that new radical group, the National Socialist Party. They also call themselves the Nazi Party. Mama, you know which group they are, that bunch of misfits and rowdies. It was a real mess down there when I left."

"Well, I'm glad you're home," Mama said. "What I've heard of them has all been bad."

"They were tonight, that's for certain. They were calling for the end of our present form of government and a bunch of other radical ideas. Even worse, they had signs about Jew-Pigs and all their usual garbage. And, right in the middle of that crowd was Rudy Hoess carrying a sign with a terrible message about Jews on it."

Mama and Van spoke at the same time.

"What did the sign say?" asked Mama.

"Was it really Rudy?" chimed in Van.

"Wait a minute, you two. Not so fast with your questions. Yes, it was definitely Rudy Hoess and I won't repeat what his sign said."

Mama directed an "I told you so" look at Van. Van chose to look at the pattern in the carpet. Papa was ready to end the subject and go to bed. As they left the sitting room, Van felt that it could no longer be the smile room.

Sheila lay in her bed in the deep darkness of the night, still awake. Two hours had passed since she had faithfully said her prayers and retired for the night. She was exhausted from the dancing and the excitement and her legs and back actually ached.

It had been a grand success. All her long hours of work and effort had certainly been worth it. When she was leaving the Spring Party, she had heard comments that it had been the best party ever held in Baden-Baden. Her parents thought so, and Sheila agreed. It had been perfect.

The sound of the approaching spring storm could be heard through her open windows. The outside was bathed in an eerie white light and then the rumble of thunder rolled like a shock wave over the valley where Baden-Baden nestled. The interval between the flash and its accompanying thunder became shorter and shorter until the two were finally happening simultaneously: booming explosions of thunder and brilliant flashes of blinding lightning. When the rain first began, it rode upon the wings of strong, fierce winds, carrying the rain farther into her room and making her curtains wave in the flashing light. Sheets of rain battered the house, forcing Sheila to get out of bed. She quickly closed the windows and ran back to bed, pulling her blankets over her head.

In her makeshift tent formed by the bed covers, she felt warm and secure, safe from the passing storm. The tapping on her windows, a sound similar to that made by someone throwing pebbles at the glass, increased in volume and intensity. The rain, mixed with hail, beat clamorously against the windows. Sheila became frightened by the increasing fierceness of the storm. She heard her mother and father shutting windows. Her door opened and her mother slipped in to close Sheila's windows.

"You've already closed them, haven't you? Are you all right, Sheila?"

"Yes, Mother," she replied from within her tent.

Her mother quietly closed Sheila's door, leaving her alone with the storm and her thoughts. She felt better then, less alone. Her thoughts wandered back to the dance and to Van. Instead of Ernst, she danced with Van, holding him as close to her body as she could. When she looked up into his face, his dark countenance towered above her, his black piercing eyes melted her soul. She pressed her young body to his, feeling every contour and curve of him mesh and flow with her yearning body. It was all a fantasy. Van had only danced with her once, holding her a respectable distance from him all the while.

Why was Van like that, she wondered. Somewhere, from deep within her feminine being, the answer came. She could not put it into words, but she knew, all of her knew, and the realization that for some unspeakable reason Van was never to be hers was as though Van had died. Her heart pained her, tears trickled from the corners of her eyes. Why Van? She sobbed quietly for a few minutes.

A gigantic clash of thunder, forcing the glass in the windows into shaking, quivering panes of reverberation, and a blinding flash of lightning combined to shake the whole valley. Hail fell more noisily than ever, the sounds and answering echoes of the storm were almost deafening.

Sheila heard none of it; her mind was full of her Van fantasy. Together, they waltzed through her reverie that night, living out her wishes and desires in the setting of the Spring Party as they did other nights in other settings. She struggled to keep her newly realized reality about Van from her mind, to preserve the lovely world of her dreams. It would not go away. It lingered on the fringes of her fantasy, threatening to destroy the beautiful pictures forever.

Others were having difficulty sleeping that night, but the storm was not entirely the cause. At the Bertholds home, the family had gone to bed after their strange night; a night that had begun with the mirth and celebration of the Spring Party and had ended with Papa's experience at Baden-Baden's first Nazi demonstration and the sobering conversation in the sitting room.

Papa slept fitfully and briefly that night. What was once a tiny group of radicals had grown in numbers and influence very quickly. He felt a foreboding concern for the future; a future of dangers that he believed the Nazis posed for his family and all Jews. He spent the night worrying and praying.

Mama was also worried about the future: her family's more than Germany's. She knew that Papa, although appearing jovial and care-free, worried too much about politics, concerning himself about things which he had no power to change. She also knew that he worked too hard in the cafe. She promised herself to get Papa to work fewer hours and to persuade him to stop fretting about world problems and enjoy life more.

Her biggest concern was Van. Although Van was already taller than Mama, she still considered him her little boy. His strange question about being Jewish was unexpected, and his association with that Rudy Hoess was the worst possible development. She promised herself that she would do everything she could to put an end to that, without hurting him. His friendship with Sheila Gebhardt was still another matter. Mama loved Sheila, but she and Van were approaching the age where the friendship they enjoyed could easily change into something more adult and serious. Van must find a Jewish girl, Mama decided. She felt that she could, with a little effort, help solve these problems. After coming to that conclusion, she was able to sleep most of the night.

Van lay in his bed in the darkness of his room, wondering what he was going to do. The night's events had combined to make him miserable and afraid. The sudden revelations about Rudy greatly troubled him: his having been in trouble, his not being a Jew—a bad thing according to Mama—and his participation in the Nazi Party. Mama wanted Van to stop seeing Rudy altogether. He would have to do as Mama wished and stop seeing Rudy. "We'll see," the inner voice said to him and laughed at him in his misery.

Ignoring that wretched voice from his hated tormentor, he switched his thoughts to Sheila. He found no comfort there. Again, he ached to love her sexually, but he could not. He fantasized about sex with her and it was like two wooden mannequins: mechanical, devoid of any emotion or feeling. "Stupid dreamer," it said and laughed at his efforts.

In desperation he tried to remember Mama's explanation to his question about being Jewish. He prayed, "God of our people, please help me, one of Your Chosen People. You know what I want. Please answer my prayer."

"Don't hold your breath until He does," it screamed out to him.

Van jumped from the bed and went to the window, opening it and gulping the cool night air, listening to the sounds of the approaching storm. After a few moments at the window, he went back to bed. Unable to find a solution for any of his problems, he worried and tossed all night, hardly sleeping. The spring storm rolled over Baden-Baden, unleashing its fury on the valley. Van gave it little notice, his mind preoccupied with his many problems.

4

"So YOU WANT AN APARTMENT of your own?"

"Yes, I do. Now don't tell me I'm only sixteen and can't handle it by myself. You know I've been practically on my own all my life anyway."

"Why do you want your own place? Aren't you happy here at the Adlon?" Tatina asked him, placing her cigarette in the overly long cigarette holder.

Franz watched her delicately fitting the cigarette into the end of the holder and, when she was ready, he walked over to the chaise lounge and, using the lighter from the table, lit the cigarette for her. He placed the heavy lighter back on the table and seated himself in one of the plush Queen Anne chairs placed around the room. Tatina blew smoke in Franz's direction and waited for his answer.

"Tatina, you know I'm happy here. I love the Adlon; it's home. But I need my own place so I can practice my dancing and my singing without bothering anyone. And besides . . . " He paused, searching for the right words or the courage to use them.

"And besides what?" Tatina interrupted, secretly enjoying every moment of the conversation.

"I have already taken a place," he blurted out to her. "It's a small apartment in the Westend. The building is on one of the highest spots in that area and, from my front window, you can see almost all of Berlin. It's really nice, and also inexpensive."

Tatina smiled slyly and asked, "And just how will you pay the rent and your other expenses?"

Franz fumbled nervously with a small statue from the marble coffee table. This was one of the few times in his life that he had been afraid to answer his mother.

"Franz, put that statue back on the table before you break it. You know it is quite valuable, and you are so damned nervous, you're going to drop it any minute now."

Tatina snuffed the half-smoked cigarette out in the ash tray, never taking her eyes off Franz. The entire conversation was a delight for her. She loved being in command of every situation, and there was no doubt about who was in command of this one.

Franz placed the statue back on the table, knocking it over as he released it. It fell clattering loudly on the marble top but did not break.

"See. Just as I said," Tatina said triumphantly, pinching her stomach with two of her long fingernails to keep from breaking into peals of laughter.

"I have a job," Franz finally said. "I start Monday at a cabaret. It's only a small job, but it's what I want. I will be singing and dancing in the chorus. It's the chance I've been waiting for."

Tatina did not reply immediately. She watched him squirm for a while longer. Then she got up, walked over to the window and looked out for a few moments. Franz watched and dreaded her refusal that was surely coming. She turned from the window and looked at Franz, checking her hair with her right hand, making certain every strand was in place.

"Marvelous!" she finally said, her face beaming brightly. "I think that is a wonderful idea. And you say you have a job as a performer in a cabaret?"

"Yes," Franz was able to reply. He was so shocked and relieved that she approved, he could hardly speak.

"Well, I'm truly pleased you have decided to do this. I think it will be an exciting experience for you and you'll probably be a star before the year is out. And, of course, I will supplement your wages."

"Really?" he asked. "That would be nice. At least until I'm a star and then you can stop."

"Well, let me know if you need anything, dear," she said, looking at her watch. "I really must be running, Franz. I am on my way to the Imperial Palace for a party honoring some professor. I believe his name is Einstadt. No, that's not right. It's Einstein. Albert Einstein, whoever he is. Never heard of him, but we're going to an affair in his honor.

"Let me know how things go. Call me and tell me where you'll be performing."

She was gone. Franz sat in the chair somewhat befuddled. He had not expected her consent, in fact he had rehearsed all of his arguments for days. What a waste of time that had been, he concluded.

Franz had worried about his height when he went for the tryout at the cabaret. Only five feet, ten inches tall, he felt he might be too short for the chorus. As it turned out, he was just the height they were looking for. That was fine, he thought, also feeling that he had grown as tall as he would ever be.

His job in the chorus was not easy and the hours were long. It was usually near sunrise before he got home. Tatina had voiced no objection when he stopped going to school. Tatina never objected to anything he did, not even his very private life. She knew about his sexual life, but it never concerned her. After all, Berlin was full of men that were "that way". It was in vogue, she told her escort one night. They had stopped by The Eldorado to watch the female impersonators perform. They both thought it would be such fun.

During an intermission, Tatina turned to the Prince, her escort, and matter-of-factly said, "You know, of course, that my son is . . . How do you say it? Inverted? Inversion? Bent? Well, whatever the term is, that's what he is."

"You mean he likes men?" the Prince replied casually.

"Yes, I do believe you found the exact phrase."

"That's nice," the Prince said and proceeded to order more drinks.

Yes Tatina thought, it *is* nice. Whatever Franz does is perfectly fine and acceptable. In Berlin, anything is acceptable as long as it's fun and entertaining. Such a cosmopolitan city Berlin is, she thought. How I love it.

Franz walked from the subway station down Charlottenstrasse on his way to the cabaret, working his way through the crowds. The weather was warm and it seemed to Franz that everyone was on the Berlin streets. He wore a simple blue polo shirt and light beige corduroy trousers. The blue of his shirt made the green of his eyes appear darker.

The area near the subway station was crowded with beggars and people whom Franz considered low class. He walked faster to get to the better section of the city. An old man wearing a tattered and torn great coat that dragged along the ground approached him and asked if he had any money he could spare. Franz felt embarrassed by the question. Of course he had money, he always had money. He almost gagged when the old man's odor filled his nostrils and throat, the taste of the smell like rotted potato peelings.

Digging in his trouser pocket, Franz pulled out a little more than eight marks. Placing the money in the old man's filthy hand, he smiled and hurriedly went on his way. The old man stared unbelievingly at the large sum of money, those were marks, not pfennigs. When he looked up, Franz was about twenty feet from him.

"God bless you, Sir! God bless you forever!" he wheezed out as loud as he could.

Franz barely heard him, just enough to understand what he had said. He *has* blessed me, Franz thought, looking at the multitude of sad people all along the street. Germany was full of such people, but they were not so evident in the Berlin that he knew. Conditions were desperate all over the country, and yet the elegant life flourished in Berlin. Within the midst of the poverty and hardship Berlin existed, an island of wealth, social amenities, new-found freedoms and previously unheard of liberties. It was the antithesis of almost the entire rest of Germany in these years following the Great War.

Franz turned down Unter Den Linden. The number of people on the sidewalks of the broad street was just as great as on Charlottenstrasse. The great difference was that these people were not poor and wretched but well-dressed and urbane. People carried parcels out of the stores, shopping and enjoying the day. Women walked together chatting merrily, some arm in arm. Men and women walked along together, some holding hands, obviously convinced, Franz thought, that they were in love. This was Franz's Berlin, his city of excitement and culture. He went by the Adlon to visit with Tatina for a short while, but she was not there. He should have known that she would be out, he thought. Coming out of the Adlon, he spoke to the doorman and crossed the street. He turned left on Friedrichstrasse and walked a few blocks, passing the Winter Garden Theater, the main subway terminal and the Comic Opera. After walking across the Weidendammer Bridge which took him to the other side of the Spree River, he turned up a narrow side street. About three blocks more and he arrived at the cabaret.

He stood and looked at the rather shabby exterior of the building. There were no windows; they had been bricked up years ago. But still hanging above the closed-in windows were gaudy green and white awnings which matched the one over the main entrance. Over one entrance was a large lighted sign: CABARET. Looks like hell from the outside, he thought. But inside—how different it was! His spirits rose and the blood rushed more quickly through his veins as he thought about the crowd that would pack the cabaret for the all-night entertainment. He walked down the narrow alley beside the building to enter through the stage door.

When Franz opened the door and stepped inside the cabaret, the familiar smells of the place and the sounds of the other performers practicing or merely talking among themselves affected him like a strong drug. He was immediately caught up in the atmosphere of the place: a feeling of happiness beyond expression engulfed him. This is where I belong, he thought. Here, in this place of such fun and excitement in this great and beautiful city of Berlin.

5

V AN BUSILY PILED THE TRASH from the cafe into the garbage cans in the rear of the kitchen. Working more at the cafe with each passing month, he had little time for much else other than school and the athletic activities in which he participated. It was spring, almost time for another annual spring party. His mind wandered back to the last spring party, the one that had been held the same night the Nazis held their first large demonstration in Baden-Baden. Everything had been different then, Van thought, as he scraped the piles of leftover food from the plates into the garbage can. Most of his friends that were not Jewish had drifted away. They wanted nothing to do with him except when he excelled in a sporting event at school. They cheered him loudly, but seldom talked with him or associated with him. They were really cheering for Baden-Baden, not for him, Van realized. He was Jewish, and he was finally beginning to realize some of what that meant.

"It's the Nazis' doing!" he remembered Papa telling him when he had asked about the strange way his friends were acting. "They are growing strong and more numerous each day. You wouldn't believe how many there are even here in Baden-Baden." Van recalled how red Papa's face got any time the Nazis were mentioned. He wasn't happy anymore, Van realized. Since the night Papa had seen the Nazi demonstration, he had changed so much. Never joking with the customers at the cafe as he had always done before, he looked worried and sad all the time.

Van stuck his foot on top of a garbage-filled can and pushed the trash down, packing it tightly. His loss of so many friends bothered him, but he had other secret problems that troubled him more. The closely guarded emotions within him were taking over a larger part of his life. He caught himself looking at other boys or men, the horrid inner feeling of desire growing stronger. Each time this happened, he tried to push the despised feeling back to its dark hiding place.

This has been a terrible year, Van thought. He placed the lids on the garbage cans, still thinking about the past year. He realized that he had only seen Rudy once or twice since the night of the spring party. It upsets Mama so much, he thought. I have done my best to avoid him. I still don't understand why she thinks he's so bad. He lifted one of the heavy garbage cans and took it out into the alley behind the cafe.

He sat the can down among the other cans and piles of garbage from the businesses around Papa's cafe. Wiping his brow on his shirt sleeve, he thought he heard someone call his name in a low barely-audible whisper. He looked around and saw no one. Again, he heard his name whispered. This time he realized it was coming from behind a large pile of empty boxes at the end of the alley. He approached cautiously. As he rounded the pile of boxes, he saw Rudy, looking completely out of character, crouching down among the boxes like a homeless dog trying to hide from the dogcatcher.

"What are you doing hiding in there, Rudy?"

"I need help, Van. They are looking for me everywhere. I can't go home, even if I wanted to. They are there waiting for me. I've seen them every place I've tried to go for help. You are the only one I could think of to help me."

Van remembered Mama telling him that night in the sitting room that Rudy had been in trouble before. He could still see her "I told you so" look when Papa told of seeing Rudy in the demonstration. In his mind, she gave him the same look now.

"Who is looking for you, Rudy?"

"The police."

"What for?"

"I killed a traitor. He needed killing and I killed him. I should be a national hero, not hiding from the police in an alley!"

Never having talked to anyone who was an admitted murderer, Van was frightened but also a bit curious. This was the first time he had seen Rudy in months. He had missed his childhood hero. Although Rudy said he had committed murder, he still stirred something within Van.

"Rudy, you know I will help. But what can I do?"

"Meet me down at the creek tonight after dark. You know, the place where we fish. I must leave Baden-Baden as quickly as I can. I need a little food and some money. Do you have any money, Van?"

"Yes," Van lied, "I have money."

"Can I borrow it? I need as much as you can spare."

"How much do you mean, Rudy?" Van asked. He knew he had only a few marks and he had no idea how much Rudy expected.

"Four or five hundred marks, at least. I've got to get away from here and I only have about forty marks."

Van was stunned by the amount Rudy wanted. He had never in his life had that much money at one time, except after his bar mitzvah. Not yet having the slightest idea where he could possibly get that much money, he still replied boldly, "Yes, I'll get it for you, Rudy. I'll meet you at the fishing place about seven. Where will you go when you leave Baden-Baden?"

"I have a lot of friends in the Party. I'll contact them. They'll help me, I know. I can't contact the members of the Party here in Baden-Baden because they are also being watched by the police."

"What Party are you talking about?" Van asked even though he knew perfectly well.

"It doesn't matter, Van. Just be there tonight, with the money, please!"

"I'll be there, Rudy. You can count on your Little Brother. I've got to get back to the cafe or Papa will be out here looking for me. Be careful, Rudy. I'll see you about seven."

Van started for the back door of the cafe, leaving Rudy concealed among the empty boxes. He thought about what he had agreed to do. Was it right or wrong? Mama and Papa insisted Rudy was bad and would harm Van in some way. He felt that they were probably correct. Van was old enough to realize that something was happening in Germany, something connected with the Nazi Party that meant bad times for his family. However, he was unable to resist Rudy's request. Had it not been for his secret yearnings, he knew he would probably have told Rudy that he had no money and could not get any. Instead he had stood there, talking to Rudy, yearning to grab him and hold him and cry.

Papa did not understand why Van left work right before the dinner business. Van told him he had to leave to do something important. Papa consented, of course, because it was rare that his son did not work when he was supposed to work. The only time he was not working was when he was either at school or taking part in some athletic event.

Van reached home nearly breathless, having run the entire distance. Mama was not there. In his room he was able to get about one hundred marks together. Those marks that had been put back for a rainy day were dragged out of their hiding place. If Rudy needed them, that was as big a flood as there would ever be. A few marks more than one hundred was all he could find. "Not enough," he sighed aloud. Then he remembered where Mama kept some money for emergencies. He raced downstairs and into the sitting room, going straight to her sewing basket. She had about fifty-five marks. He borrowed it, scribbling an I.O.U. and leaving it in the basket where the money had been.

Van walked slowly down Lichtentaler, trying to think where he could find more money. Before he had left the house, he had hastily made a few sandwiches for Rudy, and he carried them now in a sack wrapped in one of his sweaters. He dropped his bundle and, bending down to pick it up, his gold watch caught the sun and glinted brightly.

"That's it!" he exclaimed in excitement. "I'll pawn the watch! It should bring two or three hundred marks from old Kern. It's an expensive watch, very valuable."

Three elderly women, taking the sun along Lichtentaler, heard him talking to himself and shook their heads knowingly in unison.

"Bertholds boy," one said.

"Yes, pitiful, isn't it?" the second replied.

The third old woman went into a racking, coughing spasm.

"Quick, give Aunt Olla a cigarette before she coughs to death!"

One fumbled in her bag, found the cigarettes and gave Aunt Olla one. She lighted the cigarette and the coughing subsided. The three of them stood silently, watching Van as he hurried down the Avenue.

"Mr. Kern, Mr. Kern, I have something of great value I need to pawn," Van said as he entered the pawn shop.

"Oy vey! Another one yet with something of great value to pawn in my poor shop."

After much haggling, old Kern gave Van two hundred marks, and Van was on his way to Rudy's Secret Place.

He was more than thirty minutes late and was afraid that Rudy would have given up on his bringing the money and be gone. There was no moon and it was already dark in the dense forest. When Van finally arrived at the fishing spot, he could not find Rudy. He called his name over and over, but no one answered. Van's heart ached. Rudy would think Van was not going to help him. His Little Brother had betrayed him.

"Van, over here. In the trees. Hurry!"

Van rushed to the sound of Rudy's voice. His foot caught in the upraised roots of a large tree and he fell forward to the ground, sandwiches scattering in all directions.

Van did not know if he had hurt himself. Rudy was at his side helping him from the ground. He could have broken every bone in his body and not known or cared. Rudy held him, his right arm around Van's back and his hand holding him at the waist. Using his other hand, Rudy checked to see if Van had broken any arms or legs.

"Are you hurt, Van?"

"No, I don't think so."

Rudy released him and Van wondered if he had to break a leg for Rudy to hold him.

"I brought the food. It's here somewhere. I also brought the money you wanted. It's only three hundred and eighty marks. That's all I could get. I'm sorry it is such a small amount," Van babbled as he tried to wrench control from his private monster.

"That's not a small amount, Van. It is more than I really expected. I appreciate what you have done for me. I won't forget it. I must go. Take care and don't tell anyone you've seen me."

"Rudy, when will I see you again?"

"That's hard to say, Van. I just don't know. I'm not even sure just where I am going. I really won't forget what you've done tonight. I can't talk any more, I must get away. 'Bye, Van."

"'Bye, Rudy. Be careful."

He was gone. He didn't even try to find the sandwiches. Van felt as though part of him had died, a debilitating sensation of great loneliness and emptiness. He knew he would never see Rudy again.

"Rudy, I love you," Van murmured in the darkness of that fateful night.

No one heard his declaration but God.

Rudolf Hoess did not elude the authorities for long. When he was captured and tried, he was sentenced to life in prison for the murder he had committed. Germany was not yet ready to recognize his act as heroic.

Papa's friend, old Kern, the pawnbroker who had purchased Van's gold watch, managed to let this fact slip in conversation with Papa. Papa bought back the watch for Van, but when Van refused to tell him why he had needed the money, Papa would not return it to him. He placed the watch in a glass case and kept the case prominently displayed in the sitting room as a reminder to Van of his transgression. His refusal to tell why he had needed the money hurt Papa much more than the pawning of the watch. He never completely forgave Van for pawning his bar mitzvah gift and then refusing to confide in him.

While Rudy was confined by the walls and iron bars of prison, Van continued to create his own prison, not constructed of mortar and rock or bars of iron and steel but of the two handmaidens of total despair, fear and ignorance. For fear of loosening his secret desires, he limited his participation in so many youthful activities that he became almost a recluse. His only real social contact other than school was sports.

He engaged in every sporting activity available. All of these activities, being socially acceptable, filled his parents with great pride. As a means of escape, he became an outstanding student and one of the best young athletes in Baden-Baden.

Van did not consciously choose the direction his life was taking. He exerted extreme effort to change the secret part of his life. Nothing he tried worked. He seemed to be condemned to the abnormal, he concluded. All he had been taught and all that he had experienced merged together to properly classify exactly what in life was normal and what was abnormal. The classifications were already made for him.

In desperation, still struggling to find clearly defined, black and white answers to his questions, he decided to try new methods. During his last year of public school, he dated several girls, but never Sheila, always choosing Jewish girls to please Mama. He purposely avoided any association with his male friends.

One of his temerarious efforts resulted in complete disaster. He had shyly approached one of Baden-Baden's ladies of the night in the older part of the city, near Rudy's home. Predictably, she accepted his halting, stuttering invitation. She led him to her sparsely furnished room. Van's mouth was so dry that his tongue felt like one of Mama's powder puffs. A sickening, acidic taste flooded his mouth and seemed to spread throughout his body. His joints ached and his knees turned to gelatin.

Completely naked, the woman was lying upon the bed, her legs spread open, one hand massaging her breasts while the other seemed to Van to disappear between her thighs. She was not homely but actually quite attractive, both clothed and without clothing. Her breasts were well formed, pert and standing erect, the nipples taut from her manipulations. She breathed rapidly, a husky sort of breathing, causing her small rounded belly to move, rising and falling noticeably. Her pubic hairs were dark brown providing stark contrast to her too blonde hair. One leg was raised, the knee obscuring part of her face from Van's view.

"Well, and what's a young Adonis like you doing out on a night like this? Did your girl get you all excited and then pull the plug?"

Van felt it coming but he was powerless to prevent it. In great body-racking heaves, he threw up and the vomit splashed on her and on the bed. He could not stop or turn away. Finally, when he was able to stop the horrible retching, he fell to his knees on the floor. Leaning his head on the edge of the bed, he tried to regain his spent energy.

Having leaped from the bed and Van's line of fire, the woman now stood on the opposite side of the bed. She had taken a towel from her night stand and was wiping Van's half-digested dinner from her legs.

"What's wrong with you?" she screamed at him. "Are you sick or insane?"

Van felt small and insignificant: a microscopic creature thrust into the adult world and expected by all to perform as a full grown man. He could not even raise his head from the soiled bed to look at her. Physically ill and embarrassed speechless, he did not know what he was supposed to do. She told him.

"Get out of here you rotten fag!" Her shrill voice sliced through the room and penetrated him with the force and pain of millions of sharp, thin daggers. "You are perverted! That's it! Get out of my place right now or I'll beat the hell out of you!"

Van rose to his feet. His head was about to fall from his shoulders, his stomach was turned inside out and the room was suddenly filled with thousands of tiny, sparkling stars.

"I'm . . . I'm sorry, Ma'am," he said slowly, backing toward the door.

"You god-damn right you are! You're a sorry specimen of a man. You're not a man at all," she continued, her rage feeding on itself. "You come in here all big and good looking and it's all an act. You were pretending to be a man and you fooled even me for a while, but no more. I'll tell you what you are. You are slime; a nasty and repulsive something that crawled out of the sewers."

He ran from the room and out of the shabby building. Not until he got to Lichtentaler Avenue did he stop running and try to calm himself before going home. The foul odor of vomit was on him but he was only concerned with what was inside of him. He walked around to one of the back doors of his dark house. Thank God everyone is in bed, he thought while he stole up the winding stairs to his room. Safely in his room, he silently closed his door and heard the old familiar voice say to him, "Fool! Did you enjoy your masquerade tonight?"

He sat on his bed in the dark room, reliving the night over and over again. "Enough!" he said to himself. "Enough!" He finally had to face what he felt were the realities of his situation and condition. He did not understand all of the things the woman had said to him, but he understood enough to arrive at some conclusions and ideas that would guide him for the remainder of his life, or so he thought that night.

His moral upbringing and the teachings of his Jewish faith and heritage predetermined his conclusions. He could not separate himself from the influence of all those years with Papa and Mama. The Sabbaths stretched in endless succession from that day backward to his earliest recollections. The classes with Rabbi Eschel repeating and repeating the tenets of true Judaism reverberated throughout his conscious and subconscious mind. All those forces working feverishly within Germany to push him into the grasping, clutching, all-encompassing arms of his Jewish heritage were so strong and so ever present that he could not resist.

There was no one to guide him or answer his questions. Answers had been planted in his mind years ago. He sincerely believed that he was the only person in his beloved Baden-Baden that had the secret monster within. It was his and his alone. Not once did he consider that there might be even one other; the possibility never occurred to him. Van experienced an almost unbearable loneliness in trying to deal with his torment, never being able to discuss it with another person, an understanding human being. The tragedy in Van's plight was not so much having to cope with the problem, but having, or perhaps choosing, to cope with it alone.

Alone, Van searched and found what he believed to be fundamental truths. He was evil, he concluded. The desire within him was, in some strange way, connected with Satan. Sexual things must forever be taboo for him. Had the Jewish faith provided the sanctuary of celibacy for its rabbis, he would have escaped to that. Since it did not, he imposed upon himself his own form of rigid celibate self-denial. He pushed his unnamed emotions and desires to the farthest part of his mind, completely unaware of the self-hate that replaced them.

6

U PROARIOUS APPLAUSE PUNCTUATED WITH hearty shouts of "Bravo! Bravo!" and "More! More!" clamored in his ears as he rushed from the floor of the cabaret to the performers' dressing area. Applause, he thought, the performers' narcotic. Crowding around him like bees swarming the hive sheltering their queen, the other dancers and singers congratulated him and shared his triumph with hugs, kisses and squeezes. The diners continued their applause, sincere in their desire to hear him sing again.

"They want another encore, Franz!"

Franz Richter walked briskly and happily back to the cabaret's huge circular dining room, weaving his way among the tables, dodging waiters, busboys and adoring, over-zealous fans. Hands were all over him, patting their congratulations while a few feminine hands grasped and grabbed for more. Finally, feeling as though he had just come through the enemy lines, he made his appearance in the circular performing area in the center of the room. The house lights were once again dimmed and the man on the uppermost balcony operating the largest klieg light in the place turned the huge light on the entire central performing area, gradually decreasing the spot until it was a thin beacon of pure white light shining only on Franz. Bathed in the high-intensity light, his white, skin-tight trousers hugged every crease and curve of his lower body. His blue lamé blouse opened to his waist revealing his bare chest. His smiles sent the women in the crowd into a delirium of screams and more applause. He bowed gratefully to the large crowd packed into the room and stood upright again. Assuming an erotically suggestive pose, he pretended to attempt to quiet the audience. His wavy blond hair seemed to capture the spotlight and send it rushing outward from his body to the audience. Countless darts of light accompanied the suggestions of pure animal lust shooting from his countenance. The effect was electrifying, seeming to place the entire assemblage under his power.

Once again he raised his blue lamé-clad arms for quiet. The silence was so sudden and complete it was deafening. Franz thought, God, you could hear a change of heart. Then he began singing; his crystal fine tenor voice splitting the smoke-laden air with wave after wave of melodic beauty. The old German ballad he sang was known by all those crowded into the cabaret, but Franz brought it to life as they had never heard it before. He used no instrumental accompaniment; further emphasizing the clarity, tonal perfection and beauty of his voice. There were few in the gathering that did not weep.

When he finished the last note, he went immediately into one of the newer, more risqué songs, allowing no time for applause. He was joined by the full orchestra, the other singers and the dancers filling the floor with frenetic activity. The spotlight at first was on Franz alone and then grew to the size of the cabaret, constantly changing colors. Ten additional spotlights joined the original one. Circles of light, endlessly alternating colors, exploded from a pinpoint size to flood the entire cabaret and then, just as rapidly, dwindled back down to pinpoint him.

Franz relaxed in the small dressing room, too exhausted to change the clothes he had worn in his performance. He decided to wear them home. His bronzed body was covered with perspiration, as was the blue lamé shirt hanging over the back of his chair. His white trousers, rendered transparent by the moisture, clung more tightly than ever to his body revealing more than during his performance. The details of his lower body appeared; he clearly wore nothing but trousers, his matted dark body hair visible through the sheer fabric.

He slumped in the straight-backed chair with his legs extended forward, his lower body forming a straight line slanting from the floor upward to his waist, and swallowed great gulps of beer from the large stein provided by the cabaret's owner. The cabaret's steins always reminded him of Munich and the Oktoberfest. So much beer, so many people, such laughter and gaiety. It would be fun to go again this year to the annual beer celebration.

Franz was alone in the dressing room. He looked around the room, making certain no one was there, and reached under the top of the dressing table. Blindly searching with his hand, he found the package and brought it from its hiding place. He opened it, took out a cigarette and put the light green pack with the red circle back in its secret place. American cigarettes, Lucky Strikes, best cigarette in the world, he thought. He found a match on the table top, struck it on the bottom of his chair and lit the cigarette. Sucking in a large draught of smoke, he held it for a long time, relishing the sensation of his first cigarette of the day. My one and only vice, he mused. Nothing like a good cigarette with beer, or coffee, or after eating or sex.

He was not supposed to smoke. "It will ruin your voice and your career," his voice instructor had told him. When he did sneak a secret smoke, he felt guilty, the only real feeling of guilt he ever knew.

Taped to the wall of the dressing room, directly in front of Franz was the current cabaret poster. An artist's impression of a performance similiar to the one Franz had just given filled the poster; the spinning dancers encircling the much larger central figure of Franz.

He looked at the poster while he smoked the cigarette and relaxed from the tremendous physical and emotional exertion of performing. He had made it, he thought, He was at the top. All those long hours of voice lessons, practicing, dance lessons, exercise, dieting and hard work had finally paid off. It seemed he had been working for this success every day since he was born. Now he had it, and he loved it.

Franz was a unique man. Not only was he successful in his work, a labor he enjoyed so much he had never considered any other; he was also a completely happy individual with no apparent problems or burdens. He lived each day with such zestful fervor that many thought it was all a pretense. It was not. Franz was genuinely happy. He accepted his sexual desires as healthy and natural. God may not have made him this way, but He certainly did not bother Himself one way or the other about it.

"Are you ready to go, Franz?" Michael yelled through the dressing room door.

"Be right out." Franz answered. He snuffed out the cigarette on the inside of a make-up tin lid and flushed the butt down the filthy sink. Waving his arms to disperse the smoke, he hurried back to the dressing table and dusted the air with a can of powder to hide the smoke odor in case Michael came into the room. Franz had told friends about his not smoking with the idea that they would be his conscience. He regretted having done this because they all seemed to thoroughly enjoy the role.

He wrapped the blue shirt around his shoulders, grabbed his rumpled street clothes and left the room.

"You've been smoking," Michael chided as Franz shut the dressing room door.

"Oh, God!" Franz mumbled almost inaudibly, "here it comes."

They left through the back alley and walked down the narrow side street. Michael Schmidt, one of the dancers at the cabaret, lectured Franz every step of the way on the evils of cigarettes. Franz had heard this particular speech so often he was almost able to say it in unison with him.

"Deliver me," he said shortly, "from so many consciences."

"What did you say?" Michael said, forgetting at which point his sermon had been interrupted. Oh well, he was bored with the lecture also.

"Don't look back right now, but I think some brown shirts are following us," Franz whispered.

Michael turned and looked behind them immediately.

"Oh, hell! Now you've done it. I suppose if I had told you to look at them this instant, you would have waited an hour or two," Franz whispered, his voice revealing that he was provoked with Michael for having looked back so suddenly.

"They *are* brown shirts and I think they really are following us!" Michael said, terror pitching his voice higher than usual.

They began to walk faster. The brown shirts were well known to both of them—a sordid collection of unemployed ruffians who had a license to commit any crime now that they were members of the Nazi Party. They roamed the streets of Berlin spreading terror and fear. Franz and Michael were justifiably afraid.

They walked faster, but the faster they walked the faster the brown shirts walked. It was not long until they were all running.

"Catch the dirty sons-of-bitches!"

"Don't let those queers get away! Get them!"

The brown shirts constantly harrassed Jews, homosexuals and anyone else who was not exactly like them. Being different automatically made one a target; being different was the unforgiveable sin. Michael and Franz had left the cabaret that night without changing their costumes or removing their stage make-up. The brown shirts, wandering the streets looking for Jews and other "misfits", had seen the cabaret costumes as a bull sees the waving cape, a simple case of the book being judged by its cover.

As pursued and pursuers neared the crowded and well lighted Unter den Linden, Michael and Franz were caught and dragged into a dark alley. They both struggled mightily with the six men, fighting as best they could against the overwhelming odds. They had no weapons, they were tired from the long night's work and neither of them was consumed with burning hate as were their assailants. Using clubs, their fists and their heavily booted feet, the six brown shirts beat them savagely, showing no restraint, no compassion, no concern for the fact that they were human beings. Franz was beaten and kicked until he lost consciousness. The last faint, hazy thing he remembered was a fat brown-shirted man kicking him in the groin.

Franz was brought back to consciousness by a bucket of water thrown in his face.

"Two rotten queers," he heard a man say. When he was finally able to open his eyes and see through the matted blood, he realized that he was surrounded by at least four policemen.

"This one's dead," one of the policemen said, turning Michael's body over roughly with his booted foot.

"Come on you filth! It's down to headquarters with you."

They pulled Franz, feet dragging, to the police car and took him to the neighborhood police station. At the station, Franz was treated as a common criminal. They took his papers and made elaborate entries about him in a large ledger. No one inquired about his physical condition although it was obvious that he had been either beaten or hit by an immense truck. No mention was made of Michael, and Franz had been too dazed to comprehend the muttered remark about the other one being dead. After a prolonged period of painful waiting, he was taken to a large cell with some twenty-five or more men in it. The police handled him like a piece of garbage as they threw him into the cell.

"Here's another faggot, men. He's just dying for a good banging," said one of the police who pushed him into the crowd of prisoners. Franz had some recollection of hands pawing at his clothing. As the new pain being inflicted upon him became more and more unbearable, he again mercifully passed into the welcome world of unconsciousness.

He woke the next morning without clothes, his body covered with bruises and blood-encrusted gashes. Caked, dried blood was on most of his body and the floor where he lay. He ached all over so badly that he hardly noticed the cold. Moving caused him excruciating pain. When he was able to pull himself up to a sitting position, he was viciously slapped by a grimy, hulking man. The man then spat and urinated on him, eventually joined in this task by practically all the men in the cell.

Franz felt defeated; on the verge of death or insanity; earnestly wishing for either. Anything to end this unbelievable nightmare. He fleetingly thought that at least the urine was warming to his cold, naked body. As the pain from his many injuries, both those inflicted by the brown shirts and by the other prisoners, became strong enough to plummet him into oblivion again, he mumbled, "Oh God! Help me, God!"

His prayer was unanswered for many hours. About mid-morning Franz was shook awake by one of the policemen and thrown an old, filthy, torn blanket. He wrapped the tattered piece of stinking cloth around his naked, injured body. The policeman opened the cell door and told him to come with him. He walked behind the officer, his entire body feeling like one giant festering boil. His pain increased so much that he stopped and leaned against the wall, his vision blurred, near exhaustion. Grabbing him by the arm, the policeman literally dragged him to the central receiving room of the station. The blanket, draped around his shoulders, gaped open and flopped loosely. When the policeman got him into the main portion of the police station, he shoved him forward to the rail where Kurt Hiller, a leader in the German struggle for homosexual rights, was waiting for him.

"Franz! What in God's name has happened to you?" Kurt asked when he recognized the stooped, draped man. He hurried around the railing to Franz's side to help him walk to the main desk. The police behaved as if they did not want to touch him.

"Kurt, I'm so glad to see you," Franz said weakly. "It's a long story. I'll tell you later. Let's please get out of this place as soon as we can."

"We'll go as soon as I pay your bail," Kurt assured him.

"My bail! What bail? You mean I have been charged with a crime?"

"Yes, disturbing the peace, I believe that's what they called it."

"Disturbing the peace! Me? What about those . . ."

Kurt quickly interrupted Franz before he said too much, "We'll talk about all this when we get out of here."

Kurt paid the bail and they slowly walked from the police station to Kurt's car.

"Better find another corner to work, Girlie," one of the policemen yelled laughingly at them.

Kurt looked at Franz when he heard this parting comment. He shook his head dejectedly, started the car and merged into the traffic.

"Do you think that other people will ever realize that we are humans with feelings just as they are?" Kurt asked, really thinking aloud more than asking Franz a question. "I'm about to give up all hope. Why must they continue to do things like they did to you?"

Franz did not reply. He felt no pain from the parting remark. New emotions for Franz, hate and real anger—not the anger of a mad or disappointed child—were swelling to the point of overflow and he was in too much physical pain to try to express his new animosity and rage. He rode along with Kurt through Berlin in absolute silence.

Franz stared vacantly out the car window as they rode along, the beauty and brightness of the crowded Berlin streets not exciting him as they always had before this day. He suddenly noticed that Kurt had missed the turn that would take them to his apartment.

"Why are you going this way?" Franz asked. "You just passed the street I live on. You should have turned back there."

"I am not taking you to your apartment. You need to be looked at by a doctor and we have a good doctor on the staff of the Institute where I work," Kurt replied, continuing his journey to the Institute that housed the Scientific-Humanitarian Committee that Kurt had co-chaired for years.

"How are you feeling now?" he asked Franz.

"I hurt all over. The pain is worse when I walk or sit," Franz answered. He suddenly remembered Michael and felt a slight twinge of guilt for not asking about him sooner. "Kurt, where is Michael? Why didn't you pay his bail? Wasn't he arrested too?"

Kurt looked at him sadly. "The police told me he was dead, Franz. Didn't you know?"

"Dead? Michael? No, I didn't know. Are you sure he's dead and they weren't just lying to you? Who did it? Did they give any details? Was it the brown shirts or the police?"

"I assumed it was the brown shirts, but it could have been the police. I've seen the police turn away and ignore the actions of the brown shirts many times. Ever since that pig, Goebbels, formed those Rolkommando units, they have roamed the streets of Berlin and other cities disrupting meetings of any group that opposed them, beating or killing Jews, homosexuals and anyone they happen not to like. They are turning Germany into a police state. I am afraid we are all in for some terrible times."

"Kurt, if Michael was really killed, where is his body? Did they mention anything about his body to you?"

"No," Kurt replied, "but that doesn't surprise me. I don't know what they are doing with the bodies of their victims, but they have some way of disposing of them. Bodies are seldom returned to the families. They just vanish. Since Michael has no living relatives, I would suppose they would try to get some information from you or me, but they didn't today and we'll probably never hear from them again, about Michael anyway. Actually, he may not have been killed. All we have is their word about that. There are so many concentration camps in Germany now, filled with political prisoners, real criminals and God knows who else. It may be that a number of these 'dead' people are really in those camps. Frightening thought, isn't it? I suppose they could literally be called the 'living dead', officially dead but really alive and being used as slave labor or for some other purpose in those camps."

Kurt parked the car behind the Institute and they went in through the back entrance. They slowly made their way to the clinic in the Institute and into the examining room. Franz was washed, his wounds cleansed and the necessary stitches were made. It was evident he would not be able to do any performing for a long time. His face was so badly bruised and swollen that no amount of make-up would make him presentable. One eye was swollen shut, he now had eight stitches on his right cheek, and his upper lip had been split. Looking in the mirror, he decided the hunchback of Notre Dame might be a part he could play with little or no make-up.

"If I can't perform at the cabaret, I will have to find some way to earn a living for a while, I suppose," he sighed to Kurt. "I am not going to ask Tatina to start giving me money again."

"Don't worry about that. I am in need of some help here at the Committee. I think I can use you until your face heals and you are able to go back to singing. The pay is low but the work is for a good cause, our struggle for human dignity. Would you like to work with me?"

"Of course, Kurt. I would be grateful for the job, but I really think we are wasting our time and energy. If it weren't for the Nazis, we might have a chance. I think most Germans would have been agreeable to the new Penal Reform law, but not anymore. It is a lost cause, for our lifetime."

"No it isn't!" Kurt replied. "Even if you are correct, it's still a cause worth fighting for because it's right. It isn't based on lies or tainted with hate but rather on truth and has to do with love. We can't lose in the long run if we fight for the truth and the freedom to live."

"You may be right, Kurt. But it won't happen in our lifetime. Maybe ten, twenty or even fifty years from now people will recognize and accept the truth and let us live our lives freely."

7

T HERE MUST BE OVER A MILLION people here, thought Franz as he stood in the main square in Berlin. Hitler was already forty-five minutes late. He was always late for his speeches, a part of his manipulation of the crowd.

Franz had never before seen such a large number of people in one place at one time. Lines of thousands of soldiers, wearing black uniforms and swastikas, surrounded the large stage. Flags were all around the square, their black swastikas fluttering in the early evening breeze; the noise of their flapping reminded him of millions of birds taking flight.

Hitler arrived. The crowd went wild. He walked to the podium and waited for the cheering to subside. When the huge assemblage was so quiet that you could hear your own heart beat, he spoke of the rights of all Germans, the destiny of the Aryan to rule the world, the greatness of the German people. On and on he talked. At first, his speech was halting and boring, but after about ten minutes, he seemed to warm to the subject. He ranted with authority and much gesticulation, banging on the podium to emphasize many points. His excitement became evident and contagious. His speech continued, loud and with emphasis on each word.

The Jew is not a citizen of Germany! The Thousand Year Reich will thrive and flower without any Jew dog's participation.

The crowd roared its approval. It was mass hysteria, a fervor bordering on madness.

Homosexuality destroyed ancient Greece. Once legalized and turned loose, it extends its contagious effects like an inevitable law of nature to the best and most manly of characters, eliminating from the reproductive process those very men on whose offspring a nation depends. It is an evil that must be forever removed from the earth.

The crowd roared again. The tumult was more deafening than before.

Franz worriedly realized that the crowd had been pleased with the comments on Jewry, but they were ecstatic with Hitler's views on homosexuality. Objectively, Franz watched Hitler and concluded that the master of deceit and manipulation had discovered two common, learned, human prejudices and used them to unite his followers in a mutual society of hate and vengeance. Franz knew that most people had been taught to despise the Jew and the queer, almost from the cradle. He watched in amazement as Hitler continued to work his evil magic.

I am today declaring a national boycott of all Jewish businesses. No German will spend one penny with the Jews. As we spit out of our glorious land those of Jewish blood, we must also rid ourselves of the scourge of mankind, homosexuality. It is against God's laws and the laws of the new Third Reich!

As he backed from the microphone, the crowd erupted with "Sieg Heil! Sieg Heil!" The voices were as one. The crowd had become one voice, one mind, one monster. Franz knew his future was no longer within his power to control. It lay within the belly of that new demon being spawned by Adolf Hitler.

Frightening as it had been, Franz was not sorry he had attended the rally where Hitler spoke. The seriousness of the situation in Germany had finally been impressed upon him with shattering force. Seeing that strutting Nazi leader move and mold the crowd as he pleased made Franz realize the power Hitler possessed. Fear and terror were changing Franz's life and his outlook on life. He was now certain of the potential danger of life in Germany, not only for him but for anyone who was the least bit different. He had considered leaving the country altogether, but that was the coward's way. He had never been a coward and he did not feel inclined in that direction now. He had been openly homosexual his entire adult life, so there was little doubt about his bravery, he reasoned. Franz had observed that most members of a minority group, be they Jews, Gypsies or members of other minority groups, have no choice as to whether they will be open about their affiliation with their particular group. Not true of homosexuals, he thought. They have the choice of living a lie, constantly denying membership in that dark, secret society, or bravely admitting publicly that they are who they actually are. No coward would even consider such a risky life of openness as a homosexual. Franz could not live a lie. Denying the truth was never a serious alternative for him.

He had attended the rally in Berlin's main square alone since Kurt was now in the Oranienburg concentration camp north of Berlin, having been arrested on the twenty-third of March by the SS and sentenced soon after. His transgression was homosexuality.

After leaving Hitler's rally, Franz decided to stop for a beer at Tina's bar. He knocked on the door, the small peep-hole opened, an eye gazed out at him, the bolt was unlocked and Franz entered one of the few places where he felt totally free. Friends spoke, calling him by name. He stopped and chatted with many before finding a vacant seat at the bar. The dance floor was crowded with men enjoying the music. Franz did not much care for social dancing. He only enjoyed dancing in his cabaret performances.

Franz sat sipping his beer and thinking about the changes in his life the Nazis were causing. As he scanned the faces around the bar and then those around the small tables, he thought how alike the faces looked in the dim light, each a smiling, cheerful reproduction of its neighbor. In homosexual bars he often felt that he was at a masquerade ball where all the guests had accidentally worn the same mask, each looking the same as all the others. Except that this night one was different. When he glimpsed a certain mask at one of the tables, that mask suddenly became a face whose eyes were watching him intently. He scanned around the room again until he had seen all the masks, then casually looked back at the face that had been watching him, and it was still watching. Franz looked more closely at the man and turned back to his beer, but the face continued to gaze at him. He looked back and the man began to smile.

The man was about twenty, of medium height, with blond hair and strong, well-defined facial features. Very attractive, Franz thought. Taking his beer with him, he walked over to the young man's table.

"Hello. My name is Franz."

"Mine's Wolfgang. I'm glad you came over. Won't you sit here with me?"

Franz accepted the offered chair and noted that Wolfgang was even better looking at close range.

"I don't usually enjoy drinking alone," Franz said, making conversation. "I work in a cabaret. Sing mostly. What do you do?"

"I have just come home to Berlin from England where I was attending Oxford."

"Oxford. How interesting," Franz said, smiling at Wolfgang.

"Did you graduate?"

"No, I was told to return home immediately. So, here I am."

"Who told you to come home?"

"Our beloved Führer. I have been drafted or rather I have been given a commission. My father has great influence, it seems, and I'm now a lieutenant in the Army. I report tomorrow."

Franz began to feel uncomfortable. Could this handsome, young man be a spy for the SS, sent here to take names? Such a pity. Franz rose to leave the table.

Wolfgang put his hand on Franz's arm and said, "Wait. Don't leave. I am not one of Hitler's brown shirts yet, not until tomorrow. I am here in Tina's because this is where I want to be."

"Well, Wolfgang," Franz replied, sitting back down, "let me ask you a pointed question. Are you homosexual?"

Wolfgang flushed, his handsome face became a vivid red. After a moment of silence, he said, "Yes, I am . . . but I don't go around advertising it."

"I don't advertise it either; however I have nothing to be ashamed of. It was not my choice. It was my gift, I believe, from God. If I had the chance to choose whether I would be homosexual or otherwise tomorrow, I would choose to be homosexual!"

"I wish I were that free," Wolfgang replied.

"A man's freedom is sometimes in his own mind. If you think you are free, you are free."

"I don't find it that simple. I have lived a pretense so long I would not know how to change."

They talked and drank two more beers. Near midnight, Franz decided it was time to go home.

"Do you have a place to stay tonight, Wolfgang?"

"Yes, I'm staying with my parents."

There was a long pause as Franz got up from his chair to leave. Somewhat like an afterthought, Wolfgang said, "I don't have to stay with my parents. They have already gone to bed and will not know one way or the other." He looked at Franz like a frightened puppy. His pale blue eyes were one of his most striking characteristics.

Franz managed to say, "Would you care to spend the night at my place?"

"I think I'd like that."

They left together and walked in the cool, spring air of the Berlin night. Few people were about and the city was quiet at that late hour. They passed the square where, a few hours earlier, the nation's leader had warned the multitudes of the danger they faced from the very thing that was happening between Franz and Wolfgang. Franz was not thinking of that speech, however. His mind was filled with Wolfgang, not Adolf Hitler. His thoughts were of life, beauty, love and joy; not death, prejudice, hate and sadness. They walked together past the square, smiling at one another and talking of small, insignificant things. The hundreds of swastikas around the square flapped protestingly in the breeze.

At Franz's apartment they talked a while before preparing for bed. Franz loaned his new friend a pair of pajamas. Wolfgang was already in the big double bed when Franz came from the bathroom. He turned off the light and got into bed beside him. They both lay there silently, side by side, not touching for a seemingly endless while. The fingers of Wolfgang's right hand lightly touched the fingers of Franz's left hand; the touch was soft and gentle, bringing to Franz's mind Michelangelo's painting.

Franz awoke about nine the next morning. He was alone in the big bed. Wolfgang had slipped quietly away before dawn. Gone off to fight Germany's wars, Franz mused as he stretched, scratching his scalp vigorously through his disarranged, rumpled hair, and nestled snugly among the blankets and the downlike mattress. Reaching to the bedside table, he switched on the radio and settled in for more sleep. Slowly at first, as the radio warmed, the volume of the music finally reached full sound. The singer's voice was immediately identifiable. It could only be Marlene Dietrich gravelling out her song from *The Blue Angel*. Franz knew the words of the song as well as most everyone in Berlin, but he listened closely anyway.

> *Falling in love again*
> *Never wanted to . . .*
> *What am I to do?*
> *Can't help it*
> *Love's always been my game*
> *Play it how I may*
> *I was made that way*
> *Can't help it*
> *Men cluster to me*
> *Like moths around a flame.*

Franz smiled contentedly. She's singing my song, he thought. She's singing about me.

8

Berlin, Germany—May 10, 1933

F RANZ'S WORK WITH THE COMMITTEE had lasted for months, work he felt was pointless since he had no hopes for any success. He was ready to sing and dance again. His face had healed, leaving only a scar about three inches long on his right cheek. It really didn't look bad, he thought. In fact, it was a bit dashing.

Approaching the Institute where he worked, Franz noticed an SS man in front, obviously guarding the Institute building. The guard sneered at him as though Franz were an abomination.

"What is that SS man doing outside?" Franz asked Anna who worked in the office with him.

"We don't know. He was out there when the first one of us arrived this morning. We are afraid there's going to be trouble today," Anna replied.

The office was in a turmoil; under siege. All the workers were moving books to different locations, stacking the more valuable ones on a large table. It was clear that everyone was concerned about the books.

"What kind of trouble are you talking about, Anna?"

"Three or four days ago, there was an article in the paper stating that Germany was to be purged of objectionable books, those that are 'un-German'. If they burn all these beautiful books, it will be the end of all our efforts."

Anna was sincerely concerned about the prospect of someone damaging a book. She had always loved them; they were her friends. Franz, however, was not a "book person". Never the intellectual type, he seldom thought much about books. He never considered where they came from, they were always around.

One of the men who worked with Anna and Franz carried a stack of the more valuable books out the exit at the rear of the building, trying to slip away with some of the priceless editions. The guard saw him, however, and immediately arrested him, confiscating the books.

Trucks arrived at the Institute around nine thirty and unloaded about one hundred students and, to Franz's amazement, a brass band. The students rushed into the building, broke into all the offices, poured ink on manuscripts and then carried the books out of the building and piled them in the back of the trucks. The ridiculous brass band played during most of this activity, while the crowd of curious that had gathered gaped at the students loading the books into the trucks to the accompaniment of the brass band. This continued until around noon when more trucks arrived with storm troopers, who also removed books and anything else they wanted. They took more than 12,000 volumes that day and loaded them into the trucks. The trucks proceeded to the University of Berlin where more trucks, filled with still more books, were arriving. Darkness had descended upon the city by this time. Their numbers having swelled to thousands, the students formed a torchlight parade and, with the storm troopers, marched to the square on Unter den Linden, across from the University of Berlin. There, with much flourish and fanfare, the books were burned. Those who perpetrated the book-burning were so proud of what they were doing that they had news film made of the glorious event. Franz and Anna were among the crowd. Anna felt she was in a time warp; book-burning had been a practice of the Middle Ages. Surely this couldn't be happening today in the civilized nation of Germany.

The band played while people sang patriotic German songs and danced around the bonfire. The whole tiring day and tragic night were ridiculously ironic. The Nazis were all powerful in Germany and yet they were afraid of books. What could possibly be in a book that would prompt the leaders of a modern nation to burn it, Franz wondered. He was now convinced that the Nazis were not only dangerous, they were insane as well.

The building that had housed the Institute was seized and converted into an office building for Nazi lawyers. Franz was again without work. He had no difficulty finding a job in one of the many cabarets in the city. Over the years, Franz had become well-known as one of the best cabaret performers in Berlin. When he stopped by to see the manager of "Night Sounds", one of the largest cabarets in the city, he was hired immediately. Although the manager wanted him to start that night, Franz preferred to wait until the next day.

He knocked lightly on Tatina's apartment door at the Adlon. He had come to tell her where he would be working. The maid ushered him into Tatina's dressing room.

Tatina was standing in front of one of her large closets, holding an evening gown in each hand.

"Franz, dear! You're just in time to help me decide which of these two would look better on me tonight."

Franz walked over to her and placed his arms around her waist, clasping his hands together behind her back. He kissed her wetly on the cheek. "Hello, Tatina. How are you feeling today?"

"Good God Franz! Be careful! You'll muss up the gowns. And you just slobbered all over my cheek! Now, I'll have to do the make-up job again. And it takes so long to put all that camouflage over these wrinkles. Each year, it takes me longer and longer to apply all of that stuff so I will look like a twenty year old vixen instead of a fifty year old dowager."

Franz released her from his arms and stepped back to admire her. Although she was fifty, she certainly did not look that old, he thought.

"Which gown for tonight?" he repeated her question. "That is the big problem for today. Well, tell me where you are going and I'll decide."

"We're off to see Lotta Lenya in *The Threepenny Opera*. It will be my third time, but I love it so."

"The brownish one, that's the one you should wear," Franz said with conviction.

"Good! I had already decided on that one anyway. I was just trying to see if you have good taste."

Tatina hung the other gown back in the closet and placed her choice on a large chair. She walked over to Franz, took him by the hand and led him into the living room. All the while, Franz was thinking how young his mother looked. People would think we were sweethearts if they saw us holding hands like this, he decided.

She sat on one of the large sofas and patted the seat next to her. A troubled look came on Franz's face. Something is wrong, he thought. I have never seen her serious about anything. He sat next to her and mentally braced himself for the bad news.

Tatina was staring out the window, not looking at anything specific. Franz watched her, waiting for her to begin the conversation. Something else about her was unusual. Around her neck, she wore a gold chain. That was not the strange part. But from the chain hung a gold Star of David.

"Tatina, why are you wearing that Star of David? We aren't Jewish."

Her face slowly turned from the window to Franz. There were tears in her eyes, he noticed. I didn't even know she could cry, he thought.

"Franz," she began, speaking slowly and with extreme deliberation, as though she were carefully choosing each important word. "Life is going to get very rough, very soon. That man, Hitler, is not a good man. In fact, I sometimes think he is not really a man but something sent from some dark place to make Germany suffer."

"I agree with all that, Tatina, but he isn't going to do us any harm. We are not Jews."

"He won't stop there. Jews are just the most obvious ones he is after. This Star of David you asked about was given to me by a dear friend who has, I hope, managed to get out of the country. Of course, I can't wear it in public, but it makes me feel better to wear it when I can."

Franz took her hands in his and tried to console her. "Nothing bad is going to happen, Tatina. Not here in Berlin."

"Yes, Franz, it is," she replied. She removed her hands from within his, taking his hands in hers and holding them dearly.

"I must tell you something, Franz, before it is too late. You are my son, my dear son. I love you so very much. I want you to know that I have never disapproved of you or the way you live. Do you know what I'm referring to?"

"Yes, of course I do. You are talking about my sex life, aren't you?"

"That is what I am talking about. But I am talking about your whole life, not just some parts of it. You have been a treasure to me. I would not change one thing about you. It occurred to me that I had never told you any of this. So, now I am telling you."

Franz felt like she was saying farewell and good-bye. "Are you going away or something?"

"No, Franz. I felt a strong urge to tell you these things. I have been wanting to talk like this for a long time. Now that I have told you, I already feel better. I'm glad we have had this talk and glad that you understand.

"One other thing. Always be yourself. Don't pretend. And don't let them change you. Don't let them win, even if it means great sacrifice. Be yourself and be true to yourself. I think Shakespeare said it best, that is if I can quote him correctly. 'This above all,—to thine ownself be true; and it must follow, as the night the day, thou canst not then be false to any man'."

9

Baden-Baden, Germany—November 1938

H E SAT ALONE beside the little River Oos, thinking about various incidents that had happened in his life the past few years; dreaming of the way it could have been were he not so different. He sat motionless on the marble bench so worn by the years that it appeared to be coated with a thick layer of butter. He appeared to be some thirty years of age. His dark hair, with just a hint of white near the temples, was too long. It fell over his forehead and covered his dark, deep-set eyes. His neatly trimmed mustache made him appear older than he actually was. His suit was also black and sprinkled lightly with specks of white, as though a painter had shaken his wet paint brush at it. Although he was dressed as a businessman, he looked more like he belonged in the mines, digging in the earth, or on some large sailing ship, harvesting the bounty of the sea. He was a big man: tall, brawny and hardy in appearance; a working man who looked a little out of place in the business suit.

The changing autumn foliage surrounded him. Stirred by wisps of a fresh cool breeze, the leaves twisted and turned on their branches, revealing still more and different shades of colors. Some held on to their source of life for a little longer while others surrendered to the inevitable and released their hold, falling to the ground to be snatched up and carried away by the winds to a new adventure. From their only home along the banks of the Oos, they would fly with the currents to new and distant places. They swirled around in circles and then rushed down the river only to turn and hurry back for one last visit before leaving, dancing around the man on the bench before flying off on the wind forever.

The warm autumn colors along the river vividly foretold Nature's reclining for the season. The air was full of the sweet smell of roses and chrysanthemums and the slightly moldy odor of middle autumn, not at all like the new-life fragrance of spring.

Van crossed his legs and brushed the hair back from his eyes. Deep in thought, he was unaware of the beauty surrounding him. Mannheim and the classroom where he taught science were not kilometers but eons away. He had come back to Baden-Baden for a short visit and memories were everywhere.

Rudy, Papa, Mama, Sheila, Ernst, old Kern and even Rabbi Eschel were all reliving the past in Van's thoughts. His last year in public school had been terrible, he was thinking. Track had been all right, also the body-building classes, but the rest of his memories of that year were not pleasant. Rudy was away in prison and Van had seldom seen Sheila in his effort to please Mama. Those Jewish girls he had dated were all hazy and blurred, finally slipping from his recollection altogether. His encounter with the prostitute had been such a turning point that he still tended to date everything as having happened "before" or "after."

He felt that most of life's joys and happinesses for him and all other Jewish people somehow became lost about the time Rudy left Baden-Baden. He realized that, in his case, this was partly true because Rudy had gone. But it had also been a worsening time for all of Germany's Jews. Of course, he knew it had nothing to do with Rudy Hoess being away in prison, but there was a connection.

When the Nazis gained control of the government, they passed many new laws directed against the Jews. Van thought about the absurd laws and how they had changed Jewish life. Jews could not hold public office or civil service jobs. It was not long until it was against the law for Jews to farm or work for the press or radio. All Jews that had moved into Germany had their citizenship taken from them. In 1935, they stopped Jews from coming into Germany. Van wondered if there really were Jews that wanted to move to Germany with the Nazis in power. He thought about more of the unfair laws. No Jew could marry a non-Jew or have extramarital relations with persons of German blood. What are we if we're not German blood, he wondered. Laws were passed denying Jews the right to vote, making it illegal to transfer property out of Germany or employ Aryan women.

He had seen how Germany's Jews were being treated progressively worse each year. The only homeland most of them had ever known made it plain it did not want them. The official attitude was that all Jews should emigrate from Germany immediately. No one cared where they went as long as they left. Many Jewish people did have enough foresight to get out while they still could. However, the majority of the German Jews refused to leave. They read the hand-writing on the wall, but they could not or would not believe the message. Germany was their country, their home. Why should they leave? Papa and Mama felt this way and had expressed their feelings many times. Van had agreed with them.

Van's thoughts drifted to his college experience at Heidelberg. He remembered the day he was to leave Baden-Baden for college. Papa had come to his room where Van was doing the final packing.

He could still see Papa standing in the doorway, looking pleased and proud that his son was going to the university. Van also remembered how sadly changed Papa had looked then. There was a sickness about him, in his eyes and his lack of color. He had lost much of his sense of humor, seldom joking the way he once did.

"Van, you will never believe what I heard today at the cafe. Rudy Hoess has been released from prison under a general amnesty. He is a free man. Some justice we have here in Germany," Papa had said bitterly.

"You mean they let him out of prison even though he killed that teacher and then boasted about it at the trial? He wasn't in there two years!"

"Yes, free to kill again, I suppose," Papa had replied angrily. Papa was often bitter and angry.

As he sat now in the quiet park along the Oos, Van wondered about Rudy, where he was and how the years had changed him. He wanted to see Rudy and hated himself for wanting to see him. Upon reflection, he realized that he had spent a lot of time hating himself.

The nation was in chaos, Van thought. The unemployment, the economic depression, the inflation, the feeling of the German people that the Treaty of Versailles had been unfair to Germany and the many social problems had simply paved the way for the Nazi depravity that had taken control of the country. He knew that the Nazi Party was the real threat, but he did not have time to concern himself with that posturing little Austrian and his hoodlums. Van's energies were spent dealing with his own personal turmoil; he could do nothing about the turmoil around him.

"Van! Van Bertholds, is that you?"

He was summoned back to the present, his reflections interrupted, by the attractive woman who had spoken to him. He eventually recognized her. Nearly ten years had passed since he had seen her, and she had become a beautiful woman.

"Sheila! What a surprise! How good to see you!" he said, rising and embracing her warmly. Always the closest of friends, the reunion gave both of them a joyously warm, glowing feeling.

"Van, how have you been? I have thought of you so often. Oh, you don't know how glad I am to see you."

As she held him warmly, the smell of her hair filled Van's head. Her hair glistened in the late autumn sun, her warmth seemed to penetrate Van and heal his soul. He felt elated that she reacted so spontaneously and affectionately.

"I'm doing all right, all things considered. Let's not talk about me. Tell me about yourself and what you have been doing since public school."

Van was still thinking how wonderful it was that she had embraced him and shown a sincere affection. In the past few years, his Gentile friends had withdrawn from him because he was a Jew. He had begun to understand how a leper must feel.

Sheila smiled broadly, her blue eyes paling the blue of the sky into insignificance, and replied, "There isn't much to tell. I've become the typical housewife. We live in Munich where Ulrich has a good position with the I.G. Farben chemical firm. He advanced rapidly in the company when he was on the team that developed buna. That's a new synthetic rubber. Anyway, they have a plant going full time at Schkopau producing imitation rubber. Isn't that funny, fake rubber. I suppose we Germans can do anything in the world."

"Yes, I suppose so," Van murmured thinking the Germans could do anything except love their fellow man.

"Ulrich is a good man. I love him so much and we are both very happy. We have two sons, Ulrich Junior and Vance. Ulrich has always reminded me of you, Van. I think that's why I came to love him."

Van turned away from her and pretended to remove something from his eye. He did not want Sheila to know that he was removing a tear. Her comparison of her husband with him had touched something in him and the tear seemed to come of its own accord.

Sheila noticed Van's embarrassment and quickly changed the subject. "Van, have you heard about the Führer's new automobile for all the people? It's called Volkswagen and it costs only 990 marks. Isn't that wonderful? They are already building the plant in Fallersleben to make them."

They were walking down the path along the river, going no place in particular. Thinking about what Sheila had said about the new automobile, Van wondered if "for all the people" included Jews also.

He doubted it.

"Have you heard from Ernst Hoffman lately, Sheila? You know, of course, he had a terrible crush on you."

"Yes, I knew that he liked me a great deal. But he was Jewish and my family nearly died when . . . She stopped in midsentence and looked at Van, but he turned away again, watching the ducks in the nearby river and thinking, "Not her too."

Sheila blurted out: "Van, I'm sorry! You know I didn't mean that the way it sounded. I don't know why I said it. I think it's the times. All I ever hear any more is how terrible the Jews are and I know it isn't true."

She placed her hand on Van's arm and squeezed it with genuine warmth. Van knew she loved him as much as a sister would, and he knew that her comment did not come from her heart. It was a result of the mass propaganda that constantly bombarded all of them.

"Sheila Gebhardt, don't concern yourself about what you said. I've heard much worse, believe me. I know you are not one of them. We grew up together, more like brother and sister than friends. Forget it. I will if you will."

"Van, you are still my dearest friend, my brother as you say. I do love you and always will," she said quietly and matter-of-factly, looking down at the path as she spoke, not looking at Van. She then looked at Van, smiled broadly and said, "And my name is not Gebhardt, silly. I told you I was married. The name is Sheila Stempfle, Munich housewife."

Continuing their leisurely pace along the path beside the peaceful river, they approached an empty bench, surrounded by beds of different colored chrysanthemums. They sat down and Sheila took Van's hand and held it warmly in her lap. They were surrounded by the many different kinds of trees in their autumn colors. It all blended together, creating a romantic tapestry; two young people holding hands, looking lovingly at each other and talking softly.

They were not two people seriously in love as the scene suggested; they were the closest of friends renewing their lifelong devotion to one another. Van's being Jewish while Sheila was a Gentile had no bearing on anything. That day was as it should be. Van imagined God was smiling, just like all those smiling Buddhas he had seen.

Sheila remembered that Van had asked her about Ernst. "You asked about Ernst, didn't you. I believe he's in Berlin at that big synagogue, the main one. He has become a rabbi and is in some type of internship there."

"A rabbi!" Van exclaimed. "Ernst Hoffman, a rabbi! And at the Great Synagogue in Berlin. The age of miracles has not passed after all. We were kids together and I still think of him the way he was then. It sounds funny. I can't visualize him as a rabbi."

"Well, he is. So you will have to get accustomed to calling him Rabbi Hoffman, not Ernst. Now, tell me about yourself. I understand you are teaching in Mannheim now."

"Yes, I teach science and enjoy it. I finished the University in Heidelberg and started teaching immediately. I still love Baden-Baden and would rather be here, but there never seem to be any openings, especially for Jews."

Oh yes, I feel the same way about Baden-Baden, Van. Munich is a wonderful city and I like living there, but Baden-Baden is still the most wonderful place in the world." Sheila wanted to ask Van a question but she was not sure if she dared. He had already expressed some of his feelings about the Nazis and she thought it might be better not to ask. Then she changed her mind, deciding to ask even though she knew it was a dangerous subject. "Van, what do you really think about Hitler and the Nazis?"

She released his hand to push her silken hair from her face. The breeze had loosened the strand of hair, creating the illusion of a flaw in her beauty. She quickly repaired the damage.

"Hitler?" Van snarled. "He is a bastard of the worst kind. He will eventually destroy all that is good and decent in Germany. I hate him! I really wish he were dead!"

"Van, not so loud! Someone might hear you."

"The truth should not be heard? He is an evil man, a nothing inflated into a windbag by his own noxious emissions. I despise him!"

"Van, I never did understand politics. It has always been so confusing to me. I hear so much I never know what to believe." She looked around to see that no one was near them. "Do you remember how I told you that my father was always telling me 'lies are the termites in the house of life'?"

Van thought a moment and, smiling slightly, replied, "Yes, you used to imitate him saying that. You really did sound like him."

"Well, now I understand what he meant. It may have been a trite little expression but it was true and still is. I try never to lie and you must believe that what I am going to say now is not a lie. The real truth is that most of us who are not Jewish do not feel the way the Nazis do about Jews. No one I know does, anyway."

"Sheila, I believe you feel that you are telling the truth. However, my experience has been that the non-Jewish Germans I know will have nothing to do with me, and purposely avoid me. Papa's business is so bad he can hardly meet expenses. Mama's money is all that keeps the cafe open. He can't employ any non-Jewish German women. Things are bad and getting worse. It appears that no one will stand up against Hitler or the Nazis."

As Van spoke, his voice became more strident. Sheila knew that she must change the subject before someone heard him.

"I didn't realize it was all that bad," she replied softly. "Let's not discuss it any more. It is all so depressing. How is your mother, Van?"

"She's fine. I don't come to Baden-Baden often enough. Mama worries about Papa and the nation and when I am going to marry a nice Jewish girl. I'm going to Berlin the ninth of this month to attend a teachers' conference. I tried to get her to go with me but she said she was needed here at home. The conference will be boring, but I'm looking forward to Berlin. I haven't been there since Papa took me when I was quite young. Hey, I just realized. I'll get to see Rabbi Ernst!"

"Yes, you must see him. I wish I could be there when you two meet. Do give him my love." She glanced at her watch and a pained expression came over her face. "Van, I really must leave now. We are going back to Munich tonight. The next time you come to Munich, you *must* come to visit. I want you to meet Ulrich and the boys. I know you'll like Ulrich, but I don't know about the boys. They are little terrors!"

She wrote her address and phone number on a small slip of paper from Van's wallet. When they rose from the bench, she put her arms around Van and kissed him on the cheek. He hugged her warmly and she was gone.

She walked up the gently sloping bank of the river, paused, turned and waved to Van. The gathering twilight lent an aura of sadness to the parting on the river bank, a sadness they both felt but could not quite define.

Van returned to his seat on the bench and lightly laid his hand where Sheila had been sitting. He returned to his thoughts about the way things might have been were it not for his sexual inversion. Yes, he had finally said it to himself. The term he used so hesitantly to classify himself was much in style then, particularly in the larger cities and on the university campuses. Van had read of demonstrations in Berlin and other cities for the rights of these people, and laws had been passed for them, before the Nazis came to power.

He had read reports of the liberation movement, but he found it impossible to identify with any of that. To Van, his was an evil and an evil could not be legalized. He closed his mind to the whole concept and prayed that he would have no contact with the movement when he went to Berlin. Once again, his fear overpowered his desire for information, understanding and compassion.

10

Berlin, Germany—November 9, 1938

"RABBI HOFFMAN. RABBI ERNST HOFFMAN. It just sounds so strange. I don't think I'll ever get accustomed to calling you that."

"Yes, I know what you mean. It even sounds strange to *me*," Ernst said, shaking his head in agreeing disbelief. They were drinking wine in a quiet bar in a neighborhood near Berlin's Great Synagogue. Van's first full day in Berlin had been occupied with the teachers' conference. This, his second night in the city, was his first opportunity to see Ernst.

Short, fat, funny Ernst was gone, Van thought. Little about this rabbi even hinted of the stumbling-his-way-through-life teenager that Van remembered. In the rabbi's face and eyes Van did see a veiled resemblance to the Ernst of Baden-Baden. Van briefly wondered if he were actually talking with Ernst Hoffman or some rabbi using Ernst's name, trying to deceive him. During the recent years, the thought had increasingly crossed his mind that all rabbis had been deceiving him. The idea that his man was not Ernst was, of course, ridiculous; a consequence of the times and Van's state of mind. This *is* Ernst, Van concluded, but a radical change has occurred in him since I last saw him.

Berlin had also changed since the time Papa had brought him to the city as a small child. The mental pictures he had retained over the years were originally views seen through the inexperienced eyes of a child. Van's memories of Berlin were of the lofty buildings reaching the clouds; the great train station with thousands of trains all going off in every direction at the same time; tremendous throngs of people moving along the sidewalks and stopping in unison as though they were controlled by one mind. There were numerous bicycles and automobiles, moving with such speed and abandon that they must surely be rushing to a spectacular accident at some predetermined intersection, Van had childishly speculated. The stores were supplied with so many desirable things that the entire world would not be able to deplete their wares, and there were millions of people who had all worn the same face to the city to confuse one another.

The Berlin Van was seeing through the eyes of an adult was not at all the way he had pictured it for those many years. It was still a great city, but the buildings did not really reach the clouds and the traffic moved more slowly than he had remembered. The merchandise in the stores was not as plentiful and the people of Berlin were not all wearing the same mask. Quite a number of these people were always looking down at the ground, not holding their heads erect as the others did. It took little effort to realize that those walking like cowed dogs, gazing only at the ground, heads tilted in an almost prayer-like position were, like Van, Jews. He noticed that eye contact with them was rare. The few with whom he managed to have eye contact had a strange, bewildering sameness of expression in their eyes. It was not a look foreign to Van; he had seen it often during the recent years. He recognized his old companion, fear, looking back at him from each pair of Jewish eyes into which he chanced to glance.

"So, Sheila, my old girl friend, told you where I was and what I am doing."

"Yes, and I thought she was joking when she told me you were a rabbi. It is so ironic when I recall the Ernst I grew up with and the Rabbi Hoffman I see now. Had you become a priest, it would have surprised me no more than this."

Ernst laughed at Van's strange analogy. He did not look like a rabbi. Of medium height, he was thin with a darkly sad face, even when he was obviously enjoying a good joke. Although he was Van's age, his appearance was that of a much older man, a man more experienced with life's difficulties, perhaps. He, too, had the same look of fear in his eyes. Van wondered why a rabbi should be afraid. Rabbis, the faith's teachers, knew all the answers. Were these answers so frightening?

They talked of Sheila, of Baden-Baden and the fun of their youth.

"I really thought I would marry Sheila when we were grown," Ernst confided soberly, gazing into his wine. "I was a mixed-up kid, wasn't I? Can you imagine my marrying a shiksa and then becoming a rabbi?"

"Marrying a what?" Van asked, not familiar with the meaning of the Yiddish word.

"Rabbi Ernst Hoffman smiled and said, "A girl that is not Jewish. I am surprised at you, Van. As old as you are and you still haven't learned any of our language."

"I do well to speak German," Van laughingly replied. "I suppose I should learn Yiddish. Mama uses it a lot, but I just never picked it up. When I was a kid, I thought it was a language for old gossipy women. So, I ignored it."

"Well, Van, my friend, you were certainly wrong about that," Ernst told him in a more serious tone of voice. "Yiddish is one of our rich cultural heritages that should be learned, used, passed on to each generation and even revered."

Ernst became more serious with each word. He sincerely believed what he was telling Van and his expression left no doubt about that. Van watched him, still amazed at the change in him. He decided to find out how Ernst felt about the Nazis and what they were doing to the country.

"Ernst. Pardon me, Rabbi Hoffman, what is really happening in Germany? I know what I see and what Papa and Mama say, but you should know more about what is happening than we in Baden-Baden or Mannheim. Are things as bad as they seem?"

"Van, things are not simply bad, they are on the verge of disaster. What the Nazis have been doing to Jews in Germany is insane and criminal. Jews are being beaten, robbed of their possessions and even murdered. The killing of a Jew is becoming an heroic accomplishment rather than a criminal act. Just this past month, the Nazis expelled over fourteen thousand Polish Jews and Poland would not readmit them. I fear they will soon be expelling German Jews as well. I believe their objective is a Germany free of Jews. We will be gone but what wealth we have will remain in Germany."

"Do you really think it will come to that?"

"Yes! I certainly do. Their objective is racial purity. They are striving for a Germany of Aryans, even though they have changed the meaning of that word to suit their designs. And being an Aryan won't save you if you are afflicted with some physical or mental handicap. They are attempting to create their idea of a perfect Germany: no Jews, no physically malformed individuals, no mental defectives, no homosexuals or other peverts, no criminal element and no opposing political views."

Van shuddered interiorly as Ernst sealed his doom with a dual damnation.

"You see, Van, the Nazis have finally obtained absolute power in Germany. There is nothing to stop them from doing anything they want. Have you heard what happened two days ago in Paris?"

"I remember some report of an official being shot by a Jew," Van replied.

"It is not just some official and a Jew. It was von Rath, the Third Secretary of our Embassy in France. The man who shot him was a young Polish Jew, seeking revenge for the treatment of the Polish Jews in Germany. However, that is not the important part. You can forget all about him except for one fact. He is a Jew. That is the only fact they will remember and I am afraid they will use this shooting as an excuse to take even more radical actions against us. But it is not just a shooting any more; von Rath died late today. It is now murder of a high German government official by a Jew."

Looking at Ernst's grim face, Van understood why he appeared to be so thin and ill. He was worrying for all the Jews in Germany.

They continued to talk, leaving the bar shortly before two in the morning. They decided to walk a while before going their separate ways.

Their walk took them near the Great Synagogue area, into streets dotted with many Jewish businesses.

Their silent passage through the early morning hours of Berlin was abruptly shattered by the rumble of many large trucks off in the distance, but rapidly coming closer to them. When they rounded a corner onto the Kurfurstendamm, they could see the trucks stopping a few blocks down the street. There was a slamming of doors and shouted commands. The trucks were parked in a row, and soldiers poured out of them. Also getting out of the trucks were many people in civilian clothes. The only clue to their true military nature was the manner in which they moved and followed the orders of the uniformed men.

A loud crash echoed in the caverns of the city when one of the civilians threw a stone through one of the larger glass windows on the street. All of the civilians began throwing various items through the store windows. The violence was so sudden and unexpected that Ernst and Van stood like statues, unable to speak or move.

Broken glass fell from every side. Not only did they break every store window, they destroyed everything else: street lamps, windows of homes, any cars in the area and everything else that was breakable.

"What's happening, Ernst?"

"Exactly what I was afraid would happen, but sooner than I expected!" Ernst replied as the wave of destruction advanced.

"We'd better get out of here!" Van shouted.

"The synagogue! We'll go there. I don't think they will bother us there."

The entire street was in ruins. They could hear the same sounds, muffled by distance, coming from other parts of the city. It seemed as if the whole city was under attack.

Running from block to block, they worked their way to the Great Synagogue, with Ernst leading. Many detours were necessary to avoid other groups of civilians, destroying every Jewish establishment on each street. The Star of David was being painted and scrawled on the buildings, doors and walls of all Jewish concerns or Jewish residents.

The residents of these neighborhoods came out of their buildings to investigate the chaos that had awakened them. Many were seized by the civilians and also by the Nazi soldiers. They were kicked, beaten and loaded into the trucks.

Van wanted to help the residents fight off the gangs of soldiers and civilian-attired soldiers, but Ernst urged him to keep moving. Ernst knew what would happen to the two of them if they were caught.

When they reached the Great Synagogue, Ernst was horrified to see Nazi soldiers coming down the steps with the scrolls of the Law, already damaged, which they proceeded to destroy. Ernst fell to his knees and Van heard him faintly, praying for deliverance over the noise of destruction.

"God of Abraham, save your Israel."

His prayers were drowned by the thunder of a huge organ dropped from an upper balcony of the Synagogue, which splintered into millions of pieces as it hit the street. Van could no longer hear Ernst's prayer. He wondered if God could. If He did hear, the answer to the prayer was a resounding "No!".

People were swarming over the Great Synagogue like maggots crawling through a dead carcass. Van's view became fuzzy, a picture slightly out of focus, as his eyes filled with tears. Huge candelabras were being hurled from windows on the upper levels. Pavement stones and other objects were thrown through the windows of the great temple and all the other buildings. The Great Synagogue was the real synagogue for all German Jews, the symbol in Germany of their faith. To see it destroyed by a horde of such little men was a sight no Jew should have to witness.

Petroleum cans were carried into the synagogue. Van had never seen so many cans of petrol at one time. From every direction, as though prearranged, Nazis approached the synagogue. Surely they were not going to burn it. In a few minutes, the maggots all came running from the carcass. It exploded with a tremendous noise and flashed into flames which leaped upward from every opening, pointing toward the beautiful domed Star of David atop the building. The dome was soon bathed in flames. Like a dying giant, the Great Synagogue began to fall into itself. Crumbling, burning and, Van imagined, moaning and screaming, the building became a heap of smoldering rubble.

The Great Synagogue was transformed from the center of German Jewish culture into a flaming pile of memories right before their eyes. Had he come all the way to Berlin for this?

Ernst was prostrate on the ground, still praying. Van moved to get him away from the area as quickly as he could; the Nazis were loading Jews into the trucks. Van had become entangled in the limp fire hose that was all around them. No one had even bothered to turn the water on. The firemen had stood and watched the synagogue burn, making no effort to save it. While Van was trying to untangle himself from the hoses and the gathered crowd, two Nazis grabbed Ernst by his feet and dragged him to one of the trucks. People were spitting on him and throwing stones and other things at him. He was bleeding on the pavement stones of the street, directly in front of the shell of the Great Synagogue. Fleetingly, Van thought that Ernst would probably have been proud his blood was shed there, if it had to be shed.

Fury and rage swelled within Van. He would kill those goddamn Nazis. Knowing he was physically able to handle enough of them to make it worth the effort, he started for the truck where the Nazis were about to load Ernst.

Before he could take the first step, his right arm was grasped firmly. The suddenness and firmness jerked Van backward.

"Don't! They'll kill you if you interfere! You've got to get out of here and hide before they take you away with the others!"

Van turned and looked at his captor, their faces close, Van seeing his own reflection, surrounded by the flames of the Great Synagogue, in the man's eyes. He saw something more, a look he recognized. He had seen this particular look most of his life. It was not one of fear but a unique look that was most always in the eyes of a certain kind of person. Van felt he knew the look well; it was in his own eyes. It was a look of searching, one that seemed to reveal the loneliness of the soul. He had, in the years since Baden-Baden, come to recognize the look as belonging to him and to the people he felt were like him in some unusual way.

"Do you live near here?" the man asked.

"No, I don't."

"Come with me, quickly! If we don't get away from here soon, those Nazi shits will take you for certain."

Slipping through the confusion, they ran from the area of the Great Synagogue. Van followed as his rescuer led him through the streets of Berlin: running, hiding and running again through the streets and alleys of the city ablaze with pockets of flame and vibrating with the sounds of destruction.

They eventually arrived at his rescuer's apartment building, located in a slightly higher part of town, providing an unobstructed view of the city. Flames were everywhere, burning other synagogues or Jewish neighborhoods. Glancing at the fires scattered over the city and hearing the noises of so much breaking glass, Van realized that it was all directed at Jews.

They went up two flights of stairs to the man's apartment on the upper floor of the building. When they entered and he switched on the lights, Van saw that the apartment was small but pleasant and welcoming. The largest room, the living room, had a big window that looked out onto the city, furnishing a good view, not a pleasant sight that night. On the left of the living room was a dining room with a connecting kitchen. On the opposite side of the living room were the bedroom and bath.

"Won't you have a seat? Could I get you something to drink?"

"Yes, I would appreciate something cold to drink, if you have it," Van answered, breathing heavily from the exertion of their long run.

Van seated himself at the dining table which was directly in front of the window. The man went into the kitchen, leaving Van alone at the table. He did not look at the room or its contents but stared out the large window at the broad expanse of Berlin with its many scattered fires. His vision of the Berlin night blurred as his mind raced back to Ernst on the street in front of the Great Synagogue. Ernst was lifted and thrown into the truck, landing in an unrecognizable heap, his lifeless form like a puppet with no control wires. Was he dead, Van wondered. Where were they taking him and for what purpose? Van tried to blink back the tears and wiped his eyes as the man came from the kitchen with two beers. He looked away to hide his tears from this man who had rescued him.

"My name is Franz Richter," the man said to Van, pretending not to notice Van's tears or red eyes.

Van turned from the window and looked at the man, replying, "I'm Van Bertholds and I'm grateful for your help tonight." Noticing that the quaking sound of his voice hinted that he had been crying, he paused and cleared his throat. "If you had not pulled me away from them, I believe I would have killed some of them and gotten myself killed for the effort. You probably saved my life tonight."

"Well, I was glad to be of help to anyone having trouble with the Nazis. I hate those sons-of-bitches!"

"So do I," Van agreed. He turned back and again looked out the window, not actually seeing the scene but trying to conceal his sorrow and concern. His thoughts left Ernst at the point where the truck was being filled with more people, obscuring Ernst from Van's view entirely. He turned his face from the window, giving Franz Richter a closer scrutiny than had been possible before.

He was about five feet, ten inches tall, not as tall or as muscular as Van, but attractive. His wavy blond hair was the shade of the dark golden centers of daisies highlighted with random strands the lighter color of the sparkling yellow rays of the sun. Franz's eyes were a pale green, reminding Van of the eyes of a cat Mama once had. The scar on his right cheek did not detract from his looks, it seemed rather becoming, Van thought. He swept these thoughts from his mind as he realized to what point they might eventually lead him. "Down! Down! Back in your cage! Leave me alone! I want nothing to do with you," he told himself.

While Van struggled with his all too familiar inner feelings, Franz was watching him closely. I *was* right, he thought. He is the tall one from Baden-Baden. After all these years, I still recognized him sitting there in that bar with his friend. He is much older now, even has a little gray in his hair, but I still knew he was the one from Baden-Baden. How strange that I have run into him again in the midst of all this madness tonight. Should I tell him, Franz wondered. Not just yet, he decided. The silence between the two of them was becoming awkward. Franz felt he would have to lead the conversation since Van was so upset by all that had happened. He sat in the chair across the small dining table, facing Van.

"I was just wondering where you live," Franz began, "since you told me you didn't live near the synagogue neighborhood. Do you live in Berlin?"

"No, my home is Baden-Baden, but I now live in Mannheim where I teach."

Baden-Baden, Franz thought. Yes, I was right. He is the one I saw there. "You are a teacher?" he asked, looking more closely at Van's large, well-built body.

"Yes, I teach science."

"With that build? You certainly could have fooled me. What is your secret?"

Van felt uncomfortable with the conversation and was not sure what to say. He replied, "When I was in school and at the university, I was always involved with sports. Since then I still run a lot and work out with weights."

"I can tell. You are really a nice looking man with a marvelous build. God, the muscles! I suppose you could have handled a few of those Nazi bastards by yourself."

Van blushed noticeably.

"You are blushing," Franz said. "Hasn't anyone ever told you that you are an attractive man? I meant it and I should know. I've seen my share."

"Well, no," Van replied falteringly. "At least, not another man."

Franz smiled, his eyes twinkled and he said, "Well, you have been told by one now."

"Wait a minute. What kind of conversation are we having? I don't understand," Van said, ready to run for the door. The fear he had experienced in the streets of Berlin was mild compared to his need-to-escape feeling during this conversation. He felt he had to get out of that apartment immediately, or his darkest thoughts and desires would take control. He looked closely and deeply into Franz's eyes and realized that he could not leave. Finally surrendering, he admitted to himself that he had lost after fighting so many years. He could not fight his monster *and* this man, Franz, at the same time.

"Van, you act like this is all new to you. Are you not experienced in these things?"

"No," he replied timidly. He paused, giving his words serious consideration before continuing. "I have always had certain feelings, but I classified them as evil and sinful long ago. I have spent my adult life hiding my true feelings and seeking God's forgiveness for these evil thoughts."

Van could not believe what he was saying. Why was he so truthful with this man? Why, after suppressing his innermost thoughts, his secret despised monster, for such a long time, did he suddenly speak so openly? It had to be a combination of many things; it was nearly four in the morning, he had been drinking heavily, the burning of the Great Synagogue and the arrest or abduction of Ernst. These conditions and events, all new and unexpected, compressed within such a short period of time, had torn down most of Van's old protective barriers. The determining influence, however, sat across from him. He had a strange inexplicable feeling that this man was special. He had only known him a short period of time, yet he felt he would become an important part of his life. He suddenly thought of Rudy. This man, Franz Richter, was what Van had wanted Rudy to be, understanding and sharing Van's feelings. Van believed that when he spoke to Franz of heretofore unspoken things, he would understand.

"Van, you look so tense and nervous. Relax. Just in case you haven't realized it yet, I am like you in many respects. The major difference between us seems to be that you have denied the truth while I have accepted myself as I am."

I must be careful, Franz thought. If I am to help Van understand more of the truth about himself and his life, I must be extremely careful. If I say the wrong thing, it could reinforce his mistaken views. I wonder, should I even try? I may do more damage than good. God knows, I only want to help. *Someone* needs to help him. Someone should have helped him years ago. Can I manage it without really hurting him?

Franz was on the verge of dropping the subject, obviously a dangerous one for Van. He decided, however, to try his best to help Van see the truth and, perhaps, enjoy his life just as he, Franz had always done.

In an effort to lessen Van's fear and nervousness, Franz began with an account of his early life and how he learned to accept his identity. He told Van of the months with the Committee and the incidents surrounding the book-burning. He also tried to explain why things were so difficult for people like them.

Van listened closely and with much interest, almost hanging on every word Franz said. Although he was near exhaustion, he realized that, for the first time in his life, someone was finally discussing the very thing that he had so avoided and denied all those years. Franz was talking about the unmentionable, and Van felt the wraps and bindings of the restrictive strait jacket unwinding from around him. The new feeling of freedom was both exhilarating and frightening.

Franz continued, "If a man is born different in some way, most enlightened cultures have learned that this is not a sin against God or a crime against society. This is generally true with one major exception. My homosexuality is the human difference that remains a sin or a crime today even in the eyes of our society."

Franz went toward the kitchen to get another beer.

"Would you like another one, Van?"

"No, I don't believe," Van stopped without finishing the sentence. He did want another beer. Why say no when he wanted one? "Yes, I do want another one."

While Franz was getting the beer, Van was considering what he had said. Franz's explanation about people that were different sounded logical, but Van was so confused and tired he could hardly think. He was still worried about Ernst. Where had they taken him and for what purpose? He tried to think of something he could do to help him.

Franz returned to the living room with the beer and resumed speaking; "Because society does not understand us, we are classified as an evil, a crime, an affront to God, an illegal act or condition, a forbidden subject—not even permissible for discussion or consideration. This attitude has been transferred from generation to generation, gathering false ideas and myths all the while. Man can understand blindness, deafness, insanity in its various forms, and most of the other human differences.

"Today, in the world as we know it, man does not understand me or my homosexuality. I am, therefore, an evil, a criminal and something to be despised or not mentioned.

"The basic idea behind the Committee was to help other people gain an understanding of us. But I personally never fully agreed with this theory about understanding and acceptance coming with education. I've always felt that men who are not homosexual cannot understand us at all. Instead of wasting our time and efforts trying to gain understanding, we should direct our efforts elsewhere. Since they will *never* fully understand us, we should instead try to convince them how important, how basically humane, even how Christian it is to accept us as members of the human race who are not evil, criminal or sick but merely different. We obey the same laws, pay the same taxes, wrestle with the same problems and strive for the same things in life that they do. We should be accepted as a part of their society. We are here! We are everywhere! Let them be aware of our difference but not hate, criminalize, institutionalize or kill us because of our difference.

"If I could, this is what I would tell the world. To me, it seems ironic that we are hated and despised because we love, yet differently, not because we are evil or full of hate.

"I will stop preaching now. I hope I haven't bored you."

It was a long time before Van replied. "Bored me? Not at all. I suppose you have put into words what I've thought within myself for years, with one exception. I've always felt I was breaking God's laws by having this difference."

Franz smiled. "You see, I *am* right. All your life, you've been taught by your Jewish heritage that your desires are evil, an affront to God. Didn't you ever wonder if these teachings were really truth? Didn't it ever occur to you that God made you, yes, even you, and thousands more like you? Why would God, all knowing, all powerful, totally perfect God create an evil like you and the rest of us?"

"I thought Satan had done it," Van tried to argue.

"You were taught to think that. Do you really believe that?"

"I don't know anymore. I am confused by all you've said. It all sounds so rational, so true, so real. And yet, something deep within me tells me you're wrong."

"Now you have put your finger on Satan's real work. As long as evil is in control of men's lives and minds, our situation will be used for an excuse to persecute us. Being a Jew, you should certainly see the parallel there. The evil within men is what makes them seek other men who are different to vent their rage upon. We, like Jews, are society's scapegoats. If something bad can't be blamed on the Jews, then it must be our fault. Being different, belonging to a minority, thinking a different thought from the majority is not wrong. You must unlearn all those lies that were taught you over the years and learn the truth, starting tonight."

He sounds like Sheila talking about lies and truth, Van thought. And he uses Mama's scapegoat example. How strange that people use the same words and arguments to justify things that are so different, so opposite.

"Van, you continually speak of our feelings being evil. You have, I assume, indulged your evil whims many times. I don't understand how you can call them evil."

"Franz, I have to confess that I have never . . . been with a man." Somehow he managed to say it.

Franz looked at Van, at first in disbelief, then in wonder. Sadly, he mumbled, "This damned life has been harder on you than it has been on me the past few years."

Franz stood and started toward the light switch. Slowly approaching the switch, he said, "May I please be the one to introduce you to the 'world of evil'?"

Van surrendered. "Yes, Franz, I don't think I have any alternative.

86

I don't think I can live much longer the way I have been."

The lights off, darkness engulfed the room. The only light within the room came from the flames around the city, captured in the large window glass and reflected from other glass objects in the room. Van wondered why Franz had turned the lights off. Was this required so God would not see their sin? In the darkness, Van, who was still seated, was not sure where Franz was. He could not hear him.

He jumped when Franz's hands touched his shoulders. He had come up behind Van, and, since Van was not expecting that, it had startled him. Their breathing was the only sound within the room. Muffled, but discernible, the sounds of the breaking of glass and destruction from outside filtered into the room.

Franz's hands began to caress, not just hold, Van's shoulders. Slowly, cautiously, his right hand glided along Van's neck to his head and worked its way to his hair. Shivers and goose bumps travelled over Van's body. Franz pressed Van's head to him, it rested against Franz's stomach. Both hands were now on his face, feeling the contours blindly. Dropping his hands from Van's face, he let them rest upon his chest, not feeling or holding, simply resting there on the upper part of Van's chest.

Franz gently removed his hands and moved in front of Van. He was silhouetted against the window and Van could discern only his outline. He took Van's right hand in both of his and pulled him to his feet. Standing there, not knowing what he was supposed to do, Van felt him breathe on his face as he came closer. Releasing Van's hand, he methodically began to unbutton his shirt. Each button resisted his efforts but they were eventually undone by his insistent fingers. Van's shirt fell to the floor around his feet.

Again Van jumped nervously when Franz's hands worked to loosen his belt. Each garment was removed as if Franz were disrobing a king or royal person. Not once did Van assist. His mind seemed to hover above his body. Had Franz needed Van's assistance in removing his clothes, Van did not think he could have given it.

When Van was completely without clothing, Franz left him standing in front of the window. The flames and noise of Berlin were subsiding.

Franz returned to his side. He, too, was naked. Again, he took Van's hand and led him to his bedroom. They were standing beside Franz's bed. They were on his bed, his arms around Van and, Van realized, his arms were around Franz.

For the first time in his life, Van felt a new and wonderful bond with another man, with Franz. He thought about his years of loneliness and emptiness. Now, perhaps, they were over. It was as though his shroud of celibacy had floated from him and vanished into the Berlin night, freeing him forever.

Van was awakened by the November morning sun. He looked at the strange room and wondered where he was. He saw Franz next to him, still sleeping, and remembered.

His thoughts turned to the night just ended and to Ernst, bleeding and limp, being thrown into the back of a truck. Van felt an overpowering urge to jump from the bed and do something. But what could he do? Where would he go to find Rabbi Ernst and what would he do if he found him? Maybe Franz would know what to do.

Franz lay next to Van, his lower body covered by the thick blanket. Van looked at him closely, seeing him for the first time in the light of day. Asleep, he looked so peaceful and content, different from when he had rescued Van from the soldiers or lectured to him the night before. His wavy blond hair was all tousled, giving him the appearance of a small child, a cherub.

A strange new feeling of warmth engulfed Van from within, starting in one small pinpoint somewhere deep inside and, like concentric eddies of rippling water from a stone dropped into a peaceful pond, radiated outward until he was entirely consumed. Never had he experienced such a sensation before, not even with Rudy. As he continued to look at Franz, the feeling mellowed and became less intense.

What is this I feel, he wondered. Am I going to be sick? No, he just felt strange and different. Then the realization fell upon him in much the same way a waterfall cascades over the lip of a sheer cliff and lands on the earth below.

"Is this love?" he questioned aloud, quickly placing his hand over his mouth so he would not speak again and wake Franz.

Am I actually in love with this man beside me, he wondered. Is it possible for a man to love another man? He had once said he loved Rudy, but he knew that that was a completely different feeling. There had been something about his feeling for Rudy that made it seem evil, an embarrassment to God. This was not true of his feeling for Franz. It did not bring any evil with it.

Van lay there beside the sleeping Franz, watching him with a new concept of life, beauty and love. He thought about all that had happened to him the past night and realized that it would change his life forever. He felt another new and delicious sensation. He felt free at last, and the sweetness of that feeling was an ecstasy he could not describe. His years of shadow-boxing with his true emotions were over; he was a free man. That night, Crystal Night, would always be remembered by Van as a turning point in his life.

Franz opened his eyes and looked at Van, smiled, becoming a man again, and placed his hand lightly on Van's shoulder. Van placed his hand on Franz's hand, resting it where he felt it belonged.

"Good morning, Van."

"Good morning," Van replied.

Franz pulled himself up in the bed until he was in a sitting position, his back resting against the headboard of the bed. He placed his pillow behind his neck which was resting on the top of the headboard. He looked down at Van who was still lying beside him. "Van," he said, his face showing a look of guilt. "I have a confession to make to you."

Van turned on his right side, facing Franz, and propped his head up with his right arm, his face supported by his open palm. Turning his head upward to better see Franz's face, he said, "A *confession*? A confession to *me*? . . . What *are* you talking about?"

Franz did not answer immediately. He seemed to be weighing his words carefully or trying to decide if he actually did want to "confess". When he did speak, his voice squeaked a little at first. "Well, Van, it's like this." He paused again. "Before last night at the Great Synagogue, I had seen you someplace else."

"You mean you saw me drinking at that little bar with Rabbi Ernst?" Van asked, pulling himself up to a sitting position and placing his pillow behind his head.

"No, before that. Years before that," Franz answered.

"Years?"

"Yes, years. I would say about fifteen or sixteen years before last night."

"Fifteen or sixteen? What are you talking about? I would have been a kid, a teenager, that long ago! It couldn't have been here in Berlin. I think I was only six or seven the last time I was in Berlin."

"No, it wasn't here in Berlin. It was in Baden-Baden. Let me explain," Franz said softly. "My mother, Tatina, has been going to Baden-Baden two or three times a year for ages. I never went with her except once. Oh, she did take me a few times when I was a baby, but that doesn't count. The one time I had to go with her was when I was fifteen. I remember it was early in the year, before the Baden-Baden season was really going strong."

As Van listened in amazement, Franz told him about the Hirschfelds house where they had stayed, how miserable he had been and how he had watched Van and the little chubby boy walking home from school that last day he was there.

"That was the same Rabbi Ernst you saw last night!" Van interjected.

"Well, I didn't recognize him at all," Franz said. He continued, telling Van about seeing him again later that night when he and Tatina were boarding the train. "You were walking so fast and you looked afraid. Do you remember?"

Van thought about the fishing spot and Rudy. He looked away and answered, "Yes, I remember."

"What were you scared of that night?"

"Nothing. Nothing important anyway," Van replied quietly. He turned back to Franz and asked, "But how did you recognize me last night, after so many years and after seeing me only briefly twice?"

Franz looked intently at him and said, "I really don't know. I only know that I saw you last night and was almost positive you were the tall, dark boy from Baden-Baden."

They looked at one another for a long time, neither speaking. Franz wanted to tell Van more, but he decided that he had said enough. He reached over to the radio on the bedside table and switched it on. The voice on the radio started as a whisper and soon filled the room.

. . . are coming in from all across the nation. Details are still not complete but from all reports, it appears this has been a spontaneous outburst of German wrath against the Jews, brought on by the senseless assassination of Embassy Secretary Ernst von Rath in Paris by a fanatical Jew. Cities reporting incidents of major violence are Berlin, Karlsruhe, Heidelberg, Stuttgart, Baden-Baden, Frankfort, Nurnberg

"Baden-Baden! Even there!" Van said, shocked at hearing the name of his home, never having thought of Baden-Baden or his parents. Nothing bad ever happened in Baden-Baden, he thought.

"God-damn! It sounds like it happened all over Germany. I thought it was just here in Berlin." Franz was already out of bed and had started dressing.

"I have to get to Baden-Baden as soon as I can. What time is it, Franz?"

"It's nine-fifteen. How are you going? Do you have an automobile?"

"No, I'll take the train. You mean it's nine-fifteen in the morning? Of course it is. It's light outside. We didn't get much sleep, did we?"

"I didn't sleep much," Franz replied.

They were practically shouting at one another to be heard over the news on the radio. When Franz and Van stopped talking a moment, they heard the announcer say,

> *... carried away. No figures are available but the estimates of Jewish prisoners removed to the camps are high.*

Franz turned the radio off. Van dressed quickly as he could. As he walked toward the door, Franz caught him.

"Van, I had better go with you to the station. You'll never find it without me. You should take the back way. Do we need to go by your hotel and get your luggage?"

"Damn! I forgot that. Yes, I need the clothes and papers I brought with me. My ticket is in my luggage. The hotel is only a few blocks from the train station. It won't take too much time. Let's go."

"Wait, Van, just a minute."

Everything was happening too fast for Van. The horror of the night in the streets of Berlin, the newness of the night in Franz's apartment and the sudden realization that his parents could be in danger—all of these things had come too quickly. The upheaval of the night had shaken Van's reason and logic, which could have been of little help anyway, since he had no experience with this kind of parting. The advisability of saying farewell to Franz before they left the apartment, before they actually parted, never occurred to him.

"Van, I know you are in a hurry so I will make this short. I want to see you again. Actually, I think I want to see you forever. I feel the world is suddenly going to hell. Don't forget me. Write to me, come back to Berlin, do something."

Van could say nothing. Franz reached for him. Van's hand was already on the door knob. He turned it, not consciously, it just turned. Franz's reach froze, receiving a message, although none was intentionally sent. Silently, they left the apartment and went down the stairs.

They travelled a route Van could never have travelled alone. They avoided all major streets, walking along alleys and deserted streets to avoid the Nazis. At the hotel, Franz insisted they use the stairs, not the lift. None of it was humorous, but Van chuckled to himself when he thought about their secretive manner. His humor was short-lived. The door to his room was open and his belongings were gone.

At the station Van bought another ticket to Baden-Baden. Waving to Franz from the train window as the train left the station, he noticed that Franz's wave was a weak gesture. Had his haste to leave for Baden-Baden been misinterpreted as haste to leave Franz?

Franz's hand fell to his side dejectedly as the train disappeared from view. He stood there a long time, gazing down the empty tracks.

Van's hand drifted slowly from his parting wave and rested in his lap. The distant speck on the horizon that was Franz eventually melted away and became part of the horizon. He sat there still straining to see the speck that was no longer there.

The train arrived in Baden-Baden about dusk. During the trip, Nazis had boarded the train at every stop, searching the faces of the passengers and removing each Jew. Van was amazed at the Nazis' ability to determine a Jewish person by his physical appearance. Friends had often told him he did not look Jewish. Although he never really understood what they meant, he began to understand that day on the train.

The moment the train pulled into the station, he jumped from the door, not waiting for it to stop completely. He started for the Augustaplatz, hoping to get to the cafe before Papa closed.

Dusk was becoming darkness, but something was different. Baden-Baden was changed. Van couldn't determine its nature, but in two days there had been a change and it dd not feel right. A pall seemed to hang over everything like a brewing spring storm.

11

V AN HURRIED FROM THE STATION to Papa's cafe. By the time he reached the Augustaplatz, it was fully night. The changes in Baden-Baden that he had sensed when he first left the train were becoming clearer to him.

It was much darker than usual; he could not remember a night in Baden-Baden as dark and lonely. Resort city of the wealthy and aged, Baden-Baden had always been radiant at night with thousands of lights dotting the city like jewels in a crown. Tonight the lights were missing, as though the jewels had been stolen. Early evenings had always found the streets filled with people going to the Casino, particularly in the spring and summer, rushing home from work or taking a leisurely stroll. The streets were now as desolate as some plague-ridden city of the Middle Ages. Those few people he had seen on his walk from the station had all been in a great rush, keeping their heads down, avoiding contact with anyone, anxious to arrive at their destinations. Baden-Baden had a veil of fear draped over it. He could feel it and almost taste it in the heavy oppressive air.

Standing in front of Papa's cafe, the reality of Crystal Night finally hit Van with its full impact. The tragedy of that night became genuine to him only when it became his own. Papa's cafe was no longer there. Only the shell of that wonderul gathering place remained. Like the lights and the throngs of happy people, Papa's cafe had also vanished.

The shock caused Van to look more closely about him. All the Jewish-owned stores and businesses were damaged. Some had received only minor damage: broken windows, damaged store fronts and large hastily scrawled Stars of David; others were completely ruined.

Where was Papa? If he had witnessed the destruction of his cafe, it would surely have broken his heart or possibly killed him. Papa loved that cafe. Van hoped that his father had not seen what had happened here.

He started home. The time for walking had passed, he ran. As he passed the Catholic church, he recognized Sheila's mother coming from the church and hurriedly running to her car, where her husband waited for her. The motor was running and he appeared anxious to drive away.

"Mrs. Gebhardt," Van called to her as she approached the waiting car.

"Van, it's good to see you! I have wondered about you today. Get in the car. We can talk as we ride home."

They both got into the car. She locked her door and, seeing her do that, Van locked his, an unusual thing to do in Baden-Baden. Mr. Gebhardt spoke rapidly and nervously, shaking Van's hand.

"Isn't all of this terrible," he said, driving off in a lurching way. The car jumped down the road, sputtering and coughing along until Mr. Gebhardt managed to clear it of the congestion and the ride became smoother.

Mrs. Gebhardt, who had evidently been crying, dabbed at her eyes with her handkerchief. "I lit some candles for those poor people that have had all this grief today. I prayed and prayed to every saint and the Blessed Virgin. John says it's too late for prayers, but I don't believe that."

Mr. Gebhardt shook his head in a hopeless way.

"Have you seen my parents since all of this started?"

They looked at one another with pity, sadness and pain. Neither answered Van's question.

"I have been in Berlin the last two days. It was terrible there but I had no idea it was happening here in Baden-Baden. Papa's cafe is gone! What happened to it? Who burned it? Where are Papa and Mama?"

Mr. Gebhardt finally decided he would have to be the one to tell Van what had happened because his wife, usually the more talkative of the two, was too upset to speak. She was sobbing into her handkerchief.

"Well, Van, you are right. This terrible madness has been happening all over Germany. It started last night in every city and village in the country, so I hear. Spontaneous I believe is the word they are using to describe it.

"Here in Baden-Baden, nothing started until about seven this morning. Do you know why it didn't start until seven? I'll tell you!" Mr. Gebhardt said, not waiting for Van to answer. "Because they didn't want to disturb the sleep of the tourists. Isn't that the height of

94

spontaneity. You see, all these foreign guests spend a great deal of money here and the Third Reich needs that currency.

"Early this morning they arrested all the Jewish people and locked them in the prison courtyard. About noon they made them all march in orderly ranks down the streets of the city. Two men in front of the march were forced to carry a large Star of David with the words, 'God, do not abandon us' written on it. The whole ridiculous thing reminded me of little boys playing soldier.

"They wanted large crowds along the streets but none of the good people of Baden-Baden were there. I was at my office and watched from the windows. The crowd that gathered was nothing but trash. They yelled awful things at the people when they marched by. Van, you must believe me when I tell you it was not condoned by the real people, the good citizens, of Baden-Baden."

"Mr. Gebhardt, I believe that. The Nazis are doing this, not the people of Germany, and especially not the people of Baden-Baden."

"They marched them to the synagogue," Mr. Gebhardt continued. "That is where it really got bad. I went to the synagogue to see what they were going to do. But I did not consider myself a spectator.

"When they arrived at the steps of the synagogue, they stopped. Someone had a prayer shawl and they spread it on the steps and forced your father to walk on it as he entered the synagogue. Your mother was crying during this terrible thing they made your father do. I am not familiar with the significance of prayer shawls, but it was a pitiful sight when your father had to walk on that one. It must have been a hard thing for him. I thought I could see the life leaving his face as he climbed those steps, walking on that shawl. Terrible! Terrible!

"I did not, of course, go into the synagogue, but I did watch from nearby. It wasn't long until I could hear all the people inside singing one of those dreadful Nazi songs three or four times. After the singing, those of us outside that were close enough could hear someone reading something or preaching from the pulpit. When they were forced by the Nazis to speak louder, I recognized it as being from that piece of garbage, *Mein Kampf*.

"They stayed in the synagogue a long time. I had almost decided to go back to the office when a group of the men came out into the synagogue courtyard. The Nazis forced them all to face the synagogue and urinate on the wall of the synagogue, or in that direction. I did not see your father in this group. I wondered then where he was.

"Later, all of the people came out of the synagogue and were marched back to the prison yard, and this afternoon they were all loaded in buses and taken to the train station. A special train came through, stopped, loaded all of our Jewish citizens on board and took them away."

"Took them away. Where?"

"Van, I am not sure but the talk is that they were taken to Dachau."

"Dachau," Van dared say the word. That place, even the mention of its name, always conjured up visions of hell to most Germans. Even before Crystal Night, it had become a synonym for hell.

"My Papa and Mama are on their way to that place? What can I do to help them and stop the Nazis from taking them there?"

"Van, I haven't told you the whole story yet. Your mother was put on the train with the others. If Dachau is really their destination, that is where she is going now, or perheps she's already there. I am so sorry. I know that doesn't do any good but I still have to say it. I am so terribly sorry."

"What did you mean you haven't told me the whole story? What else is there? Why did you say Mama was put on the train and not mention Papa? Where is Papa?"

Mr. Gebhardt sighed sadly while his wife cried even louder. He told the rest of the story. "Van, your father died sometime, somewhere in the synagogue. I do not know what happened but they brought his body out when they marched out and went back to the prison yard. Your rabbi, Eschel I believe is his name, reached down and picked up the prayer shawl your father had been forced to walk on and laid it over his body as they came down the steps."

Papa, dead? Van thought, the two words together forming a question. They did not belong together in the same sentence, they did not fit, they were so far apart in meaning. Papa was a happy, loving, wonderful man, so much consumed with the vitality of everyday living that the prospect of his dying had never been considered. Van knew, intellectually, that everyone dies, but emotionally he had never had to deal with death; its cold embrace had never reached this close before. He could not grasp the reality that Papa was beyond his reach forever. The only thing Van could think about was that Papa had never forgiven him for selling the watch and then refusing to explain why. He would never have the chance to explain. This brought the sorrow, not the realization that Papa was dead. That would come, but it did not come with the two words Papa and dead welded together in one sentence.

"Where is Papa's body, now?" Van asked. He did not know what else to say. To him, it sounded wrong to add the word body to his question, but he had often heard the same question asked when other people had died.

"I don't know why, but they loaded it on the train where they put all of our friends to take them away. I didn't see them load your father's body but a friend did and told me about it later."

Mr. Gebhardt's car had now come to a stop in their driveway. They wanted Van to come in with them but he told them he could not. He felt that he had to do something, he did not know what, but something. Van thanked them for their concern. They waved to Van as he started for his own home. He heard them shut the door as they went into their house, and he looked back for a final glance at the warm home where he and Ernst had been so often. The house was still dark. They had not turned any lights on when they went in.

Lichtentaler Avenue was as dark and depressing as the other streets of Baden-Baden. Strangely, he still expected lights in his parents' house and for Mama and Papa to be waiting for him there. He found the house dark with most of the doors open and the windows broken out. No one else was there; he was alone.

He found that the house had been vandalized, the furniture and pictures knocked over, everything smashed or missing. It was evidently the work of a group of people, not just one or two. Every room was in such disarray that it was too much for one or two to have done. He worked his way through the broken furniture and other family belongings on the floor to the sitting room and saw the condition of that once happy place. Large words were scrawled on the walls with black paint. A large Star of David had been painted on one entire wall with the words "Christ Killers" written within the star. There were other slogans and obscene words written around the walls. He looked for the table where the glass case with the gold watch had been. The table was turned on its side, the watch was gone.

He stood in the middle of the room, and his world seemed to be falling in on him. Papa was dead, Mama was on a train somewhere between Baden-Baden and Dachau; so difficult to imagine or visualize. Dachau was hell, or so everyone in Germany believed. His mother being transported to that hell was not plausible to Van. His home, the place of his mostly happy childhood, was like a scene from a nightmare. Those words on the walls of the sitting room did not belong in his world, they never had.

The painted Star of David was not the same Star of David he had always known. This one appeared to have been painted with strokes full of hate. And those words, Christ Killers, were a lie.

Van knelt on one knee, his arm resting on the overturned table where the watch had been. Dropping his head, he looked at the floor, the carpet soiled by muddy boots. His mind was filled with all of the things that had happened that day. Was Ernst on his way to Dachau also, he wondered. He saw Ernst being dragged down the Berlin street and thrown into the truck. Franz stood beside Van, trying to help him. All of the things Franz had said to him the past night rushed through his mind.

He raised his head and looked upward toward the ceiling, not really seeing it. Looking past it to the heavens, he spoke, talking to God and also to himself.

"I am a man!" he said loudly. The echoes from the empty house repeated his words, mocking him.

"I am a man!" he said again. "They will not do this to me!"

His face had turned crimson red with his anger. His chest swelled with a feeling of new resolve and determination.

"God of Abraham, God of Your Chosen People, I swear to you, I will survive this madness that has taken power! I will survive, one way or another, I will survive!"

Van came out the front door of the Bertholds' house, leaving the door open, and stood on the porch. Feeling that he had to try to get to Dachau, find Mama and help her, he stared out across the unusually dark and quiet city. He did not know how he would get to Dachau, how he would ever find Mama or how he would manage to help her. But he knew he had to try.

"Are you Van Bertholds?"

"Yes," he replied.

"You come with us."

"Where are you taking me?" he demanded of the two Nazis that were leading him away from the house, each holding an arm.

"You are going to Dachau where all Jew garbage belongs. Now shut up or you won't even make it to the train."

Van stood in the aisle of the crowded train car, his tall, broad frame wedged tightly in one spot. Towering above the others, he was able to see the entire interior. The movements of the car from one side to the other were not violent or erratic but gentle and with a predictable pattern, thus tending to induce motion sickness in some and sleepiness in others. Those with weak stomachs, or a propensity to motion distress, were on the verge of nausea. Some few had already vomited, creating a real problem within the crowded car.

Those windows that could be opened had been opened; the cold November night air rushed through the car as the train rumbled through the German countryside. Packed within that long train were hundreds of Jews, large numbers of Gypsies and other smaller groups of people who had suddenly discovered that their differences were criminal. So closely were they forced to stand to each other that the opened windows became a welcome relief, allowing the cold air to cool them, revive them and disperse the foul odors of nausea.

Van looked at all the people in his car; well over a hundred were forced into an area that normally seated about forty. There was a solid sea of heads swaying and bobbing with the motions of the car. Mothers and fathers tried desperately to hold their small children's heads above the crush of bodies while many others nodded their heads and even laid them on their neighbor's shoulder or chest like broken sticks. He could not see his own body, for the crowd pressed around him on all sides. He watched the sea of heads move and sway and thought of a lush field of wheat just ready for harvest, the heads of the wheat rolling and swaying like an ocean in the gentle breeze.

Van tried to look through the windows at the countryside floating by. It was wasted effort. He was too tall to see anything except a dark night, occasionally mottled with streaks of light as he briefly glimpsed them from the moving train.

When Van was taken from the house on Lichtentaler to the train station, he had been herded in with about twenty others, brought there by the Nazis. Van concluded that most of the Baden-Baden people had been taken on the train with Mama and Papa. Papa's body, he corrected himself. The small group was standing on the station platform and Van was pushed into their midst by the two Nazis who had brought him there.

"Professor Neumann!" Van exclaimed, recognizing his aged art teacher from public school.

The bent, withered, old man looked up at this tall, younger man who had called him. Now, what is this goy doing down here with us Jews, he wondered. Who is this big man with the sharp face and square cut to his features? He would be a good subject for a painter. Perhaps he is someone who posed for me years ago.

"Hello," Professor Neumann replied to Van. "I don't remember your name, young man."

"Professor Neumann, it's me, Van, Van Bertholds. I was in your art classes for years and you don't remember me?"

Professor Neumann squinted over his glasses, head tilted upward, and looked more closely at Van. Yes, he did remember the strange boy from the Bertholds family whose father, old Papa Bertholds at the cafe on the man plaza, always claimed was left by a band of Gypsies.

"Bertholds? Yes, I remember you. And here I stood wondering what one of the goyim was doing down here with us. Thought for a minute you might be a Gypsy."

The two talked about the past day's terrible events in Baden-Baden. The old teacher had also been out of the city, back in the mountains and the forest, engaged in his true interest, painting. When he returned to his home late that night, he had found much the same thing Van had found at his parents' home.

Professor Neumann was known in the area and in most of Germany for his ability as an artist. His attention to detail was unsurpassed. Often painting minute figures of intricate and complicated design on small objects such as china plates, scrolls and fine parchment, he was said to be able to accurately portray a multitude of angels dancing on the head of a pin if he were only informed as to their exact number. His fame as an artist was so widespread that he had often been summoned to paint for the Kaiser.

"What are they going to do with us, Professor? I know they are taking us to Dachau, but why?" Van asked the old man. He had to be at least eighty, Van thought. Why did he have to endure this, at his age?

"We are Jews, Bertholds. They will do with us whatever they like and no one will notice or care the slightest bit."

"But we are Germans too. This is our home, our country. We fought for it and many of us died for it in the war with the Allies. What were we then, just Germans and not Jews?"

Professor Neumann looked away, watching the approaching train, and tried to find the answer for this young man's question.

"Did you not study our history and heritage when you were young? Look at our history and see the answers to your questions. It is there in our yesterdays and all you have to do is study it and you will know how our tomorrows will be."

The small group from Baden-Baden was shoved, pushed and packed into an already full passenger car after the train had stopped. Van was the last to board. He was pushed and packed even more by the closing doors. Professor Neumann was deeper in the car, out of Van's reach and the sound of his voice.

The train puffed on through the night, stopping at many villages and cities, each providing still more people, and those pushed Van deeper within the sea of bodies in the car.

The train Van was on was not the only one making such a journey that night. All over Germnay, other trains, like many poisonous serpents, slithered their way to Germany's newly found solution to difference, diversity and uniqueness: the concentration camp.

Van's train moved steadily onward, slowly diminishing the kilometers that stood between normalcy and Hell: between Baden-Baden and Dachau.

12

T HE TRAIN SLOWED AND STOPPED, the Nazi guards opened the doors, and the exhausted, sick and frightened masses of passengers poured out like grains of wheat from a punctured bag. The very old and the very young were no match for the force of the freed mob. It swept them forward, carrying them at its own pace to its own mindless destiny. Those poor ones who stumbled and fell in the ensuing panic were trampled to death in many cases.

Van's size allowed him to move with minor difficulty, but Professor Neumann would have surely fallen and been killed had Van not grabbed him around the shoulders and, protecting him from the frantic rush, led him out of the mob. Supporting him became easier when Van grasped him around the waist. Lifting him up, he actually carried him, resting the frail, old body against his hip. As he struggled to escape from the mob's movement, Van stumbled over a small bundle that screamed its protests and began crying loudly. Glancing down, he saw that it was a small girl, about four or five years of age. Leaning over, Professor Neumann's body tilting the same direction, his feet and legs pointing outward, Van reached down and scooped the child up with one arm. She screamed louder into Van's ear as he held her within the cradle of his arm and made his way out of the crowd.

When the dear, old friend and teacher was released, he tottered a bit and finally collapsed. Van handed the small girl to the professor, who clutched her to his ancient chest, quieting her screams and howls.

"Well," the professor said, drawing the word out long and emphasizing the last part, thus making it sound like an exclamation of discovery. "Not only do we have a Gypsy but a hero also. We are truly blessed today, this small young one and myself."

Freed from the cramped closeness of the train, Van took a deep breath of air. It smelled strange, musty and damp, like moldering leaves thrown into a pool of stagnant water. When he breathed through his mouth, he could taste the swamp lying like a dense fog in the air. Dawn's first hint was peeping over the unfamiliar horizon.

The Nazi SS men, members of the Death's Head Battalion, began restoring order to the mob. The skull and crossbones they wore provided no comfort to anyone. Their reputation was already well established in Germany. Their objective was to form the people into ranks, a lofty ambition considering the size of the crowd and the physical and emotional state of the people. However, they did not rely only on the usual military procedures; they used brute force.

Van stood and watched in complete disbelief. Never in his life had he actually seen women, children and elderly people treated so inhumanely. The SS men beat them, kicked them, pushed, shoved and dragged them; anything to get them formed into military ranks. The oldest and weakest were the ones that least understood the commands screamed at them from every side. They were, therefore, the ones last to fall into place or to move at all. They did not hear, understand or care.

During one terrible moment when an old woman with no teeth and poor hearing was being kicked by two brutes in Nazi uniforms, Van started toward them, his fists doubled, his adrenaline pumping at a furious pace. Van imagined the Nazis doing to Mama and Papa what they were actually doing to the old woman. The old woman, Mama and Papa merged into one.

Professor Neumann grabbed Van's trouser leg and held him. "Don't," he whispered. "There is nothing you can do to help her. There are too many of them. Forget it! Look away!"

Van realized that Professor Neumann was telling him the truth. He slowly turned away from the scene and looked at the professor and the small child asleep in his arms. I must fight them, he thought. I am a man and I must fight. I must, I am a man.

Eventually the entire throng of people were formed into ranks and were marched a short distance to the entrance of Dachau, the Jourhaus—a two-story structure with an archway through the center. The paved road ran through the archway into the actual camp. On either side of the building was a set of double entry doors. A wooden watchtower, with an antenna atop it, rose from the center of the tile roof. Had it not been for the watchtower and the road running through the middle of the building, the Jourhaus would have appeared ordinary. A tall stately poplar flanked each side of the road.

Passing through the Jourhaus, the marching column was actually in the prison compound. A wide thoroughfare ran down the center of the camp through two rows of prison barracks. Van assumed one row was for men while the women were kept on the other side. He was not altogether correct; the divisions for barracks occupancy were based on other criteria. Generally, the prisoners were segregated according to their crime. Jews were housed together, Gypsies were in a separate area, hardened criminals were segregated in another and so on, the number and size of the areas having to be increased as the categories increased.

The ill-formed troop from the train was marched to a large open area near the back of the Jourhaus, just inside the main compound walls. There they were separated into two groups for processing. Men were processed in the area where they stood while the women were taken to another area. Struggling to stay together, family members received the quick attention and wrath of the Nazis. They pulled men from their wives, fathers from their daughters, sons from their mothers and brothers from their sisters. The rule was irrevocable and no exceptions were allowed.

Van watched the many small tragedies happening around him. Each was heartbreaking by itself, but with so many occurring simultaneously, the effect was overwhelming. A single parting of two loved ones destined for some unknown, terrible fate is grief enough for the soul, but hundreds of such partings, and in many instances more than one within each little family group, provided a thick pall of sorrow and emptiness that became a part of the low-hanging, thick fog engulfing the whole area.

Professor Neumann's sleeping girl child was wrenched from the loving cradle of his arms. He stood, arms extended and empty, pleading for the return of his small angel, tears slowly trickling down through the valleys of his wrinkled old face. The child cried noisily, joining a chorus of other cries, moans, pleadings and shrieks. Tears slipped quietly from the dark eyes and down the smooth plane of Van's face. He sobbed, thinking of his own emptiness without Papa and Mama.

The men were processed in lines leading to a large table staffed with Nazi clerks. Van stood behind the professor, waiting his turn. He tried to see the camp more clearly, but the fog still lay thickly over the entire area. He wondered how he would find Mama and, if and when he did find her, what he would do to get her out of this place.

The camp stretched as far as Van could see. It was surrounded, in some places, by a tall concrete fence with barbed wire on top of the concrete. Climbing the fence seemed out of the question, and getting through the strands of electrified barbed wire would be impossible. Spaced along the fence were watchtowers, and guards with machine guns. In some places, there was no concrete fence, just a thick tangle of rolled barbed wire, forming a high-voltage electric barrier. Between the electric fence and the compound was a moat, filled with water.

Van observed it all closely. He had never imagined that there would be so many people in Dachau. As far as he could see, there were crowds of people coming through the fog and disappearing back into it. They all moved at the same pace: a lethargic, lifeless shuffle, the picture of hopelessness. He was reminded of a line from Dante, "Give up all hope, you who enter here." The prisoners, looking all alike, seemed to have done just that. With so many prisoners and the men being separated from the women, Van wondered how he would ever be able to find Mama. She may not be here, he thought. They may have taken her to one of the other camps.

"Name? You, big one, what's your name?"

The clerk was talking to Van. He had reached the processing table without realizing he had been moving. His name and offense, "Jew", were recorded in a large ledger-like book. A number, 24967, was placed beside his name.

A Nazi grasped his left arm and held it down on the table, the inner part of his arm up. A little short man tattooed his number just above his wrist. It stung and smelled of burning flesh and paints. Van looked at it closely and felt a finality, a sealing of his fate. Everything was official now, he thought. I am here and I am 24967.

He was yanked back to reality by an SS man who grabbed him by the arm and kicked him to move him on. The Nazi's boots were big and heavy with metal imbedded in the toe portion. He kicked Van on the back of his legs, mostly in the calves, and finally in the buttocks.

Van turned on him to crush the little uniformed official. Standing over the rather short, dumpy SS man, Van raised his arm to try to knock his fat head from his shoulders. The short Nazi rammed his club into Van's groin. Excruciating pain shot through Van's body and he fell to the ground, doubled up in the fetal position, his hands cupping the injured area.

"Get up, you swine! You ever raise your arm to a Nazi uniform again and you'll be a feast for the maggots. Those goddamn maggots don't care if you're kosher or not. They eat pork, so you better watch out."

Professor Neumann helped Van to his feet and then supported him as they walked into the building. Inside, Van leaned against a wall while a harried man behind a counter quickly took his measurements by looking at him head to foot. He threw him some ragged clothes and directed him on to another smaller room where Van removed his clothes and put on the dirty rags. All the men had been given the same uniform. Some were more filthy and ragged than others, but they were all alike: trousers and a shirt with large, alternating black and white stripes. There was also a beret-like cap. On the left side of the shirt or blouse, the yellowish-gold Star of David had been attached. More Stars of David made with hate, Van thought.

The Nazis did not do all of this processing. Most of the real work was done by prisoners called Kapos, more hated than the Nazis. Van was to learn that these men had sold their today for one more tomorrow.

They were led to their assigned barracks. The outside of each was dreary and bleak, much the same as the entire camp. Professor Neumann and Van were not housed in the same barrack. Van entered his barrack noting that the interior was more depressing and dismal than the outside area. A row of bunk beds flanked each side of the large middle aisle. The beds were stacked three high, with two tiers pushed together to form a clutch of six beds. In the aisle were a few benches and tables. The ceiling rafters were exposed and the roof was visible. Two or three large black cans sat in the center aisle. The foul odor was thick from the cans, and Van soon discovered that they were substitute toilets. During the night, prisoners were not allowed to leave the barrack to use the toilet; thus the black pots were provided.

With no luggage, clothes or personal belongings of his own, he stood looking at his new surroundings. Was this Hell, he wondered. All his life, until Crystal Night with Franz, Van had had his own secret hell that he dealt with alone. Now he wondered if this new one would be as bad. He thought not.

When he entered the barrack, he was told which bed he was to occupy. It did not appear to be long enough for his tall frame. He went to his bunk, wanting to test it and see if it were big enough. No, he thought, I must go look for Mama. Perhaps one of those Kapos can help me. He found it difficult to think, he was so completely exhausted. He would lie down for only a minute.

His bed was the middle one in the stack of three. The mattress was about three centimeters thick, a greasy, filthy rag circled and spotted with human waste or blood or the tears of time. He lowered himself onto the mattress in spite of its sickeningly soiled condition. It was so greasy it was slick. Stuffed with rocks and pebbles, Van thought.

Something was crawling on him. Lice! He bolted from the bed and stood beside it, scratching himself in a near fit of panic. Leaning against the wooden structure that held the three levels of beds, he looked for the minute insects that had suddenly taken up residence on his body. The parasites were so tiny he could only find a few of the larger ones. From the darker corners of the barrack, the rats watched him intently, their beady eyes shining from the shadows. Van had never seen a louse much less had one on his body. The entire place was nothing but filth. He was so tired and sleepy that he could not think or do anything; he felt he must lie back down, lice or no lice. Scratching his scalp, arms, legs and all over his body, he fell into a fitful sleep, his first since that short sleep on Crystal Night.

It was not a restful, refreshing sleep; it knitted none of the ravel of Van's life. His was a sleep filled with fitful dreams. He dreamed of things that had been, reaching deep within his subconscious to retrieve stored images that had become distorted and altered by time. The future crept into his dreams in some unexplained inversion of reason and sanity, taking on the guise of the present. As the dreamer, he was unwittingly the entire production crew: author, director, stage hand, scenic designer, casting director, censor, and both star and audience.

Ephemeral images and hazy pictures drifted languidly or rushed at a maddening pace through his restless sleep. The dream was of Mama in the middle of the sitting room, the painted obscenities on the walls around her. She tells a young Van about his Jewish heritage, God's laws and the mandatory requirement that he keep the race pure by marrying a nice Jewish boy. She said boy! She knew! God had finally whispered Van's secret to her.

Papa enters the room, floating, not walking, wearing one of those ridiculous shrouds, a long, grayish sheet wound about him and floating through the air behind him. Rabbi Ernst Hoffman appears as though by magic and he and Papa dance a deathly somber dance while a Nazi military band plays the *Horst Wessel Lied*. Mama continues to lecture him over the noise of the music about marrying a Jewish boy.

Everything in the scene, like many toppled cans of paint, suddenly begins to run and mix together, creating a vivid, multi-colored abstract painting. The music being played by the band slows, sounding like a recording whose playing speed is gradually decreased until the sound becomes a garbled, deep-throated moan and, finally, the sound melts away completely, the low-pitched bass protesting its death.

The dream has become a void, a speck of empty cosmic space replacing the mixture of colors. In the midst of this nothingness, a large bed materializes, eventually occupying the entire area of an immensely large room, the school concert hall, which is gaily decorated for the annual Spring Party. Franz, Van's Franz, enters and is followed by hundreds of Nazi soldiers. Methodically, in the middle of the tremendous bed, Franz unbuttons their shirts, their belts and their trousers. He completely undresses them all in slow motion. When all of their clothes have been removed, the bed becomes a mass of naked bodies, arms, legs and torsos, entangled in a weird orgy with Franz serving all of the men, sometimes one at a time, sometimes en masse.

Van struggles to awake, desperate to escape the nightmare created by his own subconscious mind. He feels as though he is slipping into the very pits of hell, the depravity of the dream corrupting and vulgarizing all those he has loved and held dear with the terrible secret torment he has tried to hide for so long. The dream has loosened his tormentor and it is controlling him, destroying him and all the decencies of his world. He cannot escape; the nightmare holds him captive.

The entangled mass of humanity continues its movement with Franz the central object. After a seemingly forever period of time, the soldiers all meld together into a giant phallus. It lies across the bed, pulsating with a life of its own. Franz is no longer in the bizarre scene, but Mama and Papa enter and look disgustedly at the object. They both spit on it in revulsion, turn and spit on Van who is on the very edge of the scene. The spit becomes a torrent of liquid, washing the vision away.

Sheila stands alone on a tall pedestal, completely nude. She holds a gold crucifix in front of her, her arms extended full length. She glows and radiates beauty, her naked body a marvel of God's handiwork.

"Van, come to me! I love you. Let us wed and become one. I don't care if you are one of the Christ Killers. I still love you."

Mama and Papa are heard screaming in unison, "She is not a good Jewish boy!" as Sheila flies away on wings of pure down, pink and fluffy, a vision of heaven.

Professor Neumann ushers in another woman who stands in

Sheila's spot on the pedestal. Van recognizes her. It is the prostitute in Baden-Baden. She is without clothes, a Star of David hangs around her waist on a thick iron chain, the Star hanging in front of the juncture of her legs. She beckons to Van with hands drenched with blood, her extended arms dripping it on her body. She comes toward him gliding, not walking, as on a cloud. The closer she gets, the more horrible she looks. She is face to face with him. Her breath smells of sulfur and is hotter than anything he has ever imagined. Her arms encircle him, pulling him to her blood-splattered body. In an instant she is no longer the prostitute, she has become Rudy. He embraces Van tightly, holding him as a man holds a lover. He kisses him, his tongue in Van's mouth reaching to the back of his throat. They fall to the soft mush of the floor and billows of cloud swirl around them. Ripping Van's prison stripes from his body, he roughly attacks him. The pain is unbearable. Rudy grunts like an animal; then he is still. He helps Van from the marshmallow floor.

Van looks up at him as he rises from the floor. He is no longer Rudy. Now he is Franz. Touching Van, he heals all his pains and wounds. His touch is one of love. Rudy reappears behind Franz. In Rudy's upraised hands, high over his head, he holds an oversized battleax. As though in slow motion, he lowers the battleax and splits Franz vertically into halves that fall in opposite directions to the floor. Instead of blood and the expected internal organs, butterflies, thousands of butterflies, escape from Franz's halves and fly heavenward. They are of every shade and hue, dazzling to the eye. Rudy opens his mouth to speak, and a nauseating fountain of blood and pus pours out, drenching Van and the crowd that has gathered around him. In the crowd are Mama, Papa, Rabbi Ernst Hoffman, Rabbi Eschel and Professor Neumann. Swastikas fall on them from the skies above. They strike painfully as they fall like large hail. Rudy's fountain seems endless. It floods Van's dream. They are all swimming and drowning in a thick pool of blood, pus and swastikas. Van begins to sink in a vertigo of reds, whites and blacks. He falls downward with increasing speed toward the pits of Hades.

13

S HAKING VAN ROUGHLY, the Kapo finally got him awake, rescuing him from his nightmare-dream and bringing him back to the nightmare-reality of Dachau.

"Wake up, you lazy Jew!"

"I'm awake. What time is it? How long have I been sleeping?"

"Time you don't need to worry about. In this place, we take care of all things to do and when to do them. You don't need a schedule or a clock."

"Is it still morning?" Van asked as he pulled his aching frame from the misery of the bed and the fright of his dream.

"It's morning. And you don't sleep in the day here. Day is for work. 'Work Makes You Free' as they say. You come with me."

Still not awake, almost trance-like, Van followed the man, who he assumed must be the Kapo for the hole in which he was to stay. They approached a small building near the Jourhaus with lines of men leading into it, and Van was pushed into one of them.

"You got by without getting your head shaved. Everyone must have his head shaved. Lice and other creatures love all that hair, especially thick hair like you have. Well, enjoy it because off it comes as soon as you get in that building there."

Five or six lines of men stretched for long distances. The lines moved quickly, convincing Van that there must be many barbers in the small buildings. While he waited in the line, almost steadily walking toward the building, the man who had brought him there talked to him.

"My name is Golt. I am the Kapo of your barrack. When I say, 'shit,' you better shit or you'll never shit again! You're a big strong one aren't you? Sure you're a Jew?"

"Yes, of that I am positive," Van said, beginning to wonder if he really had been left on the Bertholds doorstep by a band of Gypsies.

"Well, I never seen a Jew as big and strong as you look. What kind of work did you do?"

"School teacher."

"School teacher! What did you teach? Logging?"

"No, I taught science. In Mannheim," Van added. He did not think much about adding the extra bit of information concerning where he taught. It was a response he almost always gave when asked what he taught. He would soon learn to volunteer no facts in that place.

"Science, eh. That is good. We need a big man like you to help in the infirmary. Since you taught science, you can work in the infirmary. Yes, that is the job for you. Need to dip some people to get rid of lice. They don't want to be dipped. You dip 'em! No matter what, you dip 'em!"

The mere mention of lice launched Van into a fit of scratching. The little bastards seemed to be all over him.

When he entered the building where he was to have his head shaved, he was shocked at what he saw. It was more like an assembly line than a barber shop. One group of men had electric razors which they used to remove all the hair on each man's head in less than thirty seconds. Their speed was phenomenal. Van was reminded of men shearing sheep, each trying to do the job faster than all the others. The hair literally flew, creating the illusion of a cloud around the activity.

A second group of men had straight edge razors and took the shorn victims as soon as the ones with the electric razors finished. Patting the stubbled heads with a little water from a large pail beside each one, they would then shave the heads. A few members of the second group used a dish of soap and a brush, thus making the shaving easier and less dangerous. Those that used only water were constantly wiping the blood from their razors.

Van looked at the busy workers in the small building, noting that most of them did not wear the gold Star of David. Instead, on the left chest of their shirts or jackets and also on the outer right trouser leg, there were chevrons or triangles of different colors. Some were red while others were green. Many of the different colored triangles had letters in the center of them, an "F" on one or two and a "P" on some. How strange, Van thought. They must not be Jews. He wondered what the different colors and the letters on some of them meant.

Before he realized what had happened, his head had been passed over quickly a few times with the electric razor and the other man was applying dabs of lather. He also finished in less than thirty seconds, cutting Van only twice.

Kapo Golt was waiting for him and took him immediately to the infirmary. They walked through the building to the back where large tubs or vats were filled with a foul smelling thick, whitish liquid. It smelled of Mama's bug-killer that Van had always been warned of as a child. Men, women and children were huddled together in a corner part of the area behind the infirmary.

"Get over here you lice-bait! This'll get rid of those little buggers!" yelled an SS guard at the woeful group. Evidently fearful of the pungent dip, no one in the group wanted to be first, second, or at all. An SS guard struck a woman in the back with his rifle butt. She fell senseless to the ground. Her clothes were removed by the guards and she was lifted by four of them and dropped into the huge vat. Quickly reaching into the murky dip to pull her head above the liquid, Van's hands burned as though he had stuck them into a bucket of fire. The dip was too concentrated, he thought to himself. Her screech shattered the waiting group and startled Van, her pain almost unbearable. She came out of the vat so fast it was hard to believe she was as rotund as she was. Her fat body was bright red. Around the yard she ran, screaming her misery and burning pain. A guard grabbed her and inspected her blistered body.

"No lice on this one!" he announced.

They dipped them all, an experience in efficient German absurdity. As soon as they reentered their barracks, they were infested again. They were not treated to rid them of lice and make life more endurable, but rather out of a sadistic desire to see human suffering.

When the day finally ended, Van had helped treat what must have been hundreds of people. His energy and strength were gone. Helping to force his Jewish brothers and sisters into those vats of near-lye liquid had been the worst thing he had ever done. His inner struggle with the right and wrong of his lifelong secret paled into insignificance.

From the back of the infirmary where Van was finishing his first day in Dachau, he could see the path leading to the building's front entrance. In the gathering dusk, he noticed an old man, probably a rabbi, and a younger man carry a woman toward the infirmary. They laid her down on the ground near the end of a long line of people waiting to enter the building.

The old rabbi straightened and Van recognized him. It was Rabbi Eschel from Baden-Baden. Van ran from behind the building to the rabbi. He called him by name. Rabbi Eschel turned and looked at Van searchingly. Without his hair Van did look different. Finally, the rabbi recognized him as yet another of his flock from Baden-Baden.

"Van, is it you? Here in Dachau too?"

"Yes, Rabbi, they got me last night and we arrived here before dawn this morning. Professor Neumann was in the same group that I was."

"My son, I am so sorry," he said sadly.

"I am sorry too, Rabbi, but surely we won't be here long. They can't keep us too long, can they?"

"No, no, that's not what I mean. Here, at my feet! This is your poor sick mother that we were carrying to the infirmary for help. I am afraid she is dying and no one will help or do anything to save her."

Van couldn't believe it. Not Mama! She had never been ill. She could not be dying. Rabbi Eschel must be mistaken. Papa's death was enough; not Mama too. Van knelt beside her and pulled the scarf from her face; she was pale and withered, her eyes sunken in her face.

"Mama, Mama," he said softly to her. "It's me, Van. Can you hear me?"

She moaned a little but did not answer.

"Mama, can you hear me? I am here to help you."

She opened her eyes and smiled weakly up at Van. In an almost inaudible whisper, she said, "Van, why are you here in this awful place?"

He had found her. He had not expected to find her so ill but he had felt that he would eventually find her. Her eyes were again closed and her every breath came with such physical effort it was tiring to watch the struggle. Wrenching each wisp of air from some unseen bellows that had almost ceased to function, her body fought for the most important of all intangibles, life.

"What is wrong with her?" Van asked Rabbi Eschel.

"I'm not certain, but I believe she has had a heart attack. If we don't get a doctor soon, I'm afraid she'll not last much longer."

While Rabbi Eschel went into the infirmary to try to get help, Van sat on the ground and pulled his mother up, between his outspread legs. Sitting behind her, his legs around her forming a makeshift lap, Van leaned her against his chest. She breathed more easily in the upright position.

He knew that she was dying. Her skin was a pallid gray while her breathing was a choked, deep-seated rumble. Was this the death rattle Van had heard mentioned? Until that day, his only direct experience with death had involved chickens, rabbits, fish and other small animals. To see a human die was not at all the same, he realized, especially when the dying person was your own.

Rabbi Eschel returned from his fruitless quest for help. The people in the infirmary had refused to listen to him. They were all so busy with the people in line that they could not possibly leave to help one more sick person.

It began to rain, changing the dreary, depressing, damp scene into one more foreboding. The cold drops fell on Van and his dying mother, her rabbi and a small group of friends who stopped for a moment, but soon moved on. Streaking dirt and grime on her face like hundreds of tear drops, the rain enhanced Mama's deathly appearance. Her lovely hair, always coiffed to perfection, fell in strings around her face like strands of limp seaweed.

Revived by her sitting position and the cold rain, she opened her eyes and looked up at the rabbi questioningly.

"Where's Papa?" she asked in a clear, firm voice.

Rabbi Eschel glanced at Van, sadness dilating his eyes. He spoke softly, "He has gone to the synagogue for a moment. He'll be back shortly, my dear."

"It's so dark!" she moaned. "Van, turn some lights up. You know I like it bright and cheery."

She squinted at Van, trying to see through her private world of growing darkness. He put his arms around her shoulders and held her close. He did not want her to see him crying. His tears mixed with the rain drops on his face. He brushed them from his cheeks and removed his arms from around Mama. Taking her cold, lifeless hand in his, he rubbed it, trying to transfer his body warmth, his life, to her.

She closed her eyes again and spoke, sounding as if she were speaking from a distant place. "Rabbi Eschel, I saw Moses. He was calling me. He is waiting for me."

"He waits for us all," Rabbi Eschel tried to console her and relieve her of any fear of dying.

Rain began to fall heavier and it was becoming much colder. Mama suddenly sat upright, opened her eyes and looked at Van, seeing him clearly for the first time that day, Van thought.

"Van, he's here. I saw him. That terrible man is here in Dachau."

"Who, Mama? Who did you see?"

"Rudolf Hoess. Here, in a Nazi uniform. I saw him. He recognized me and turned away."

"Mama, I don't think it was Rudy. You were mistaken. It is so dark and dreary here and the fog is always so thick, you mistook someone else for him. They all look the same when they wear those black Nazi uniforms."

"No, I saw him! Nothing could make him different. He's here! Here in Hell, where he belongs!"

Van drew her nearer to him and again put his arms around her, trying to calm her. She seemed to relax and forget she had seen Rudy. She took his hand, holding it tightly, and spoke, "Van, I am dying, aren't I? Remember what I told you about being Jewish. We are God's Chosen People. Don't ever forget that. Marry a good Jewish girl, Van, for your Mama, promise me, Van."

He swallowed a mouth full of nothing. Mama was waiting for his answer, but he could not promise that, not even to her. He had done with living the lie and he would not lie to Mama. Never again.

"Mama, don't worry about me. You rest and we'll get you to the doctor. You're going to be all right."

She slouched sideways in his arms, dead. Rabbi Eschel reached down and closed her eyes, the eyes that were looking at Van in anticipation of a spoken promise that never came.

"Oh, God of Israel, God of Jacob . . ."

Rabbi Eschel prayed. Van did not want to hear those lamentations to the nonexistent God that would allow this hell called Dachau to exist. He closed his mind to the prayers.

Van pulled his mother up from her position across his arm and held her to his chest, her lifeless body limp, like a large sack loosely filled with rice, lacking the essence that had maintained its form, stature, grace and dignity over the years. He wrapped his arms around her shoulders and midsection and squeezed her to his body, sobbing audibly. It was as though he were trying to receive one last something from her, holding her so close and kissing the top of her head. Pressing his lips against her soaked, matted hair, he dimly realized that she had missed the head shavers also. He felt proud of this, feeling that, in some way, she had managed to cheat the Nazis out of one final indignity.

Rabbi Eschel squeezed Van's shoulder comfortingly and whispered ages old expressions of compassion and consolation, of hope and faith; expressions deeply rooted in Jewish history and tradition.

"Van, it is not a time for sadness. She is with Abraham and Moses. Consider how much better that is than being here in this place, this Dachau."

Van did not acknowledge the rabbi's words. Sitting on the muddy ground, his mother in his embrace, he rocked back and forth with her. Rabbi Eschel stood over his pitiful charges, his words offering a balm to soothe Van's anguish. No other person within the confines of that hated place noticed the three of them. Small vignettes of death and tragedy were so numerous that they had long ago ceased to be of much interest to the other prisoners. Flowing around the small, still group of Rabbi Eschel, Van and his mother were crowds of shuffling, dreary, corpse-like figures walking aimlessly as though from their crypts to some unknown destination of horror. Like spokes from the hub of a wheel, the moving ghostly figures appeared in sharp contrast to the stillness of the central group of three. They filled the compound with a sameness of motion, always moving and never reaching their destinations. Van, his mother still cradled within his arms, and Rabbi Eschel were uniquely still, easily mistaken for statues. The haze and fog were heavier than ever and drops of rain continued to fall on the macabre gathering.

Entirely oblivious to his surroundings, Van's thoughts were of home, and of days long past. He thought of warm puppies and soft kittens, of Mama's kitchen with its many wonderful odors and of her sitting room when it had been filled with so many happy moments. He saw a field of wild daisies, their bleached faces nodding at the sun and bending this way and that with the gentle breezes. In the midst of this palette of beauty, Mama and Papa beckoned him to the spread picnic lunch and he happily joined them. They both hugged him warmly and he wept uncontrollably.

The rabbi helped Van up from the ground. Taking his prayer shawl from his shoulders, he covered the upper portion of Mama's body. He then led the silent son away. Van silently removed Rabbi Eschel's arm from around his shoulders, his fingers nearly tearing the flesh; he grasped the rabbi's arm and pushed him away in total rejection.

Rabbi Eschel looked searchingly into Van's face: he did not understand the look of rejection and hatred. Accepting the repudiation as having sprung from Van's immense grief, the rabbi turned and walked away from him. Van watched him leave, feeling a hate and disgust for him that almost rivaled his feeling for the Nazis.

Leaving Rabbi Eschel and the prayers of the damned to the god of the damned, Van walked through the faceless figures moving about the camp. He saw them only as passing blurs, occasionally blocking his path, as he walked to the edge of the three meter wide neutral-zone separating the camp ground from the wide ditch of water and the electric fences on the other side. No prisoner was allowed to walk onto the neutral-zone.

He stood at the edge of the expanse of barren land. Cold, driving rain was falling heavily, but he was unaware of it. The events of the past two days rushed through his thoughts: Papa and Mama were both dead; Rabbi Ernst was gone, maybe also dead; this place, Dachau, filled with so many of God's children, His Chosen People; his meeting with Franz on Crystal Night—a meeting that had ended so abruptly and sadly.

They had all lived a big lie for thousands of years, he concluded. There was no God. The Jews were not His Chosen People. They were, instead, chosen by the Devil. Satan had chosen the Jews to endure forever the wrath and hatred of all mankind.

Unable to make a promise to his dying mother, he found it easy to make one to himself. No more living a life of lies. He would never again consider himself one of God's Chosen People and he would never marry a good Jewish girl.

14

V AN STOOD IN THE RITUALISTIC morning formation for the third time since his arrival at Dachau. Since the night of Mama's death, he had functioned in shock, obeying the orders of the Kapos and SS guards without knowing what he was doing or what it meant. The last thing he remembered was standing in the rain near the neutral-zone, denying the existence of God and the ridiculous idea that Jews were His Chosen People. He surrendered all hope for any happiness or beauty in his future. For two days and three nights, he moved like a robot, doing only what he was ordered to do. He continued to work at the infirmary, forcing people into the vats of almost pure lye, not hearing their screams and pleadings.

When Kapo Golt jabbed him and shook the beds on that third morning, Van woke not only from the night's short sleep, but also from his state of shock.

"Where is Mama's body?" he immediately asked Kapo Golt.

"What? You're asking me?"

"Yes," Van continued, "where is she?"

"I am not on the body detail! I don't know what they do with the bodies. They come around and drag them off and no one knows where they take them. I tell you to forget it. Don't ever ask that question again. Forget it!"

Golt continued to shake other beds and yell at the men to get out to the morning formation.

Van was led to his spot in the formation by one of the men that slept in the same cubicle. He stood there, watching the activity in front of the formation. Three men stood about ten paces in front, each man's hands tied together with the ends of the rope connected to a log. The log was then hoisted up and each end placed in the fork of a tall post that had been driven into the ground. It resembled an enlarged reproduction of a structure used for heating or cooking over an open fire. The crossbar was high enough that when the men's hands were tied to it, their bodies were so extended that their toes barely touched the ground.

Three SS men, each with a long whip, approached the hanging men. With cracking noises that split the air, they popped the whips above their heads before they began the beatings, the sounds echoing through the camp like three rifle shots. They whipped the three men until all three were unconscious, their backs bleeding from the razor-like cuts the whips had made. All three hung by their wrists, their feet dangling. The ropes around their wrists were soaked red with their blood.

Morning and evening formations were used as punishment times. All offenders were brought before the formation and punished, and all the other prisoners were forced to watch. The three whipped on that day had been caught trying to steal some stale bread from the kitchen area.

The formation sometimes lasted for hours. In ranks formed into identically sized groups as in the military, the prisoners were forced to stand for long periods of time while various routines were performed. A count of all prisoners was made at each formation to see who had survived the day's work or the night that had just passed. While these formations droned on, the camp loudspeakers continuously played patriotic Nazi songs or broadcast Nazi propaganda.

Van watched the beatings and tried to sort out the past few days between the screams and shrieks of the three men. He remembered Mama dying in his arms with her lifeless eyes searching his face for a promise that never came. He also remembered pushing Rabbi Eschel away and standing on the edge of the neutral-zone in the rain. After that, he could remember nothing until this morning.

Standing in the ranks of men from his barrack, he realized that the cold rain in which he had stood on the edge of the neutral-zone had at some time during the past days turned to snow. It fell on the massed prisoners and the beating taking place in front of them, muting the sounds and enveloping the camp in a fluffy comforter of white. It softened the harsh, sharp edges of everything, giving the camp the illusion of peace and beauty.

When the formation finally ended, the prisoners lined up for their scoop of thin, watery gray liquid and piece of old bread. Each person had to have his own pan or cup for the gruel. Since Van did not have a container, he was not given any of the liquid.

He walked toward the infirmary with his piece of hard bread, bluish-green mold growing in its center. The snow fell heavily, chilling him. Gnawing on the bread while he walked, he approached three SS guards walking toward him.

Van had noticed that all the prisoners looked away from the SS men, as though it were forbidden to look at them. The camp inmates seemed always to be looking downward, their eyes seeing nothing but the snow-laced mud.

He looked at the approaching Nazis. They all looked alike to him, three copies of a master madman in hated Nazi uniforms. When he was nearly even with the three, he realized that Mama had been right. Rudy Hoess was there in Dachau, and in one of those Nazi uniforms. Van stopped and stared at him as the three passed him without noticing him; to them he was a nothing, draped in stripes.

"Rudy! Is that you?" Van said to the three uniforms.

The three Nazis continued walking, giving no indication that they heard him.

Van stood silently, watching the three Nazis disappear into the crowd of prisoners. He looks different, Van thought. He remembered Rudy as being much taller, more slender. Now he looks short and fat. He has changed so much over the years, Van thought. Nothing about him looked heroic now, most certainly not in that Nazi uniform.

Van walked on to the infirmary to continue his work with the newer prisoners. Work assignments for each day were given at the morning formation. Van's number had been called for work at the infirmary. He hated having to help the Nazi guards force people into those vats. His hands and arms were blistered and the skin was beginning to flake and peel off. Between his fingers, the cracks were starting to fester and look as if his hands would eventually be eaten away. Each time he put his hands into the lye or whatever it was, the pain was so sharp and intense he almost cried aloud. Had he done so, no one would have heard him. The cries of those being dipped would have made it impossible for his voice to be heard.

That night, after formation, Van dragged his exhausted body back to his barrack and fell into his lice-infested bed. He did not notice the lice much any more. The barrack was quiet, everyone too physically tired and emotionally drained to do much more than lie on their filthy beds.

"Hey, Teacher! Get out of that bed and come with me," the Kapo yelled as he approached Van's cubicle.

Concluding that the slimy excuse for a bed had never actually been intended for sleep at all, Van pulled his too-long frame from the confinement of the short bed and the clutches of its resident lice. He followed the Kapo down the wide aisle past the stinking black pots, which were already being used. Three men with terrible aims were standing around one of the pots, relieving themselves, while another man was hunkered on the other black pot, his feet on the rim and his buttocks hanging over it.

Kapo Golt opened the door leading outside and said, "Come on you lazy Jew! Let's go!"

Cautiously, Van followed the trusty, the worst of a bad lot, out the door. Just outside the door, he again instructed Van, "You go over there behind that long building, that warehouse near the neutral-zone. One of the SS men wants to talk to you." He pointed to a building away from the barracks area.

"Wants to talk to me? What does he want?"

"How the hell should I know! Get your worthless ass over there right now!"

Certain he would be shot for being outside the barrack, Van tried to walk in the shadows to the warehouse building. No one was there. Not knowing who or what he was waiting for, he stood back against the building, hidden by the heavy shadow, and waited. His foot rested on something that felt out of place. Bending down, he discovered that it was a large stick, about twice the girth of a walking cane and about one meter long. A perfect club, he thought, seizing the stick and holding it along his right leg. The stick, like ninety-five percent of the inmates, did not belong in the camp. How it got there he did not know or care. A cornered man becomes something more when he has a weapon. Van had his weapon and he was damned sure he was going to use it.

A Nazi guard came around the corner of the building and stood in the light from the searchlights and the other lights along the fence. He looked around expectantly. Van intended to kill him as soon as he got near enough. His short time in Dachau had convinced him it was better to die trying to escape than live trying to serve his new captors.

The Nazi moved closer to the building shadow that concealed him. Van squeezed the weapon harder, thinking only of killing the Nazi, taking one of them to the grave with him. Silently and slowly, he raised the club. He was close enough. He was looking straight at him, but Van thought that the Nazi could not see him.

Just as Van started to bring the club down with all of his force on the Nazi's head, he recognized the man in the Nazi uniform. It was

Rudy! Van dropped the club and it clattered to the ground. Drawing his pistol and pointing it in Van's direction, Rudy said, "What are you doing hiding there?"

Van stepped into the light, "Rudy! It's me, Van."

"Van, it is you. Why were you hiding like that? And what was that noise?"

"I was afraid, Rudy. I had a club and I was ready to kill you and try to get out of here. I didn't know it was you."

He put his pistol back in its holster, reached down and picked up the stick. Van realized that he intended to get the potential weapon out of the camp. Rudy leaned the stick against the building, so he could take it with him when he left.

"How long have you been here in Dachau, Van?"

"Only a few days. My mother was here too but she died two or three days ago. I can't find out where they buried her. Do you know, Rudy?"

"That is not your worry," Rudy snapped back at Van. "She is dead. She has been taken care of. Forget her! She is dead!"

Van soon realized that the Rudy that had lived in his thoughts since the night he had to leave Baden-Baden was not the same as the man standing there in that Nazi uniform. What had happened to him, he wondered. He seemed furious about Van's question concerning Mama. Van decided that he had better talk about something else.

"There are a lot of people from Baden-Baden here, Rudy. Have you seen any of them?"

"Yes, I have, but I just ignore them. Jews are Jews. Hometown Jews are still Jews."

"Does that include me, Rudy?"

"It has to. You're Jewish, aren't you?"

Van wanted to tell him that he was no longer Jewish but he knew that Rudy would consider that absurd. Van's recognition of the lie about being God's Chosen People did not truly alter the fact that he was Jewish. In his mind, he was no longer a Jew. He was a wise Jew, one who had recognized the lies and no longer believed them.

"Yes, you know I'm a Jew," Van said, giving the only answer he could.

"Don't talk so loud, Van. We can't be seen together, ever."

"Why not?"

"Because you are a Jew and I'm an SS soldier. If anyone catches me talking with you, like we are now, I would either be transferred to a battle unit or imprisoned in one of these camps myself."

"Does that mean that we are now enemies?" Van asked him.

"Yes, we are enemies. It is not a situation either of us created. It is the way things are in Germany today. We can never again be friends, in public anyway. We are enemies for the world to see."

"Do you feel like my enemy, Rudy?"

"Not you personally, Van. But the fact is, I am a sworn enemy of all Jews. Things are changing in Germany. The Führer is going to make it the greatest country in the world."

"By putting all the Jews in concentration camps?"

"You are talking too loud again. If I get caught talking to you, it will be the end of everything for me."

"What do you think it is for me, right now?" Van asked as quietly as he could.

"I cannot change any of that. No one can. I will help you though, if you'll let me. As long as no one knows about us, I can make life in this hell-hole much easier for you. I was a prisoner myself for a long time because I killed that radical. So, I know how bad it is and I also know it is going to get much worse."

Van's thoughts raced back to one afternoon they had fished together. Could he rest his tired head and sleep in Rudy's lap today? Would he really want to? The night Rudy had been forced to borrow money from Van to leave Baden-Baden was also vivid in his memory. He wondered if he could make the same declaration of love standing there in Dachau. Then the question came to him. Was there still any declaration to be made?

"Rudy, I have little choice. You are the jailer and I am the prisoner. Whatever you say, I'll have to do."

"Good. Here is what we must do. Never acknowledge you know me in public, no matter what happens. Even if it comes to violence between us, you must not say anything that would give a clue that we know one another. If you do this, I will do what I can for you."

"For your little brother," Van added, more for torment than for information.

"Don't say that! Don't ever say that again!"

They were in the shadow of the building, the warehouse for storing clothes and other supplies. He motioned Van to follow and led him to the door, which he unlocked, and they entered. The inside was so dark that nothing was discernible. Van reached for Rudy to steady himself and to use him as a guide. They advanced farther into the building, Rudy leading the way and Van stumbling behind him, holding to his arm. Rudy was familiar with the bulding and its interior.

Rudy stopped near the middle of the building. Stacks of boxes completely blocked the windows, creating a darkness so intense that neither could see anything. Rudy pushed Van's hand from his arm. They stood there, face to face in the blackness of the dark, the sounds of their breathing the only noise inside the building. An occasional rat could be heard running in and around the boxes, but rats were so common in the camp that their night noises were accepted and seldom noticed by anyone.

Rudy struck a match on the side of a box and lit a cigarette. The sudden unexpected flash of light scared Van at first. He watched Rudy light the cigarette, wave the match out by shaking his hand in the air and then drop it on the floor. Each time he drew on the cigarette, Van could see the reflection in Rudy's eyes. He could faintly see his own face mirrored in those two eyes. When the end of the cigarette glowed brightly, Van felt he could see something else in Rudy's eyes.

Lust, Van thought. I am looking at lust and it is mixed with evil. Why would Rudy be looking at him with an evil lust, he wondered. Suddenly, he understood.

Rudolf Hoess, shorter and more portly than Van, wanted something, and whatever Rudy wanted, he would get. Van was big and strong enough to have handled Rudy with little effort, except for one thing, the uniform. Rudy was an officer in the Nazi Death's Head Battalion and Van was a Jewish prisoner in Dachau. If he refused or fought Rudy, he would not live another day. He did not want to die. He wanted to survive, somehow. He wanted to survive more than he had realized.

Rudy dropped the cigarette to the floor and crushed it with his boot. Van felt Rudy's hands on his shoulder, one hand on each side of Van's head. He could see nothing, but he knew that Rudy had had to reach up or stand on his toes to reach Van's shoulders. Gentle pressure from Rudy's hands became more forceful and demanding, forcing Van to his knees on the floor. Van felt one of Rudy's hands leave his shoulder and he heard Rudy doing something with his clothes, buttons and fingernails making contact. In a moment the noise stopped and the only sounds within the warehouse were the two men breathing and the rats moving about.

Van's long years of innocent love and hero worship were reduced to sordid ministrations to what once was his idol, his hero, his love. Van knew then that he did not love Rudy Hoess and had never loved him. His long, secret love for Rudy, kept and nurtured for many years, was revealed that night to be nothing more than a lie. The lie that had deluded Van for as long as he could remember, tormenting him and making him miserable, was transformed that night from a hidden feeling of love into a pandering relationship, imprisoned within the dark and shadows of a gathering hell.

15

Dachau, Germany—1938

FROM THE BACK OF THE DEPARTING TRUCK, Van looked out and saw the main entrance to Dachau for the first time. If he had been marched through that gate when he arrived at Dachau, he had not noticed it. He looked at it closely as the truck sped away from Dachau, carrying him and the others to their assigned labors for the day.

The entrance gate was large and imposing, made of iron grillwork. Its two giant legs straddled the main road that led into the camp and were connected by a grillwork that arched across the road. Across the arch were the words, "Arbeit Macht Frei". Standing over the arch with the slogan was an iron Imperial German Eagle, its wings spread and its talons clutching a swastika.

"Work Makes Free," Van thought. Insanity, complete insanity is all it is. Why did they put that inscription on the gate? There is no freedom here and never will be.

He could see the entire camp compound now. Lines of gray figures were being marched from the camp in all directions. Some were made up of a few men while others were large groups in military ranks. In the distance the camp resembled a great ant hill, with thousands of columns of somber ants moving in every direction to gather supplies for their return trip. The covering of snow made the lines stand out even more, the dark little creatures plodding along with the same zombie gait in the grayish white. Soot and other pollutants from the industries soon turned the white snow of Dachau into a dirty gray.

Van scratched his lice gingerly, causing them to burrow in deeper. He ran his hand across his shaved head, feeling the stubble where his hair was already growing out. His other hand rubbed his new beard. He wished for a mirror to see how his beard was going to look. He had decided to grow the beard if he could keep the lice out of it. His

126

stomach ached from hunger and he stank. Filthy, nasty and un-shaven, he thought, I must look like a tramp.

Van could not smell his sweaty, dirty body because the other men's odors overpowered his own, but he knew he must stink because everything in Dachau stank. The odors were everywhere: the people, the barracks, the black pots, the dip, the food, the mud and slush and the dead and dying. The stink of the dead was the worst. Every day the death squad came around, pulling big wooden wagons, to pick up the ones who had died of starvation, typhus, suicide and un-known causes. Some of the bodies appeared to have been the victims of murder and mutilation.

Work makes free. Van concluded that the only freedom from Dachau was death. Mama had been freed of Dachau along with the many others who had died or been killed. They were the only ones in Dachau who had gained freedom.

The first morning after Van met Rudy in the warehouse, his num-ber had been called for the work detail at the I.G. Farben chemical plant, near Munich. No dipping those poor wretched people any-more, he thought thankfully.

All the prisoners at Dachau were forced to work. In those years when the camp began to fill, work was the primary function of the people, the camp providing slave labor for the industries of Ger-many. Dachau was located about fifteen kilometers from Munich and the industries around Munich used all the prisoners they could get. Large numbers of prisoners walked to and from their work outside the camp, but the I.G. Farben plant was too far. It was not too far for the prisoners to walk, it was simply a matter of economics. The time required to walk to the plant was too long, taking too many hours from the work day.

The camps were giant labor pools during the late nineteen-thirties. There was as yet no extermination policy. There were many deaths but they were not due to an official policy of extermination. The death of a prisoner usually went unnoticed by the guards and was most often viewed as a blessing. "One less Jew-dog to contend with," was the typical comment.

Survival was the real issue faced by the prisoners each day. It became evident that the work details that left the camp area and went to the civilian world were the best to be hoped for by all in Dachau. To get out, to see free people and to realize that life was still possible helped them retain a little hope.

After some thirty or forty-five minutes, the truck arrived at the chemical works. The Kapos herded everyone out and into formations. Van saw that his truck was the last of many trucks to arrive and unload. The number of prisoners formed into ranks seemed to be some two or three hundred.

The I.G. Farben chemical works used so many Dachau prisoners as slave labor, it was sometimes difficult to remember that they were outside Dachau. Because of his size and strength, Van was assigned to shovelling a greenish-blue powder into a giant vat, containing a liquid that constantly bubbled and boiled. A large fire under the vat kept it heated. The fire burned unceasingly and created a fierce heat that seared his exposed skin. The fumes burned his eyes and made him gag with each breath. A civilian, one of the Farben employees, wearing a gas mask gave him instructions and immediately left the hot, putrid air of the large room where Van worked.

The work was hard, the heat and fumes were overpowering and the entire place reminded Van of what fire and brimstone must actually be like. However, it was better than staying in Dachau. Each day that he worked there, he was tempted to thank God, but he never did. Rudy Hoess was the god he had to thank. It was difficult for Van to remember that he had decided there was no God. How could he thank someone that did not exist?

Attached to one side of the giant room, high up on the wall, was a small glass room that housed the controls and the civilian who came down to tell him what to do during the day—always wearing the gas mask. Van never saw the man's face except when he was in the glass room high above, watching whatever it was they were making. The thought often occurred to Van that the man had no face although he could see him without the mask up there in his glass room. Yes, he had a face but Van supposed he would never see it.

Green clouds of fine powder surrounded him each time he had to shovel more into the boiling tank. Green sweat rolled from his body in an endless flow. His skin got so hot he thought it was cracking, curling up and burning away, as bark on a tree branch does in a roaring flame. Tears mixed with his perspiration, becoming a green froth, and flowed from his body. A breath of clean air could not be had in that room, gasp as he might.

Van leaned on his shovel, surrounded by the thick, billowing clouds of blue-green dust. In desperation, he had tied an old rag around his nose and mouth to try to filter the air he was breathing. Without a real gas mask, it was almost impossible to breath. The shovelling made him breathe harder and deeper, taking more of the fine powder into his lungs and body. It burned his insides as the lye had burned his arms and hands. The rag around his mouth and nose helped, although it made him look the part of a bandit. When he worked, he removed his shirt, leaving him with only his shoes, trousers and mask. His entire body was green; the black hairs on his broad chest became a darker shade of green. He must look like something fresh out of a rain-soaked garden, he thought, all green and sweaty.

Van had a lot of time to think, his work being strictly manual labor, requiring no mental processes whatsoever. Major Rudolf Hoess had certainly done what he had said he would. The work was much harder at the chemical plant, but it did not require that he inflict pain and misery on another human, a most welcome change. He refused to think about the price he had been forced to pay.

From the glass room high above him, the man watched Van resting, his green-colored body leaning on the shovel. It isn't right, he thought, it just isn't right. All that business about Jews was wrong. He peered through the green fog at the man below, wondering what logic or reason put that particular man below and him above in his glass room.

Van continued to work at the chemical plant, finding that the unusual working conditions never varied from one day to the next. Other than the short periods they stopped for the noon meal, the only interruption of the routine was when the masked warden tapped him on the shoulder unexpectedly, usually scaring him. He never got accustomed to the unexpected presence of his masked boss.

When it was time to eat the midday meal each day, all Dachau laborers at the plant returned to the trucks. There, each day, they were fed the same horrible soup. Everyone in the concentration camp had a theory about the secret ingredients of the soup, ranging from old boots to human waste. None of the suggested recipes included meat. It was a gray, water-like fluid; obnoxious to the nose, repulsive to the eye and practically terminal to the taste buds and stomach. It was consumed only because there was nothing else available in Dachau, except for the black market. Occasionally they were also given a piece of old, mouldy bread.

When Van returned to his work room after lunch each day, he usually found a sandwich, or something else equally appreciated, hidden where he could find it with ease. These bits of decent food provided him strength, hope and a renewal of the conviction that all men were not evil. A German who was not a Jew, and who knew that Van was one, helped restore his hope in those days when there was so little hope in his life.

16

A FTER WORKING ON THE I. G. FARBEN WORK DETAIL for almost a month, Van decided that Rudy had made the work arrangement a permanent one, as permanent as anything could be in Dachau. He watched the population of Dachau daily grow larger. Obviously all the people put in Dachau were being put there by the Nazis in the hope of putting an end to their survival. The Nazis wanted them out of the German nation. Ironically, the one thing the Germans wanted to end, the prisoners' survival, became the driving motivation of those in Dachau. This Nazi effort to end survival, to repress all desire to live, to kill all hope for another day, to extinguish the fires of freedom within the souls of specific types of men, to erase entire groups of people from the pages of life, andto make Germany an ultimate Utopia, by ridding it of undesirable classes of people, had the opposite effect. The Nazi efforts created a new and stronger will to live among the prisoners, an all-consuming desire to stay alive one more day. Among the prisoners, the common bond of their Jewish heritage and religion helped them struggle and endure together for survival.

Although the majority of the people in Dachau were Jewish, Van noticed that the number of people that did not wear the yellow Star of David was growing. The variety and numbers of different colored triangles seemed to increase each day. He wanted to know what all of the triangles meant, and he thought he knew where he could find the answers.

Ben, one of the men that slept in the same six-man cubicle with him, seemed to know more about concentration camp life and routine than anyone else in the barrack. He had been a jeweler in Karlsruhe before Crystal Night. Ben became the barrack authority and he seemed to enjoy this role, ready to provide the answers to all questions. Van thought that some of the answers were not necessarily the truth; they were just answers. Ben was apparently involved in the black market at Dachau because he always had more possessions than the others, and more and better food.

After the lights were turned out, Van lay on his bed, too tired and cold to sleep. There, in the dark and cold of the early December night, he thought about the symbols on the prisoners and what they meant. Suddenly, he felt something bite one of the toes of his left foot. The thin blanket was not long enough for his large frame, his feet generally stuck out. The pain was sharp and quick, as if a small vise with many sharp teeth had abruptly clamped down on his toe. He quickly reached down to the end of the bed to stop whatever was biting him. He grasped the small furry creature and wrenched it loose from his toe.

"God damn rats!" he said aloud as he threw the rat against the far wall, but not before it took a nip at his hand. In the dark, he managed to grab the rat around its back and free his toe. Throwing the repulsive thing as hard as he could in the general direction of the barrack wall, he successfully hit the wall, somehow missing the other beds. It sailed through the air, flying through a cubicle of six beds and splattering against the wall. It lay on its back on the floor, feet slightly quivering their final death kick, and died.

"Got one, eh?" Ben asked quietly.

"Sons of bitches! It's a wonder they don't eat us while we sleep," Van replied.

Both men were talking in low whispers so as not to disturb the sleeping Kapo. They were not allowed to talk after the lights were out.

"They do," Ben said matter-of-factly. "Over in Block D they are worse than they are here. It isn't safe to sleep over there. Those damn rats will eat anything that doesn't eat them first."

Van rubbed his bleeding toe with the old blanket, wiping the blood from it, and then did the same to the small bite on his hand. Wonder what kind of disease I'll get from that damn rat, he thought.

Both men were silent for a few minutes. Van decided to ask Ben about the triangles.

"Ben," he said softly, not wanting to wake him if he had already gone to sleep.

"Yeah, Teacher, what do you need?"

"Don't call me 'Teacher'! I told you my name is Van. I hate that 'Teacher'. Sounds like I'm a rabbi and I am not a damn rabbi."

"All right, Van. What do you want?"

"When I first came here, nearly everyone wore a Star of David. A few who weren't Jewish wore triangles of different colors. Now, the number of these people wearing triangles is increasing every day. What I want to know is what do the different colored triangles mean and why are there so many of them?"

"Those are easy to answer. I thought you might have some tough questions for me."

"No, the answers to those are usually too tough for me to stand. I'll stay with the easy ones. Tell me what they all mean, Ben."

"Well, the red triangle is worn by political prisoners. They are people who happen to oppose the Nazi Party. I suppose the Nazis feel like these people are poor losers or they want them in here where they can keep an eye on them.

"You know the green triangle because there were plenty of them here from the beginning. They are ordinary criminals, the people who would be in prison, even if the Nazis weren't ruling Germany. Watch out for that group. They are just as dangerous in here as they were outside.

"Purple triangles are worn by members of the Jehovah's Witness religious sect."

"Jehovah's Witness!" Van interrupted. "I thought they were Christian. Why are they here?"

"Because they refuse to pledge allegiance to the Third Reich. Isn't that a good reason to be here? It makes as much sense as the reason we are here. You would be surprised at the number of Christians in these camps.

"Seen any black triangles? They are worn by a type of catch-all group called 'shiftless elements' whatever that means. Most of them were beggars and tramps, but in here they just seem to blend in with the rest of us. They are not dangerous and some of them are quite interesting.

"Gypsies are forced to wear brown triangles. They won't bother you, but they are strange."

"Gypsies? Why do the Nazis put Gypsies in these camps?"

"They are here for the same reason we Jews are, racial purity. The Nazis are trying to create a pure race of men. Jews and Gypsies bastardize their theory of racial purity."

Racial purity? Van had heard that phrase so often from Mama and the rabbi. Jewish racial purity had been preached to him for as long as he could remember. Now, the Nazis had stolen one of their Jewish principles and made it their own.

"Racial purity," Ben continued, "is also the reason still another group is here. I'm sure you've seen them. They have the word 'BLOD' on their badge of identity. Morons, feeble-minded people and idiots are not conducive to their Aryan ideal of perfection. I think all Nazis are feeble-minded morons, but they don't want any certified nuts breeding and creating more nuts for their perfect world. That's their idea, not mine.

"Some of the triangles have letters on them, like a P or an F. These letters generally stand for the country from which the prisoner came when it was not Germany. The ones with the P came from Poland while the ones with the F came from France."

"Shit," Van moaned, "how in the world can you keep up with all those colored triangles: black, brown, purple, green, red, yellow Stars of David and 'BLOD' for the insane. Is that all?"

"No," Ben answered. "Once you start putting groups of people away that you either don't like or feel are dangerous to you, you just never seem to run out of groups. They'll probably run out of colors for the triangles before they get everyone in here that they decide belongs in here."

"Once they get everyone categorized into one of these niches," Van asked, "I wonder what they do with a person that has a double offense. Do you understand what I mean, Ben?"

"I'm not sure. Give me an example of this double offense business."

"Suppose a member of the Jehovah Witness group were also discovered to be a member of the political opposition, or a common criminal or even a Gypsy. Another possibility would be a Gypsy that is feeble-minded or even insane. The combinations seem numerous, and the more groups they create, the larger the possible combinations of offenses. Who decides which badge they wear and how is the decision made?"

"Now, you have asked one of those tough questions I mentioned. I never thought about that situation and I really don't know the answer."

"Let me ask one more question and I'll let you get back to sleep. I've seen another color triangle and you haven't mentioned it yet."

"That doesn't surprise me. There are probably some I haven't even seen yet. What color are you talking about?"

"They were pink, Ben, pink triangles, inverted like the others, worn on the left chest and the right trouser leg."

"Oh, those," Ben mumbled.

"What do they mean?"

"Pink triangles are worn by queers, the worst group here, made up of the most despicable collection of trash you will ever see. I don't agree with much the Nazis have done in Germany but they are damn right to put those people away. If it were up to me, I'd do more than put them away. Not only are they criminals, they are also breaking God's laws as well. Illegal and immoral. What a combination! I hate them all!"

His sudden rage and obvious hatred for these people who wore the pink triangle was surprising. This was the first time Van had known of any emotional outburst from him. Calm and controlled, Ben wore the original poker face most of the time. His behavior at the mention of the pink triangles was so unusual, Van wished he could see the look on Ben's face.

Darkness was best, however. Van's face felt as hot as it did at the chemical plant. He felt he must be blushing the deepest shade of red as he listened to Ben's description of the "queers," and he decided to let the subject die. Tired as his body was from the grueling work at I. G. Farben, Van's mind would not allow sleep to abate the exhaustion or relieve the tensions. What would they do if he were discovered? His Star of David, as alien as it had become to him, was suddenly very precious. In its place, a pink triangle would reap abhorrence, malice, venom and damnation for him from all the other prisoners, as well as the Nazis. Ben had stated the prevailing opinion when he observed that those who wore pink triangles were "the worst group here".

How would the Nazis handle his predicament when, and if, it became known? Would the pink triangle replace the Star of David, be worn alongside the Star of David or be ignored and not worn at all. Was it worse to be Jewish or homosexual? If it was a crime against Germany to be Jewish, how much more of a crime was it to be a Jewish homosexual, or a homosexual Jew. Which was the correct label anyway, he wondered.

Everyone in the barrack was asleep except Van. Snoring, heavy breathing, groaning, clacking of false teeth and nightmare jabberings filled the long room. Above this noise, he heard the door open and someone walk toward his end of the barrack. Just the stupid Kapo, he thought. The footsteps came to Van's cubicle. A man stood beside his bunk, which was so high that Van could just see the top of his Nazi cap in the dark. Softly he spoke, "Van."

Rudy Hoess. Oh, God, not again, Van thought.

"Yes, here I am," he whispered.

"Come with me—quietly."

He walked to the door and was outside before Van could rise from his bunk. All he had to do to be fully dressed was to slip his old worn shoes on his feet. They all slept fully clothed, for many reasons, with their shoes in bed with them.

Following him through the shadows to the old warehouse, Van thought about the change in his feelings toward Rudy. Most of his life, Rudy had been his idol. His first night in the clothing warehouse at Dachau gave birth to a smoldering hate and resentment. Rudy had never recognized Van or his feelings for him, and now he only recognized him as an instrument for his own self-gratification. Van was an object to Rudy. The line between love and hate is indeed a thin, thin line, Van thought.

In the warehouse that night, Van served as he had before and would until he got out of Dachau, if he ever did. There was no feeling or emotion involved on his part. It was an act of survival, not an act of lust nor of sexual desire and, most assuredly, not of love. He loved life, as terrible as it had become, and did everything he could to preserve his own.

17

Dachau, Germany–1938

I T ALWAYS LOOKED THE SAME, the uniform ranks of gray, gaunt men, their striped uniforms hanging on their emaciated bodies, their thin faces, with eyes deep in the sunken sockets, staring out with blank, hopeless looks; never seeing, only looking. Each day weighed heavier and heavier on the prisoners at Dachau, the length of their stay revealed by the degree of their starvation, exhaustion and loss of hope.

Van hated the formation because it brought all of the sadness and tragedy into the same place at the same time. The formations were designed and situated so that the prisoners could see the Alps in the distance. The beautiful sunsets, the view of the hazy mountains starting their lofty climb on the far horizon, and the sounds of freedom that sometimes drifted into the camp during the formations added to the prisoners' misery and sadness. The little hope, or the complete loss of all hope for the day of their deliverance, increased in intensity at those formations when a particularly beautiful sunset filled the horizon and the sky behind the Alps, or when the sounds of singing birds, barking dogs or free men passing outside the camp interrupted the usual concentration camp noises. Sometimes when people walked past the camp or drove by slowly, they could be heard talking and laughing. These were the worst sounds for the prisoners at Dachau.

Since Van was getting food at the chemical plant, he did not lose weight or look as though he were starving like most of the other prisoners. The only well-fed prisoners were the Kapos and those involved in the camp's black market activities. Everyone assumed that Van was part of the black market. When he began to realize how different he looked, he was ashamed, particularly when he thought about the way he managed to get and keep the detail at I. G. Farben. For days, he sneaked the food from the masked man back to Dachau and gave it to someone who needed it much worse than he. He stopped doing this after he gave an older man some of the food and it killed him. He would have died in a day or two anyway, Van reasoned; but to see him gorge his empty stomach on the bread and cheese, choke, heave and gasp for his last breath, clawing at Van as he died, saddened Van and filled him with guilt. He brought no more food to the other prisoners.

He found that the only way he could survive and remain sane was to ignore as much around him as possible. Standing in the formations that sometimes lasted for hours, he escaped to thoughts of Baden-Baden, of happier times with Mama and Papa, of Sheila and Ernst; of Franz and that one night in Berlin. Within this island of hell, surrounded by the natural beauty of the Alps and the Munich country-side, Van became an island himself, drifting away in his thoughts to happier and freer days, days gone forever with nothing remaining of happiness and freedom except memories.

As he drifted back from one of those warming recollections of the past, he realized thta the formation had been dismissed and he was still standing there. Kapo Golt yelled something at him, bringing him back to reality. He started for the barrack, merging with the flow of seemingly lifeless forms. Noticing a familiar, bent form in front of him, he walked faster until he was even with the old man.

"Professor Neumann, is that you?"

The thin, ghostly pale man looked up at Van and squinted, trying to see in the dusk.

"Yes, it is me, but who are you?" he said so softly that Van barely heard him.

"You never do recognize me, Professor. It is Van Bertholds, remember?"

The professor appeared to be searching his memories for the name. "Oh, yes," he replied, "Papa Bertholds' boy from the cafe."

"I haven't seen you since that day we came here. Where did they put you?" Van asked, lightly patting the old man on his back.

"I am in Block C," the professor said while they continued walking slowly toward the barracks.

"What work detail do they send you on?" Van asked. He could not imagine how the stooped, old man could possibly work.

"Just outside the walls of Dachau, I work, each day creating deli-cate things of beauty for the Nazi beasts. Like everything else they touch, they have taken my life's work of beauty and made it some-thing ugly and vulgar.

"I work in the porcelain factory on the road that goes from the camp to Munich, just a short distance from the main gate of Dachau. All the work details that go to those big industries in Munich, those details that so many prisoners go on, go right by the porcelain factory each day. We make art treasures for the Nazi leaders. They have dirtied art by making us paint their horrible swastika and other symbols on lovely pieces of crafted porcelain. Of all the things I have had to endure in this place, that is the worst. To take my greatest joy, my true love in life and turn it to their use and pleasure, to corrupt my art, that is worse than death itself.

"I really think that I am slowly starving to death and I am glad. I prefer death to what they are making me do!"

Van's resolve, like so many things in Dachau, melted away. Reaching inside his jacket, he pulled out the brown bread and slab of cheese and handed the makeshift sandwich to Professor Neumann.

"What?" Professor Neumann asked in total disbelief. "What is this? Where did you get it?"

Van looked at the poor old man, acting as though he had just been handed a stolen fortune in pure gold. Damn, Van thought, this is what they have done to us.

"Professor, don't ask. Just eat it, but eat it slowly. Take small bites and chew them until they are like mush or you'll throw it all up. Slowly, now."

"No real food in a month and he tells me to eat slowly. Ah, youth! It does tend to make you ridiculous."

They had stopped near the place where they would take separate paths to go to their different barracks areas.

"Halt there!" the SS man yelled at them.

"We *are* halted, dumb bastard," Van said under his breath.

Professor Neumann was trying to hide the sandwich in his clothes when the SS man grabbed his arm and took it from him. He had seen Van give the sandwich to the professor and he turned to Van.

"Where did you steal this, Pig?"

"I didn't steal it, Sir. It was given to me by . . ."

"Shut up! You lying Jews don't know the truth when you see it."

He wrenched Van's left arm downward and looked at his tattooed number. Taking out a pen and pad, he wrote down both Van's and the professor's number, and then walked away from them, taking the sandwich with him.

"You two get to your barracks. Now!"

Van slept little that night. He knew what the coming morning formation would mean for him, punishment for certain. Since the guard assumed that Van had stolen the food, the punishment would surely be for him alone, not for the professor also.

The snow was falling so thickly and heavily that it was difficult to see more than five meters. The temperature hovered below freezing. Snow blew in great swirls around the formations and then fell quietly for a while. Again, the wind came rushing through and brought the snow with it, adding icy pellets to its cold bite.

"Number 24966 and Number 24967! Front!" the SS man at the head of the formation yelled.

Van and Professor Neumann walked slowly to the front of the formations and stood before the SS guard. The guards tied their hands together with rope that felt like a circle of knives around their wrists. The two ropes were then tied to the giant log which was hoisted up into its place on the two forked posts. Van was barely able to touch the ground with the tips of his toes.

Van looked sadly at Professor Neumann and called to him. The professor turned his head sideways and strained to see around his upraised arm. He was barely able to see Van.

"Oh Professor, I'm sorry. This is all my fault. I knew better, but you were so hungry," Van pleaded, trying to convey with words the remorse and guilt he was feeling.

Professor Neumann looked deeper into Van's eyes, his voice louder than seemed possible. "No! None of this is your doing. It is God's will. None of this is your fault. The fault is in their hearts, not yours."

"For stealing food, the punishment is fifty lashes. These two are thieves. Watch and learn," an SS man announced to the entire formation.

Two SS men, each carrying a whip, walked to their places behind Van and Professor Neumann. They cracked the whips in the air sending snow spiraling madly in every direction from the whips' paths. The sharp, air-splitting sounds of the whips sent shivers through the bodies of all those in the formation.

They began, the whips slicing through human flesh with a force that thrust the two men's bodies forward, jumping forward and then gliding back to be met with another forward thrust of the whips. The ends of the whips wrapped around the two men, cutting not only their backs but also their chests, shoulders and stomachs. Some slashes hit the lower part of the body, the ends of the whips wrapping around and hitting the men in their thighs.

Both men's backs were covered with long, deep, bleeding cuts, until they resembled maps with dark red paths going haphazardly in every direction. Strong currents of wind blew through the area, whipping the snow around them, cloaking them in snow and obscuring them from the other prisoners' view. The Kapos and SS forced the prisoners to watch the punishment.

Van bit his tongue to keep from screaming out his pain. He vowed not to give them the pleasure of hearing his cries. Professor Neumann screamed loudly and pitifully at first. Eventually his screams became frail whispers of "Dear God of Israel, let Your People go." Van could faintly hear his prayers and he knew no one else could hear him, especially the God to whom he prayed.

Suddenly, interrupting the sounds of leather biting through flesh, Professor Neumann screamed out, "Oh, Lord, I go!"

Everyone heard this last scream. The professor's body became limp, but the SS man continued the lashes, whipping the dead body. His body did not swing forward with the same force; it just lurched forward a little and fell back as the carcass of a dead animal might.

Van looked over at his old teacher and felt a mixture of sadness and relief. His dear friend was dead, gone forever, never to paint another joyful image. But he was also free, out of their reach, never again to suffer and endure their hate and degradation.

Van faintly heard the man that was whipping him counting each stroke of the whip.

"Thirty-one. Thirty-two."

He heard no more, succumbing to the terrible pain of the whip's slices, losing consciousness.

The commonplace, almost routine, beating of two prisoners at Dachau passed almost unnoticed. So many were punished in front of the gathered formations that it became a normal activity worthy of little interest. Professor Neumann's death was not realized by most. He, like Van, had simply lost consciousness, they thought.

Kapo Golt had ordered the unconscious Van brought to the barrack. When Van regained consciousness, he was lying on his stomach in his bed. It was late and the lights were out. The barrack was quiet except for the regular night sounds. Someone had put some thick, smelly, greasy mess on his back. The cuts from the whip felt like a thousand hot irons pressed into his body. He finally slept, the sleep of a man stretched on a rack, a hundred devils slicing him into a million parts.

Van was not, of course, allowed to miss a single work detail; work would make him free. His pain and soreness were of no consideration to anyone other than himself. Riding to the chemical plant in the bitter cold of that late December, he tried to decide how he could have given the professor that food, an act of compassion that had caused the professor's death. Why had he not learned his lesson when the other man had died in his arms? His physical pain was matched by his mental anguish, the responsibility for the two men's death made him feel evil and contemptible.

The blowing snow raced through the moving truck, further chilling the already miserably cold men in the back. Van was thankful for the work in the I. G. Farben plant. At least it provided warmth and an escape from the walls of Dachau. Those in control at Dachau made no effort to provide warmth for the prisoners. The nights were so harsh that men resorted to sleeping with one another despite the fact that they did not wear the pink triangle. It was again a matter of survival.

At all costs, Van avoided the increasing number of pink triangles in Dachau. He felt sure that they would recognize him. It was not too difficult, since they were kept away from the other inmates because of the abhorrence and hatred all felt toward them. Used by the guards, abused by their fellow inmates, despised by everyone; their situation was not one with which Van wanted to cast his lot. Within the hell of the concentration camp, they lived in a deeper, darker, more terrible hell than the others, if that were possible.

A few days before Christmas, a woman came to the masked supervisor's glass room. She arrived during the lunch break and Van was able to watch her during her short visit. He had not seen many women since being brought to Dachau. A few days after Mama's death, nearly all women inmates were moved to Ravensbruck, leaving Dachau predominantly a concentration camp for men.

He watched her approach the glass room along the catwalk. Dressed in a full length coat with fur trim around the collar, sleeves and the attached hood, she was dazzling. She walked up the catwalk to the glass room, covering her mouth and nose with a lace handkerchief. When she entered the glass room, she removed the handkerchief from her face and pushed the coat's hood from her head. Her blonde hair was bunched around the inside collar of the coat. Using both hands, she pulled her hair out of the coat and let it cascade around her shoulders. The spirit of Christmas was evident in her face and bearing, especially when she hugged and kissed the man. He gave her some money from his wallet and she started to leave. Van assumed that she was his wife and that she had stopped to get some shopping money.

She saw Van below the glass room and stopped abruptly. Pointing at him, she appeared to ask the man a question. He replied and she talked to him for a few minutes and left the room. The catwalk exit from the room to the outside of the building ran near where Van was resting. When she was closer to him, he saw her face plainly. It was Sheila Gebhardt, except her name was Stempfle. She turned her face away from him and walked on hurriedly. The masked supervisor was her husband, Ulrich Stempfle. Although he had been recognized by Sheila while she was still in the glass room, Van had been ignored. He no longer existed for her; it was as though, to her, he had already died.

In the abysmal depths of those years of Dachau's hell, a vision of forgotten yesterdays of Baden-Baden's heaven had appeared, paused briefly and successfully penetrated the dense, deathlike present of Van's life with the frivolous, ecstatic, lively past. Sweet, perfumed pictures flooded Van's mind with visions of earthy hued chrysanthemums, trees shedding their brilliantly colored leaves in preparation for the approaching winds of winter, small animals scurrying to store their loot for the winter onrush. And the dearest of friends waving from the gentle incline of the bank of the River Oos, her golden hair gleaming in the autumn sun, her voice ringing clear and vibrant with love, "The next time you come to Munich, you must come to see us."

His recollections of that wonderful day were filled with the strains of the Barcarolle from *Tales of Hoffman*. The lilting, melodic roll and glide of the Barcarolle swept him with it to dreams of beauty and grace, elegance and charm, love and friendship.

Van turned aside from this memory of warmth and love and wondered if Sheila could possibly have changed into the cold, unseeing, unconcerned woman who had just ignored his very existence? Was the evil spawned by the Nazis also changing the people outside the camps? Van had never given much thought to conditions any place other than Dachau. Maybe it was not he that was dead to Sheila. Maybe Sheila, the Sheila he had known, was dead to him, another victim of the Nazi's rule of terror.

18

Dachau, Germany—1939-1940

D ACHAU'S POPULATION INCREASED DAILY during 1939 and 1940, creating more problems and resulting in even worse living conditions than already existed. The Jews were the largest of the many groups in Dachau, but all categories were increasing almost daily. People wearing pink triangles became more numerous and intimidating to Van. But by careful questions he learned more information about them.

Before the Nazis came to power, there had been a liberal attitude in Germany concerning homosexual rights. During those years of new-found freedom, many Germans were more open with that heretofore secret part of their lives. Because of the many legal freedoms gained during that period, law enforcement agencies had little authority over them except to record their names as known homosexuals. This was done in nearly every city in Germany; the police in the city of Berlin had over sixty thousand of these names on record.

When the Nazis decided to imprison all homosexuals, the lists of names were available all over Germany. It was a simple matter to arrest these people and imprison them in camps like Dachau. In effect, the law was retroactive. The taste of freedom enjoyed by avowed homosexuals in the late 1920's in Germany eventually cost them their freedom, and more.

The number of pink triangles grew in every camp in Germany. Dachau became so overcrowded, Van began to wonder if it would be necessary to make the entire nation a concentration camp. Where thirty were housed before, ninety or more were now living. Filth and disease were a constant problem. Deaths increased steadily, but the number of incoming people was far greater than the number dying; the only way out of Dachau. Typhus, pneumonia and starvation freed more people from Dachau than could be counted.

From November of 1938, when Van entered Dachau, until the late part of 1940, he endured the dreadful conditions. He bought his survival by prostituting himself to Rudolf Hoess for a payment of tomorrows. Rudy would come to Van in the night or send one of his SS men for him. Van's worst fear was not death but that what Rudy was forcing him to do would be discovered by the other prisoners.

On the day of Mama's death, he had promised himself never again to live a lie. Many promises died in Dachau; Van chose survival over total honesty.

The work at the chemical plant never changed. Whatever they were making must have been in great demand. The supervisor in the glass room, Sheila's husband, seemed more kind after Sheila's visit. Van never saw her at the plant again, but her husband was helpful to him in small secret ways, although he never spoke to Van.

Van had resigned himself to dying at Dachau. The world allowed Hitler to do as he pleased and did not know or care about a few Jews and other misfits in the concentration camps. Van could only anticipate being used by Rudy until he died of one of the many diseases in the camp, or was killed by some SS men or his fellow prisoners when they discovered his true nature.

Within Van's thoughts, the constant, gnawing, secret and private fear of being discovered combined with the real, obvious and communal fear of daily life in the camps to create an almost unbearable situation. While he deteriorated both psychologically and emotionally, he grew stronger physically because of the hard work at the plant and the daily portion of decent food provided by Sheila's husband.

Sturmbannfuhrer Rudolf Hoess admired his reflection in the mirror. His new black uniform with its insignia of his new rank gleamed with a radiance of its own. The promotion had been the proudest moment of his life. Adjusting his cap, he smiled and the image returned the smile, clear and sparkling. From the large mirror, the reverse picture of Rudy's room on the top floor of the Jourhaus framed the newly decorated reflection. For Dachau, it was an elegant room with furnishing to suit a gentleman. On the walls were a large picture of Hitler and the Nazi flag. A large iron swastika, gaudy and too large for the size of the room, hung over the giant chest of drawers. It was his crucifix, his smiling Buddha, his Mecca, his God.

Rudolf Hoess' mind was filled with the brassy sound of Wagner's *Ride of the Valkyries*, its tumultuous sharp crescendos forcing everything else from his thoughts. He heard the full volume of the music, in his imagination, and the sound transported him to an ecstasy of his own importance and brilliance. He made the final perfunctory adjustments to his insignia, smiled at his image, and turned to leave the room. The reflection smiled also, trapped by the perfection of the mirror into revealing only what was seen, and nothing that was foreseen.

Outside his room, he again adjusted the insignia and went down the stairs to the ground floor. He had sent one of the Nazi guards to bring Van to the Jourhaus. When he reached the main doors of the Jourhaus, the guard and Van stood waiting for him.

"That's the one," Rudy said to the young guard. "I need him to do some work in my room. He looks strong enough."

He motioned Van up the stairs. He didn't have to explain his actions to that guard, Rudy thought. He was, after all, an officer, an officer of high rank, while the guard was only an insignificant corporal.

Van was wary and afraid. He had never been inside this part of the Jourhaus and certainly never to Rudy's room. He had no idea what the reason for his being there was, but he knew it could be for nothing good. Rudy opened his door and went into the room. He told Van to come in, then carefully closed the door and locked it. He strutted around the room, showing off his uniform with his new rank.

"As you can see, I have been promoted to Major," Rudy said, his voice full of pride. He lifted a glass of champagne and held it up toward the ceiling, giving the traditonal toast gesture. Bringing his glass down from its toast position, he started to sip the bubbly liquid. "I believe congratulations are in order," he said between sips.

"Yes, I suppose they might be," Van said weakly, almost inaudibly.

"What?" Rudy roared.

"Congratulations, Major Hoess," Van replied in a dull, flat, emotionless tone.

"Well, it is richly deserved," Rudy boasted as he finished the glass of champagne and set it on a small table.

"I'm leaving Dachau soon, Van."

The words both frightened and elated Van. Was he finally to be rid of this man who had taken what Van thought was love for him and twisted it into nothing more than an obscenity? But would his survival without Rudy to protect him be more difficult, perhaps impossible?

"What do you mean, Major Hoess?" Van asked, not daring to call him "Rudy". His "Rudy" was dead forever.

"As one of my new duties, I am to take over a small camp in

Poland. I am going to look at a site just over the Polish border near a small, ugly town called Auschwitz. The area is a malaria-infested hell-hole. Sounds perfect to me."

"I don't know what to say, Rudy," Van said, using the old familiar name more to goad him than for any other reason.

"God Damn it! Don't call me that. Don't ever call me that again. You don't have to say anything. Why do you queers always have to talk about everything? There is nothing for you to say. Less talk and more action is what you need."

"I'm sorry, Major Hoess," Van said with no respect in his voice.

Rudy pulled the shades all the way down. He then proceeded to undress, carefully removing the uniform and placing it neatly over a chair. He smoothed and patted the uniform over the back of the chair.

He stood there with nothing on, short, fat and totally repulsive to Van. Without the uniform, he looked like the "before" advertisement for a health spa.

"Well?" he said in a stern voice.

Van knew all too well what was expected of him. He slipped out of his dirty stripes and let his Dachau uniform fall to the floor. He looked at the bed and thought how nice it would be to sleep in a real bed, with clean linens.

"What happened to your back?" Rudy asked, a sneering quality in his voice.

The question surprised Van, until he remembered that he had never been forced to be with Rudy in a lighted room. He had always met Rudy in a dark place, where no one could see them.

"The first month I was here, I tried to give some food to Professor Neumann. You remember him, don't you? He taught art in Baden-Baden."

"Oh, that old senile Jew pig. Yes, I remember him."

"I was caught giving him the food," Van continued. "They, your Nazis, said I stole it. Fifty lashes is what happened to my back." Van continued to avoid looking at Rudy. "They tried to give Professor Neumann fifty lashes too, but he died before they finished. Cheated him out of about thirty lashes, I believe."

"No great loss to anyone that that old fool died. I always hated him. 'Your colors are not just right' he used to say to me in those damn art classes. Well, your back doesn't really look too bad. I hope you learned your lesson. If I had not been away when it happened, I would have administered the lashes myself."

146

Van looked at him then, a look of unabashed hatred. Someday, he thought, I'll kill you with my own hands.

"I'm waiting, Van."

The nightmare of that first day in Dachau became real again, as it had so many times since. He took his mind away from his forced service within Rudy's room to the night in Berlin, where everything was voluntary and beautiful. What he and Franz had enjoyed had been turned into filth by Rudy. Professor Neumann had been right. The Nazis did corrupt everything they touched.

Rudy's departure from Dachau did not alter Van's existence. The only change in his routine was his release from going to the clothing warehouse when Rudy sent for him. He was thankful for the reprieve but there was no happiness within him; there was no happiness in Dachau.

19

V AN STARED UP AT THE GLASS ROOM, watching Sheila's husband eat his lunch. On the wall of the room was a calendar, barely discernible to him. Squinting to see through the bluish-green dust, layered like stratified clouds to the ceiling, he could make out the month of November and the year 1941. Three years, he thought. He'd been there three years this month. He felt it was more like thirty years and wondered if it would ever end.

The large glass wall of the room had a slight vertical slant, affording Van a dim reflection of himself. His three years growth of beard was full and black, with a thick dusting of green powder. He had been able to trim his long black hair with a makeshift razor that Ben had, keeping it shorter than a lot of the other prisoners' hair. It just covered his ears. Since his hair was straight, he tried to keep it cut so it would not resemble a girl's head of long hair.

His upper body was much more muscular than when he first came to Dachau. Looking at the reflection above him, he concluded he did not look at all like a teacher, a concentration camp prisoner, or a Jew, but more like a lumberjack, dyed green.

All the days of the past three years seemed to merge into an endless repetition of one long day. The nights had been times for exhausted sleep, nightmares and Rudolf Hoess' occasional summonings. Van hated the nights; he refused to think of them because they had so often included Rudy.

The next day he again stood in the morning formation, trying to calculate the number of times he had done the same monotonous thing. Two times a day for three years, remembering the calendar he had seen the day before. That's one thousand and ninety-five days. Two times a day, that's two thousand, one hundred and ninety times. Ninety-two, if one of the years was a leap year. How many hours was that, he wondered, with two to thee hours each formation.

His thoughts were interrupted by the SS officer saying something different in a louder, more commanding voice, not the usual monotone that they all used at formation.

"All prisoners will be ready to depart for the railhead at 0800 hours. Barracks groups will remain together. All Jews, Gypsies and homosexuals will depart today for relocation. Dachau has become too crowded for sanitary conditions. The groups named will all be relocated, starting today."

"What's going on?" Van asked a prisoner near him.

"Relocation, for sanitary reasons. You heard him."

"Do you believe that?" Van asked.

"Of course. Why would they lie to us? They have no reason to lie."

Van knew they were lying. Sanitary conditions had deteriorated more than two years ago. Why move them now? Why not let them go free? He had learned long ago to never believe anything a Nazi said. Something new and strange was happening and he had to know what it was.

"Hey, Ben, wait. I need some more answers."

Ben waited until Van caught up with him. He greeted him with, "Not only do I have answers, I even know your question before you ask it."

"Well, I'm waiting," Van replied. "What is my question?" In some two years he had yet to get a wrong answer from Ben, other than his observation about the pink triangles.

Ben actually smiled at him and gave him the question and the answer. "The question is what are the Nazi pigs really doing? The answer is simple and obvious. They are sending the worst of their collection of bads to one place and when they get all the worst of us, Jews, Gypsies and queers, in one place, the only thing we will find there will be the angel of death. That is the answer!"

There was no time to consider Ben's opinion. It was time to leave. They were actually getting out of Dachau alive.

In the huge area between the barracks and the Jourhaus, masses of people, grouped together by barracks and by offenses, were gathering. The largest group, the Jews, were first in the formation. Behind them was the much smaller group of Gypsies. A group of homosexuals followed the first two.

Van covertly watched the homosexuals. The other two groups jeered at them, pointing and laughing, and threw things at them. Those that were close enough to them spat on them. It occurred to him that the homosexuals did not look any different from his group or the Gypsy group. All were so thin and gaunt, with a look of desperation. Van was ashamed of his large, well-fed body. One of the men wearing a pink triangle smiled at him, a strange smile of recognition and sadness. Van looked away, avoiding the man's eyes; he could not bear looking into the mirror of that face. It convicted him of the lie he continued to live.

Out the main gate they marched. Van looked back at the familiar Nazi eagle and the words, "Work Makes Free". The line behind him, passing under the eagle, stretched the entire length of the long central thoroughfare of Dachau and snaked around the camp. He could not see the end of the line; the number of people was staggering. He had never seen so many gathered at the same time and place in Dachau.

A train was waiting for them at the railhead. It, too, stretched into infinity on its iron trail. Cattle cars were connected to the engines, and the doors of the first ten or twelve cars were pulled open with a grating noise. With an unusual politeness and helpfulness, the SS guards put the people into the cattle cars. Ninety to a hundred people were loaded into each car. Crowding and pushing, each scrambled for a place to sit. They were overcrowded, pushed closer together, and then closer still.

When the cars near the platform were loaded, the doors were slammed with a shattering finality, a particular sound Van would never forget. The doors were then locked, sealing the prisoners within, with no prospect of escape in the event of an accident or fire. The air was thick with body odors and an awful stench from the urinal can in one corner of each car. The train moved forward in a series of lurches that sent entire car loads of people plummeting to the floor in large heaps. The cans tipped, spilling their contents on all those near them. Many wondered why the cans were already filled in an empty car.

Once the train had pitched forward enough that the filled cars were away from the platform, another group of cars were opened and filled beyond reasonable capacity. This process was repeated until all of the prisoners in that long line had been loaded. Van had no way of knowing how long it took, he had no way of keeping time. He remembered the gold watch he had pawned to get money for Rudy. It was always in that glass case in the sitting room. He wondered what had become of it.

It seemed to those in the cars loaded first that it took hours to load all the people. Although it was November and there was a hint of snow in the air, the loaded cattle cars became unbearably hot and stuffy. Many fainted and had to be help upright by friends, if they were lucky enough to have friends. Those who fell to the floor of the car were trampled. Van tried to exercise some control in the car in which he was imprisoned. Arranging the passengers in his car in some kind of order, he was able to prevent some of the panic that ensued in most of the other cars. The people in Van's car could hear the screaming and fighting for space from the other cars.

Sometime around noon, the train moved westward. The prisoners had no idea where they were going or how far it was from Dachau. They only knew they were going west—toward Baden-Baden, Van thought. Again, as on Van's trip to Dachau, the train stopped at many towns to take on more people.

The walls of the train cars were solid, the only openings small cracks between some of the boards, or small holes made in a desperate effort to get air. The people fought for fresh air and to try to see where they were going. Van found a crack, through which he was able to watch the passing landscape.

The closer they came to Baden-Baden, the more excited he became. Looking through the small crack in the car, he began to recognize some of the countryside. Just outside Baden-Baden, he saw the area where he and Rudy had fished so often. Entering the town, the train slowed and he was able to see many things he had thought he would never see again. Additional prisoners were taken on at Baden-Baden. Van was so involved with looking at the town, looking for familiar places and faces, that he did not notice the new passengers. Slowly pulling out of Baden-Baden, after switching, the train headed back east toward Stuttgart. Van watched as Baden-Baden became smaller and smaller until he would see it no more. He wept; he could not help it. Baden-Baden was home and all his life he had loved it and its people. He still did.

They continued eastward all night, stopping many times along the journey to take on new prisoners. As the train passed through Stuttgart, Nurenberg, Zwickau and Dresden, it became clear that they were approaching the old Polish border. Since Hitler's move into Poland, the border between Germany and Poland was not well defined.

Where were they going? Why were they nearly in what was once Poland? Those questions were shared by all of the people in the train. Even Ben did not have the answers.

They crossed the Polish border. After a few miles, the train slowly came to a halt. The terrain was similar to that of a desert. The earth was a yellowish clay, with clumps of trees scattered sparsely around.

It was a desolate, dead landscape.

The doors opened, and they poured out of their putrid confinement. No food, no facilities and no exercise in over twenty-four hours had taken a heavy toll of the already emaciated prisoners from Dachau. The dead were brought from each car and stacked on the platform of the place where they had finally stopped. Van helped carry so many corpses that he could not count them. The dead were stacked three or four high. He went back and leaned against the cattle car to regain his strength. Above the platform, he saw the sign that told him their final destination. Above the wretched pile of human carcasses was the sign. In Gothic letters, it read

AUSCHWITZ

20

T HOSE WHO DIED ON THE JOURNEY were left on the railroad station platform, as the surviving thousands were marched to the main camp. Van estimated that there were ten to fifteen thousand on that train, with at least two hundred left on the station platform. Who were the lucky ones: the dead on the platform, or the living, marching the two kilometers to the main camp?

The short march was too much for many of the prisoners who had not eaten or slept in the last twenty-four hours. Many had to be helped, even carried. People fell out of the march, unable to survive a two kilometer walk. No one in authority seemed concerned with the increasing number of deaths.

Over the main gate of Auschwitz, in giant iron letters, were the familar words, "Arbeit Macht Frei". The wide main street was tree-lined and did not appear menacing. They were marched to a large clear area, where they were processed.

Processing was efficient, fast and typically German. The prisoners were first segregated by sex. All of them were then further separated into two groups. The group to which Van was assigned was clearly for the healthy, able workers. The other group was the aged, ill, very young or any male unable to work. Van knew some people that were put in this second group from the years at Dachau, but he never saw any of that group again. He assumed they were imprisoned in another area or sent to another camp.

Those healthy enough to work had their heads shaved. They were forced to strip and bathe in a solution of calcium chloride for delousing.

At long tables, officials recorded the information concerning each prisoner. Tattooed numbers and names were recorded along with offenses. The man in the white smock wrote "Jew" beside Van's name and number. Another lie, he thought. He was no longer a Jew.

But, he realized, that incorrect entry was preferable to the truth he so feared.

The last procedure was very strange. A man in authority was checking each prisoner. Apparently a doctor of some kind, he selected certain people and sent them in a different direction. Van watched him select a set of twin boys and send them with his special group. The doctor then looked at Van.

"You're a big one to be a Jew."

"Yes, sir," he replied.

"Are you a Jew?"

"Yes, I am Jewish."

He examined Van carefully; arms, legs, teeth, his entire physical structure.

"Are you as strong as you appear to be?"

"I don't know. I am hungry and tired and sleepy. I don't feel very strong right now."

He tapped Van's chest and had him breathe deeply two or three times. "I think you'll do. Sergeant, I want this one to assist me in my work. He looks strong enough to handle it properly."

The sergeant ordered Van to stand behind the table and wait. He stood there during the inspection of the entire train load of people. The doctor who had chosen him inspected every male closely. The females were routed through the inspection line, when the doctor had completed the line of men. He sent every set of twins into the special area. Van concluded from watching his selections that the doctor was primarily interested in twins, healthy men and women, particularly women with long legs. Although Van was exhausted and hungry, the selection process was a curious sight. He could not determine the reason for the doctor's choices.

Pink triangles were passing through the line and the doctor seemed extremely interested in them. They had been made to wait until all of the other men and women had gone through the process. The doctor selected many of the pink triangles. Van could see no pattern or reason for the selections. He was convinced that being selected was, in some way, a bad thing. The large number of pink triangles selected worried him. Fear was growing within him. Why had the doctor picked him and separated him from all the others chosen? What had the doctor meant by helping him in his work? What was his interest in twins and tall women? And, most worrisome of all, why was the doctor so fascinated with the pink triangles?

He was still standing alone when darkness fell, before the line ended. Lights were turned on and the process continued. He felt faint and sat down on the ground. The sergeant kicked him and told him to get up on his feet. Soon after, the processing was finally completed and the officials, gathering their paper work, started to leave. The doctor was giving orders to everyone. As he was leaving, he remembered Van and came back to where he stood.

"What you will do will be difficult work. It will require great strength and perseverance. Do it well and you will live longer and better. You will see things that won't be pleasant but the results will be astounding. I am doing medical research here that will eventually make life better for the people of the world. I have already made some tremendous advances toward our ultimate goal of a true master race, a race free from infirmities and physical deficiencies. Enough of that! I get carried away when I discuss my work.

"You will do exactly as you are told, no matter what you think about what I am doing. You will not question or analyze why you are told to do something. You will do it!

"Why do I not use an SS guard for this job? There are not enough of them. I have to have someone all the time. You are that someone."

He turned to leave but remembered something else to tell Van.

"The sergeant will tell you more about what you will do and everything else you have to know. Do you have a name? I don't like to call the prisoners by the numbers."

"My name is Van, Sir."

"Good. I shall call you Jew-Van so I won't forget you are a Jew. You certainly don't look like a Jew. I have an idea your mother must have been sleeping with some big Aryan."

Van hated the son-of-a-bitch. He wanted to kill him, crush him to death right there in front of all the guards. The doctor was the incarnation of all Van hated about the Nazis. Rudy was evil but this man was evil personified.

"Jew-Van, I'll see you right after roll-call tomorrow morning. My name is Dr. Mengele."

21

A USCHWITZ WAS DACHAU ON A MUCH LARGER SCALE. It was designed and constructed by a madman, though the actual labor was done by the first group of inmates, forced to build their own confinement.

Over a hundred barracks were built, the exteriors covered with green tar paper. The inside of the barracks was the same as in Dachau. Van was assigned to a barrack of Jews with the same six-man sleeping arrangement.

Roll-call began at three in the morning and lasted until six or seven. Rain, snow or the worst weather conditions imaginable did not cancel or shorten it. The actual calling of the roll and number check was completed in about thirty minutes. The remainder of the three or four hours offered only harassment and degradation. All of the shorter prisoners were placed in the front ranks. A different officer then reversed the order, placing the tall people in front. Another officer would take charge and reverse the arrangement again. This exercise in the ridiculous sometimes continued until seven, regardless of weather or any other consideration.

Van's first day at Auschwitz started with the insane roll-call. When that was over, he reported to the camp infirmary. Dr. Mengele was already there, studying medical books.

"Good morning, Jew-Van."

"Morning, Dr. Mengele, Sir."

"Were your new quarters to your liking?"

"They were the same as we had in Dachau. I have grown accustomed to them over the past few years."

"That's good. Now, about your work. I am conducting experiments and your task will be to keep order among the inmates who are waiting to be part of the experiments. Is that clear?"

"I suppose so. I will learn what it is you expect of me."

That first day was not busy. Dr. Mengele spent most of the day reading and working on the journals of his experiments. Van tried to stay out of everyone's way.

The workers and staff left the camp hospital about dark. Van was standing in line to get his crust of bread and mock soup when an SS officer came to him and asked if his number was 24967. Van showed the tattoo to the guard, who then ordered him to the camp commandant's office immediately. The SS officer knocked on the commandant's door. From inside the room, a voice told them to enter. The officer opened the door to let Van go in, and closed the door behind him, not entering himself.

The office was large and beautifully furnished, decorated to resemble the living room of a fine home. Seated behind the desk was Rudolf Hoess, wearing a mocking, sneering smile.

"Welcome home, Little Brother."

The words were laced with sarcasm and hate. He was throwing Van's private, secret term back at him.

"This is not my home," Van said in a firm voice. He kept reminding himself how much he hated Rudy.

"Oh yes it is. It is doubly your home. All Jews belong in a place like this and all queers belong in Hell. So, you are here for two good reasons. Shall I tell the guards to give you a pink triangle to wear alongside your Star of David?"

Van stared coldly at him, wanting to run behind the desk and pull his head from his body. He despised him, and felt he could have done it quite easily. With as much hate as he could summon, Van answered him, "I don't give a god-damn what you do about the pink triangle or anything else!"

Rudy rose from his chair in a seething rage. His face was so red, Van thought he would explode any second. He looked at Rudolf Hoess closely for, perhaps, the first time in his life. When Van was a child, he saw him through the eyes of a child. Now, he saw him in reality: a short, repulsive, little man in the even more repulsive Nazi uniform. He had also gotten fat in his new position, and was completely disgusting. Even though Van had no gods to hear his prayers, he prayed that he would live to see the day Rudy was dead, and he the one who killed him.

Rudy exploded, hurling a torrent of words at Van like daggers. "Don't you dare talk to me in that tone of voice. I am Major Rudolf Hoess, commandant of this camp. Here, I am not only your god, I am God. You live or die at my command. One word from me and your miserable, queer, Jew life is over. Finished."

He finally calmed down a bit. His outburst had relieved him and made him feel more in command of the situation. He spoke more calmly.

"I understand you are helping Dr. Mengele. That will be an education for my little Jewish dandy. I keep referring to you as little; that you certainly are not. How have you become so big and muscular? I never saw a more Aryan-looking Jew."

"Hard work and clean living, Major, Sir," Van said, with as much venom in his voice as he dared.

"The hard work is probably true, thanks to us. Clean living you have never done. It is diametrically opposed to your nature. Queers can't live cleanly."

A long lecture ensued about the basic evil of homosexuals. Van tuned him out. For Rudy to tell Van of his basic evil nature was so incongruous as to be laughable. He finally got to the point.

"I have my family here with me. My wife hates this place and runs off to Berlin at the slightest excuse, but it is nice to have them here with me. I won't be seeing you as often as I did in Dachau. I tell you this so you won't think I have forgotten you. I haven't. I'll be watching your every move. Those of us from Baden-Baden must stick together."

"Is that all, Major Hoess?"

"Yes, that is all. I will be seeing you."

His parting statement propelled Van into a well of fear. If Rudy resumed his demands on him, he did not feel he could stand it. He would kill rather than submit to him again.

During his first few weeks with Mengele, he was more a traffic controller than anything else. Multiple births were Mengele's primary experimental subject. Van had never realized there were so many twins in the world. The hospital was full of twins of every size, shape and sex. In some cases, the eyes of each individual twin were not the same color, one eye might be brown while the other was blue.

But later came full knowledge and realization of the details and extent of Dr. Mengele's experiments on the prisoners. This knowledge numbed Van to all of the calamities occurring around him. Life seemed to have ended for him with the discovery of the true nature of these experiments. He was oblivious to most things that happened. He later felt that this insulation was all that allowed him to retain his sanity. Back in Baden-Baden, in those days of life and freedom, he had thought the worst possible thing that could befall a person was death. In Dachau, and more especially, in Auschwitz, he came to the real conviction that death was not the worst of life's terrors. Auschwitz, this bedding-down with death; this embracing of evil and human suffering; this breathing in of the foul stench of man's immeasurable bestiality; this embodiment of tyranny and genocide; this place, Auschwitz, was worse than death.

Van's work in the camp hospital kept him busy from the day of his arrival in late 1941 throughout the winter, the worst winter he had ever experienced. It was as though Mengele and the elements were in a battle to determine which of the two could kill the most people. Auschwitz was farther north than Baden-Baden and the winters were more severe. For the first time, Van saw human beings frozen stiff. The barracks were woefully underheated and none of the prisoners had proper clothing.

Life was unbearably miserable for all those in Auschwitz, but the pink triangles suffered the worst treatment. During that bitter winter, Van saw so much done to so many that his conclusion that one group was treated worse than the others was similar to deciding which of the dead were most dead. Because of his intense curiosity and interest in the pink triangles, he was more aware of the things that happened to them, and he concluded that they were despised by all: the very bottom layer of humanity in the sewer called Auschwitz.

The guard shack was clearly visible from the window of the camp hospital. One afternoon Van saw two guards bring a young man to the shack and take him inside. Later the two guards came out and two more went in. He watched the shack the rest of the day, looking through the window as often as he could. Each time two guards would come out, two more would go in and stay about thirty minutes.

Near sundown, the guards brought the man outside, stripped naked. He was bleeding and could not stand alone. Beside the shack was a line of shower heads used for delousing. They forced him under one of the showers and held him there for about fifteen or twenty minutes. The termperature must have been below freezing, Van thought. After the shower, they tied him to a post, driven into the ground near the shack.

When Van came out of the barrack the next morning, the naked man was still there, his feet and hands tied to the post. After the morning formation, Van saw the guards drag him back into the shack. In their haste and obvious enjoyment in what they were doing, they left the door of the shack open and Van could see them put him under a sun lamp, keeping him there until the sweat dripped from his body. Van stood at the small hospital room window, galvanized by what he was watching. No real effort was made to conceal their actions.

They finally removed the man from under the sun lamp and brought him out of the shack. It had started snowing again and the temperature seemed to have dropped even lower. They threw the man on the snow covered ground. He could not stand without help; he lay there naked and wet with perspiration, the soft, fluffy snow covering his body like a blanket of down. The guards repeated the sun lamp-cold shower routine and then retied him to a different post in the large assembly area. Completely without clothes, a large wooden pink triangle hanging around his neck, he stood there tied to the post. In the bitter cold and blowing snow, both guards and prisoners kicked, hit and otherwise abused him. He slumped over dead, Van supposed, even hoped, after about an hour. His frozen body remained tied to the post for three days, the wooden pink triangle tied around his neck, occasionally blowing in the wind.

Van's feeling of revulsion at the excesses he knew were being committed by Mengele increased weekly. Mengele would attempt anything on the pink triangles, completely ignoring the fact that they were human beings. Over a period of some months, he injected a new type of male hormone into some of them. He used such massive doses that some other doctors were moved to comment on the unusual size of the doses. Those pink triangles were kept in the hospital for observation during the experiment.

Van supposed that the theory was that the hormone would cure them of being homosexual. Actually, it made their beards grow much faster than normal and increased their sex drives. Dr. Mengele was disgusted with the results, telling another doctor that all he had done was to create very hairy queers with insatiable sex drives.

During the experiment, the prisoners were kept in small rooms in the hospital where the staff could watch them through small spy holes. Mengele became so enraged at the experiment's failure that he ordered all of the prisoners castrated without anesthesia and returned to their barracks.

During the operations, Van watched Mengele, trying to avoid any eye contact with the pitiful pink triangles being operated upon. Their mournful pleadings before the actual cutting began tore at Van's insides, splitting his heart to pieces. When the sharp surgical blades and other instruments came into use, the screams pierced the air, ripping his soul and slicing at his sanity. Mengele, his small, piggish eyes gleaming with pleasure and joy, relished those moments, like a man tasting a prized, vintage wine. No, not exactly like a wine connoisseur, but more like one who has just slain the dragon that was after the fair maiden. He acts as if he has rid the world of some awful evil and is aglow with pride and self-esteem, Van concluded. He is totally heartless. If the wretched man ever had a heart, it has long been dead.

The winter of 1941 was characterized by increasing violence toward the prisoners, particularly the pink triangles, and a tremendous rise in the number of incoming inmates. Trains disgorged their sad contents practically every day. Auschwitz had long ago been filled beyond its capacity, and each day saw an influx of hundreds more.

Jews were the largest group in Auschwitz, and their numbers increased daily. Van observed that the pink triangles were the second largest group and their numbers also increased steadily—staggering to one who had, at one time, considered himself the only one in existence. Another possibility that he considered was the large number who, like him, did not wear the pink triangle but were qualified. There were also those who had not been sent to any concentration camp. They had managed to keep their secret and had not been condemned by being a Jew or a member of any of the other illegal groups.

When Van's group arrived from Dachau, they filled every bed in the barracks. It was not long until the guards placed boards along the beds, connecting them into one long bed that ran from one end of the barrack to the other. Since there were three levels of beds in each cubicle, there were three long wooden runners on each side of the aisle, along the tops of the beds.

The three tiers of board beds were completely filled with Germany's refuse. They were so tightly packed together on the three levels that it was impossible to change positions unless the entire barrack line also changed positions at the same time.

In the center aisle, the black pots were ever present. However, if a man got out of the tightly packed sleeping arrangement to use one of the foul, stinking pots, he lost his sleep place and was unable to find another for the remainder of the night. The result of this hesitancy to forfeit a small sleeping area was that men who had a place wormed out in the line simply relieved themselves where they lay. This practice became the rule rather than the exception.

People on the bottom level suffered the worst, as the human waste from the two upper tiers fell upon them. The middle level was nearly as bad as the bottom, while the upper tier became the most desirable sleeping places. Only the strongest men were privileged to occupy them. King of the mountain, a children's game where the strongest child fights off the others to control a hill or some other designated spot of importance, became an adult game, fought in earnest for the best sleeping spot. Van often slept on the rafters or the beams.

"Jew-Van, I have an order here that we must obey. It has come to me from the high command, therefore, I cannot question it. It is, however, one order I would oppose if I could be successful in my opposition. But, it would be a futile effort."

Van stared at Dr. Mengele in disbelief. What possible edict from on high could he be so opposed to, he wondered. It could only be an order to free the prisoners.

"You are not going to ask me what the order is?" Mengele sarcastically inquired of Van. "And you seem like such an intelligent man, for a Jew, I mean. I would have thought your curiosity would have been aroused by this development."

He watched Mengele, visibly upset with the official-appearing document he held in his hand. He paced around the small room, muttering vicious curses to himself; curses directed at those few people who had the power to order him to do anything. The sight made Van feel good, gave him some hope. Maybe there is a chance that someone is putting a stop to some of this madness, he thought, knowing that it was more a hope than a thought.

"What . . . what is the order, Sir?" Van asked hesitatingly, not at all sure he wanted to know the answer.

"You won't believe it!" Mengele shouted back at him, his rage almost overpowering Van with its fierceness. "Some idiot professor at the University of Strasbourg has gone to the very top and managed to convince them that he must have a good cross-section of eastern European Jews for his studies. He is taking over a hundred of my Jews for his worthless experiments. Damn him to Hell!"

Any hopes within Van faded with Mengele's outburst. He had been a fool to think anything good would come of any official Nazi order.

"This bastard," Mengele continued, "claims that we have skulls and anatomical data on most of our race, but we have very little on the Jew race. He wants to collect this information on Jews. He wants nearly two hundred eastern European Jews, two hundred of my experimental subjects."

Van shuddered. He had never felt so near a raging madman. Being in the same room with Mengele in his fit of fury brought to Van's mind the picture of God casting Satan out of Heaven. It had probably been a scene like this, Van thought, Satan furious and stomping around in a fit, knowing he had no alternative to the directive.

"Well, there's nothing to do but to do it," Mengele exclaimed remorsefully. "I will select his 'cross-section' of Jewry and ship them to him. He wants men and women, and he wants them alive so he can measure them first. Then he will take their skulls and complete his collection. Lunacy! Pure lunacy! Taking my subjects after I have worked so carefully to properly select and classify them. The very least he could do would be to let me send him the heads in air-tight tins so I could experiment on them first and keep the bodies. I could use them for some bone-grafting experiments I have in mind. Damn that professor! Damn him to Hell!"

Mengele stormed out of the room, his anger at losing two hundred of his guinea pigs nearly sending him into a fit of delirium. Van sat down on one of the tall laboratory stools for a long time, hunched over, his arms resting on his knees, his hands hanging lifelessly downward.

His mind refused to dwell on all that Mengele had said. It chose instead to rush back to Baden-Baden to grasp for some past beauty in the midst of the present hell. He could see Papa standing behind the counter of the cafe, his arms folded and resting on his fat stomach, a smile on his face and a merry twinkle in his eyes. Old Kern was laughing at something Papa had said. Mama was sewing in the sitting room while Hilda, the maid, sat with her, sipping tea and chatting merrily. Sheila ran down Lichtentaler Avenue, her long, blonde hair bouncing up and down on her back and shoulders. Ernst waited for her and took her books. The fishing spot was empty, now just a place, no longer a special place. In his thoughts the tinkling of glass sounded around him as Franz led him to his bedroom. The dreadful voice from Franz's radio sounded the end of happier thoughts. His mind went no farther. There was no point in thinking of anything after the voice from the radio ended the beauty of life.

He could see Mengele filling two hundred air-tight tins with their terrible load. He could not help it; he laughed. That was not to be. He had to ship them alive and unharmed. He loved that part, laughing loudly and boisterously. The sound was so unusual in that place that it could only be coming from an insane person. One of Dr. Mengele's assistants opened the door and looked at Van quizzically. Shaking his head in mock sympathy, he closed the door, convinced that Van had finally gone mad. He thinks I am insane, Van thought. He's probably right.

22

Auschwitz, Poland—February 1942

A N EPIDEMIC OF TYPHUS raged through Auschwitz in the early months of 1942 surpassing both Dr. Mengele and the unbelievably severe winter in its number of victims. The hospital was busier than usual but it was not due to any effort to help the dying prisoners. The SS guards and other camp staff fell victims to the typhus and they were the people being treated.

Dr. Mengele was visibly upset that the typhus had interrupted his experiments. Twins, pink triangles and Jewish women were his most numerous subjects. The Gypsies were also subjected to these inhumane experiments but their number in the camp was much less than the other groups, thus they were used less.

During this period Van was forced to take on new tasks. One new duty that gradually became his was that of assisting Mengele work a new shipment of prisoners. When the waiting line snaked its way all over the camp, Mengele usually said something like, "Well, Jew-Van, you have watched me long enough. Your decisions are usually the same as mine, anyway. You take that line and I'll work this line. You know what I need." Helping Mengele make the choices was very sad and depressing for Van. When a group of homosexuals came through the line, he did all in his power not to be involved in the selection process. If Mengele forced him to do it, he chose only the few he had to.

They were working an unusually large shipment from Germany during February: a train with cattle cars filled with more than a thousand people. They had started about ten in the morning and the cold, winter sun was about gone. They had been processing primarily Jewish prisoners for over eight hours. Van no longer saw their individual faces; he only noticed the yellow Star of David on each as he examined them. Glancing at the endless line that wound all over Auschwitz, his senses were jerked back to complete awareness by the vivid pink where he had been seeing yellow. Pink triangles were worn by each person in that long, snake-like line, as far as he could see. He did not see faces of people, only an elongated chain of pink triangles, hundreds of triangles. At varying heights from the ground, held together by their common destiny, their vivid pink color shocked the senses in Auschwitz's sea of blacks, grays and drabs.

"Here they come, Jew-Van. Pick me some good specimens before the guards get them. They won't be worth anything after the SS have their fun. Those SS really waste a lot of good material," Mengele said to him, just as Van was thinking of some excuse to go to the hospital for a few hours.

"Why don't you stop the SS from doing what they do to them, Doctor? You have the authority and they do kill a lot of them, or worse."

"Let them have their fun. Those SS have a hard job here. Besides, it looks to me that there are enough homosexuals for all our purposes. By God! I never thought there were this many homosexuals in the world, much less in Europe alone. How many do we have here in Auschwitz?" he asked one of the men at the table where the journals with names, numbers and offenses of all prisoners were recorded.

"Not counting these we are receiving today, we have received 83,279 since Auschwitz opened."

Dr. Mengele looked aghast at the news of such a large number of pink triangles. "There are that many already here?"

"Sir, that is the number we know we have received," the clerk answered, emphasizing "we know" and looking at Van strangely. "As you well know, Doctor, a lot of them have . . . died."

"Yes! Yes! I forgot about the typhus and all that," Dr. Mengele said.

"Yes, typhus . . . and all that," the clerk agreed with a sly grin at Mengele.

I am not the only one living a lie, Van thought. These Nazis kill together, then lie to one another about what they have just done.

The talking subsided; they were all anxious to finish since it was late and getting colder. From the length of the line, Van thought they would never finish. He rushed through the selection process, letting as many people pass as possible. They were a cold, sad group, their heads freshly shaved and most of them thin, gaunt and deathly pale. Although Van had to feel their muscle tone, inspect their teeth and touch them, he tried to make it a perfunctory inspection, never looking one in the eye, nor pausing in his examination, nor speaking to any of them and never daring to smile. He was certain they thought him either a cold-hearted Nazi beast or a fellow traveler, afraid of recognition.

As he felt the muscle tone of one, Van had the impression he knew him. He opened his mouth wide, with Van's help, so Van could check his teeth. Something about him was familiar. Van decided to check his hands, something he was supposed to do to all of them, but rarely did. He took the man's right hand, palm up, in his hands. The hand clasped Van's right hand and squeezed it. For the first time, Van looked into his eyes.

"Van! What are you doing here?" cried the man in a voice whose volume seemed to crack the walls of Auschwitz. Actually, he had spoken in a low tone but it had shocked Van so much that he thought the man was screaming. The man put his arms around Van, pressed his head against his chest, and cried. Van stood immobilized by the shock of what was happening. Then both of his arms were around the man, patting him while he wept on his chest. Van was crying also.

The entire selection process had stopped. Everyone was watching them. Van glanced at the clerk who had previously given him the knowing look; his sarcastic grin appeared to say, "I thought so!" Van then put his right hand on the sobbing man's head in an attempt to console him. His weeping became louder and he was having difficulty catching his breath, as people sometimes do when they cry too hard. Placing both hands on the man's shoulders, Van pushed him away, to get a better look at him. Even with his shaven head and emaciated body, there was no doubt. It was Franz Richter, his Franz from Crystal Night in Berlin.

"Move on! Move that line and get those homos processed!" Mengele yelled. He had seldom raised his voice to Van before that day, but he was exhausted; hurrying to finish the processing. Van could not understand why he screened every prisoner that came to Auschwitz. Since racial studies were his primary interest, Van assumed he wanted to see every human form and condition that came through the processing.

"Franz, is it really you?" Van asked as Franz was forced to move on by an SS man.

"Yes, Van. Where can I find you?"

"Barrack J-53," Van shouted as Franz vanished into a sea of pink triangles being buffeted by the contingent of SS guards, leading them away from the processing area to their separate barracks area.

"Well, Jew-Van, an old friend of yours?" Mengele casually questioned as he continued the selection process.

What could Van say? How could he tell the truth and pull his frail world in on top of him? Mengele would never understand the truth, so Van decided to lie.

"He is an old friend of my family from Berlin. I have known him since we were children. He came to Baden-Baden to visit some of his relatives there and we became friends," Van explained, his voice etched with a pleading quality. At least it wasn't a total lie, he thought.

"'Friends', you say. Looked more than friendship to me," Mengele said in a casual manner. He smiled at Van as though they were sharing some dark secret. His expression made Van want to retch. He knew the truth, and Van knew Mengele would never hesitate to use it against him.

"I don't think either of us expected to ever see the other one again, Dr. Mengele. It was just an emotional, unexpected meeting of two life-long friends."

"Yes, yes, I'm sure."

Franz moved along with the other pink triangles in near shock, the meeting with Van having been so unexpected. He had thought of Van many times since their parting at the Berlin train station the day after Crystal Night. But he had always hoped—the hope eventually turning to a reality in his mind—that Van had in some way been able to elude the Nazis and escape from Germany with his parents. The idea that Van was free—in some distant country, perhaps England—had been one of Franz's consoling thoughts through the years in the concentration camp. That idyllic picture was shattered, leaving Franz with one less solace for the terrible times he knew lay ahead.

"Form-up in proper ranks!" yelled one of the SS guards.

"Hurry up, you fags! Can't you make a straight line?"

All those that had been processed were being forced to form themselves into ranks like a military unit. The guards were especially brutal, kicking them and using their night-sticks and rifle butts to beat them into the desired formation. They had moved some distance from the processing area when the guards had decided on this course of action.

Someone pulled Franz by his shirt sleeve, forcing him into line before the guards got to him. He stood in the formation, his mind a kaleidoscope of questions, wonderment and fear. Would he see Van again? Why was Van working with those inspecting doctors? How long had he been here in Auschwitz? Not long, Franz thought. He looks so strong and well.

The formation started moving through the camp and eventually arrived at a section of barracks set apart from the remainder of the camp. When Franz's group arrived at their new barrack, they were allowed to break the formation and enter the wretched building. All of the barracks in this area appeared to be in worse condition than the others in the camp. A slum in hell, Franz thought, just like it was at Oranienburg camp. The men from the ranks of the dismissed formation ran into the barrack and fought for the best spots, the top boards. Franz was so confused and disoriented from his having seen Van that he flopped down on one of the bottom deck beds.

He lay there, thinking about his life the past few years. Before Crystal Night, he had had everything he wanted. His had been a happy, carefree life, never wanting for anything. Tatina had seen to that. Now, he had nothing. The whole of Berlin had been at his feet when he performed. Now, no one in Berlin knew he existed. He wasn't even sure if Tatina knew he was in a concentration camp. He believed that she did since she had warned him of Hitler and what he was going to do to Germany. He wept silently thinking about her.

He remembered his success at the cabaret "Night Sounds" and felt a little better. Life had been wonderful then. Franz Richter had been a star and Berlin had loved him. Happiness had filled his days and the adulation of the Berliners his nights. All that was gone now. He could barely remember how happiness felt. Perhaps, he thought, I should have felt happiness today when I found Van. But I didn't. All I could think of was that he was also in hell, just as I am.

Franz wondered if he would ever be happy again, if he would ever be free. He decided he would not. Those years in Berlin were another life, lost forever, never to be found again. And, making it still worse, he thought, Van is also here. We have both lost it all. There is nothing for us but death in this place.

When a large shipment of incoming prisoners forced them to work late, as they had that day, Mengele arranged to have the night meal sent to the hospital, after the processing. Those special meals were for the hospital staff, not the prisoners who helped them. Mengele had allowed Van to eat with the staff as he became more valuable to his unit's operation. The masked supervisor at I. G. Farben in Dachau, and Dr. Mengele at Auschwitz both provided him with a continuing supply of decent food. Without these meals, he would have become the same as the other prisoners at Auschwitz. He wanted to thank God but could not.

The staff usually treated Van much the same as they treated each other. All this changed the night he saw Franz. He was allowed to eat, but no one would talk to him or associate with him. He became an outsider, an outcast, a pink triangle without portfolio.

The scarcity of food in Auschwitz had taught him to always eat everything he was given. That night he ate very little but stole all he could hide in his baggy clothes. He was stealing the food for Franz. Van was not sure he could find him, but he would try.

When he left the hospital, it was nearly midnight and the snow was again falling. The new snow covered the old, blackish fall, creating a soft, white blanket effect over the entire camp. The light from the spotlights along the fence and throughout the camp fluttered in the falling snow and reflected it, making the night lighter and whiter than usual. Auschwitz looked deceptively beautiful and peaceful.

Van was unaware of any beauty around him as he hurried to his barrack to get the information about Franz's location from Ben. He would know. He probably already had his black market functioning among the new arrivals.

He could think only of Franz and his terrible condition. He had surely lost over fifty pounds, his eyes were sunken, the sockets outlined in black, and his cheeks were hollow. The young, healthy, muscular body that had stood silhouetted against Berlin's Crystal Night was no more. Strong hands and arms that had urged Van to discard his pall of self-denial were nothing more than sharp bones draped with skin. Worst of all, the vibrant, happy individuality that had shared with Van its uniqueness and joy of living was altered, perhaps forever.

Why did they not just kill them, Van wondered. They held them in these abominable camps and, little by little, smothered all of the finer qualities of the human soul. Why did they not end their existence completely? If there was life after death, surely the Nazis would be relegated to its most miserable levels. If this nonexistent God had created a Hell, the Nazis would fuel its eternal fires forever with their souls' tears.

Van's barrack was bitterly cold, nauseatingly pungent and weirdly quiet. The only light was the small amount that filtered through the filthy windows from the snow shrouded floodlights and searchlights outside. Immediately, he sensed that something was wrong; an eerie feeling of impending disaster could almost be tasted in the dank air.

In the dark, someone hit him in the pit of his stomach. He doubled over in terrific pain. Then a barrage of blows and kicks fell upon all parts of his body, knocking him senseless to the floor. The food he had stolen for Franz was grabbed by greedy hands as they tore at his clothing, and someone emptied one of the black pots on him, dousing him with the stinking refuse.

"You dirty rotten queer!"

"Kill the perverted bastard!"

He recognized Ben's voice. The other voices he did not know, but he recognized them as those of the people in his barrack.

"You're not a Jew!"

"Get the Star of David off his jacket. Get that one on his trousers too."

One of the hands ripped the Star of David from his jacket while another tore the one from his trouser leg. Everyone in the barrack seemed to join in the beating and kicking. They were so brutal in their assault that Van lost consciousness.

He was dragged through the snow. His clothes were torn and practically ripped from his body. He was wet and the cold snow seemed like a million tiny needles sticking into his skin. A great commotion was made by some hundred or more Jews from his barrack, but the guards did nothing to stop them. Van opened his eyes and saw the blood from his battered face leaving a red trail in the snow.

After what seemed hours of dragging, they reached their destination. A group of them picked him up, tied him to a post and hung a large sign around his neck. One of them banged on a barrack door a short distance from the post. The door opened cautiously. A few men came out of the barrack.

"You slimy queer, listen to what I got to tell you," one of those from his barrack yelled. He did not recognize the voice. It could have been Ben or the Kapo. People continued to beat and kick him while someone told him how life was to be for him.

"You are not a Jew anymore! Don't ever wear the Star of David again! Jews aren't queers! It is against God's laws! You are a queer! Here is where you belong!"

Everyone from Van's barrack filed past him, hitting, kicking, tearing at his skin and spitting in their utter disgust for him. The worst blows were those in his abdomen and groin. He fainted in a brilliant burst of millions of tiny stars, when he received a particularly well-aimed kick.

Then someone was untying him and he was falling to the snow. He was lifted and carried inside a barrack. He opened his swollen eyes as much as he could. They removed a large wooden pink triangle from around his neck. His head rested in someone's lap. He felt himself slipping away again, he could not fight it. He looked up at the man in whose lap he was lying. It was Franz.

Van was led to the formation the next morning by Franz and another man, supported by one on each side. His first roll-call in the pink triangle formation started at the regular time of three in the morning and lasted until nearly five thirty. When it was finally over, Van stood in the food line with the other pink triangles, a dirty, battered tin cup in his hand.

Standing in the blowing snow, aching from the beating he had received the night before, he looked at the new badge of identity on his left chest. The outline of his Star of David was clearly visible on the fabric. In the center of the shadow of the Star was his new badge, the pink triangle, its inverted top pointing downward. As he gazed at the new emblem, his final truth, he knew that he could at last keep his vow to himself never again to live a lie.

After eating the slop that had been dumped in the tin cup, he left Franz and the others, and reported to the hospital for his work detail. The workers ignored him. When Mengele arrived and saw Van's condition and his new symbol of identity, the pink triangle, his face changed from an emotionless mask to a scowl of utter disgust.

"Looks like a name change is in order, Jew-Van. I'll have to call you Queer-Van from now on, I suppose," he smirked. Clearing his throat, he spat on the hospital floor, something Mengele had never been known to do before.

He explained his feelings further. "Jews I can stand, if I have to. Homosexuals I cannot endure. You report back to the Kapo of your new barrack. I won't be using you here in the hospital any longer. I might need you for one of my experiments, but I don't want you around me otherwise."

Van left the hospital in search of his new quarters. Slouching along, not seeing anyone, he was startled when he glanced up and saw Rudolf Hoess and his group of lackeys. Van continued walking, trying to get past without an incident. He had not seen Rudy since the day he had been brought to his office to welcome him to Auschwitz. He did not want to see Rudy again, especially on that first day of his wearing the new badge of identity.

"Hold up, gentlemen. Here is one of my old home town friends. Have you been in an accident, Van? You look absolutely terrible."

"Yes, Major Hoess, I had a little accident last night," he quietly replied, unable to walk away and ignore him.

"Where is your Star of David? Who gave you that pink triangle?"

"It was a group decision, Sir. All of the men in my barrack decided I was no longer a Jew. They were of the opinion I should never again wear the Star of David. I think I agree."

He looked at Van closely. For a brief moment, Van thought he saw the old Rudy in his expression. Rudy started to say something but changed his mind and did not speak. Reaching out to Van's chest, he felt the pink triangle. In a whisper that was barely audible, he said to Van, "If I can help, let me know. I still remember your help that night I left Baden-Baden. I suppose I owe you, if you need it."

They walked on, leaving Van standing there in disbelief. He heard Rudy say to his followers, "Those damn queers are a threat to the Third Reich. Germany must be completely cleared of that trash and we must then eradicate them altogether."

Van decided he would never ask him for anything. Death's open arms would be preferable to Rudy's assistance.

For the first time since he had entered Dachau, he felt utterly alone. His few friends in high places were gone; he had declared his God dead and had been officially banished from the great Jewish nation. In the midst of Auschwitz, he knew that, for the first time in his life, he was free. He no longer had to live a lie.

The area where the pink triangles' barracks were situated was set well away from the others. It was easy to find the area, but he had trouble finding the right building. No one was there when he entered, so he collapsed on one of the board beds and slept, hoping for no recurrence of his old nightmare.

Franz woke him when he returned from his long day of work. They went to roll-call immediately and endured the torment of two hours of harassment by the SS. Van had slept all day and felt rested and hungry. His injuries were painful but he did not think any were serious. After they had eaten the pieces of bread and watery soup, they had their first chance to talk to one another.

Although it was dark, the barrack had not yet been locked. They went outside to find a private spot to talk, and crawled under the barrack building. It was cold, dirty and cramped, but they were alone. Above them they could hear the noises of men moving around.

"Van," Franz whispered, "when you left Berlin that night, did you find your parents all right?"

Mama and Papa. He seldom thought of them. Franz's question underlined the bitter loneliness that ate at him. A strange, bitter taste filled his mouth, a taste of gall or vinegar. He swallowed hard and answered:

"Papa was dead when I got back to Baden-Baden—of a heart attack in the synagogue. Mama died the first week in Dachau, of a broken heart, I suppose."

Neither one said anything for a long time.

"They are both better off to have died," Van finally said.

"I'm sorry they died that way," Franz said, "but you're right. If they had lived and gone through all of this, what good would it have done?

"How long have you been here at Auschwitz?" Franz asked after another long silence.

"Since November of last year. Before that I was in Dachau. I arrived there soon after I met you in Berlin."

"You were in Dachau that long? You don't look like someone who has been in a Nazi concentration camp that long. In fact, you look bigger and healthier than you did when I met you."

Van explained what had happened since he had seen him on Crystal Night. He did not mention Rudy. When he reached the point where Franz had come to Auschwitz, he stopped and Franz asked a few questions. Van then asked Franz to tell him what had happened to him since Crystal Night.

Franz had been arrested by the SS a few days after the night they met. Using a list of the names of known homosexuals that the Berlin authorities had gathered for years, the SS arrested approximately 45,000 in Berlin. The same methods were used in most cities all over Germany.

"Even before the Nazis came to power," Franz said, "the police in Berlin were keeping lists of all of us. I know when they added my name to their list. It was that night Michael Schmidt and I were attacked by that group of brown shirts. Did I ever tell you about that?"

"No," Van answered, "you didn't tell me much about yourself that one night in Berlin."

"Michael and I were followed by some five or six brown shirts as we left work one night. They beat us pretty bad, killed poor Michael, I believe. I never heard any more about him. The police came, after the brown shirts had done all to us that they wanted to, and took me to jail. That's when they got my name for the list they were making."

Franz told how those arrested in the vicinity of Berlin were sent to Oranienburg, a camp north of Berlin. Franz had been in Oranienburg since the day he was arrested. All the pink triangles were at the complete mercy of the SS and the other prisoners, just as in Dachau

173

and Auschwitz. The other prisoners considered them the scourge of the earth and killed any pink triangles they could catch alone. Before killing them, they often abused them brutally. He told Van worse things than Van had ever imagined.

During the first months of imprisonment, the sexual abuse of the pink triangles was a daily occurrence. But since all the concentration camp inmates were slowly being starved, sexual harassment gradually ceased. The struggle for survival took all of the prisoners' energies. Hated and despised, the pink triangles remained easy targets upon which others could exercise their growing frustrations in the world of the concentration camp. Nazi SS guards never tired of using and abusing them. The death of a pink triangle was not even cause for comment. One less queer to feed. The abuse by the Nazis ranged from beatings to the worst types of sadism.

Franz continued, relating incidents of a more specific and personal nature.

"One of the men that slept in the cubicle where I slept was taken away by the guards one night. I had noticed two of the guards watching him with much interest a while before they came and got him. They simply came into the barrack one night and took him away. The Kapo or no one else said a word. He was gone for over a week, so we all assumed he was dead. Then the guards brought him back and threw him in the door of the barrack. He lay there on the floor, unable to get up or walk. They had broken both of his knees because 'the queer spent most of his time on his knees'.

"Although my friend was crippled, his knees finally healed enough that he was able to push himself about on the floor or the ground.

"Behind the main camp, there was a pen of hogs, about twenty of them, I believe. Each one of them must have weighed as much as two or three men. Scraps, garbage and anything edible were dumped into this pen daily for the hogs. They fed those damn hogs better than they did us. When they fed them, the guards would stand around the pen to keep the prisoners from trying to steal the slop for the hogs before the swine ate all of it. I have seen those bastard guards shoot starving men that could no longer stand and watch the pigs eat while they went hungry.

"Late one afternoon, the guards came and took my crippled friend away again. They dragged him to the back of the camp area, next to the pen of hogs. The daily garbage was being dumped into the pen. Using a rifle butt, a guard struck him on his shattered knees, causing them to bleed. Two of the guards then placed him on the back of one of the larger hogs.

"The blood streamed from his knees and down his legs. He screamed horribly as the hogs began to go after the fresh blood, devouring his lifeless, dangling legs in the process. His screams were heard all over the entire camp. I covered my ears but I could still hear his screaming. I will never forget those screams, I hear them now still. A large crowd of prisoners, not pink triangles, gathered to watch. The pigs made short work of him. It was awful. Van, those pigs ate him alive. Never in my life have I seen anything like that. I will never forget it! Never!"

Franz began to cry, his thin, gaunt face in his frail hands. Van did not know how to console him. Finally, Franz stopped crying and began to tell Van something that he had heard whispered around the camp many times before but had not yet believed.

He described how the Nazis at Oranienburg had started using large, completely enclosed vans to transport prisoners from the camp. The vans were loaded to capacity and those taken away were never seen again. Relocation was given as the reason. However, Franz discovered the truth.

"I had been on a work detail most of the day, with a group of other pink triangles. It was a somewhat loose detail in that the guards did not watch us too closely. Since we were still in the camp area, there was no place to escape to; so they were not as alert as they were when we were sent outside the camp compound to work.

We were paving a road, hot and tiring work. We were interrupted when one of these large vans had to pass over the road where the work was being done. I knew the van must be loaded with prisoners because the weight made the tire tracks much deeper in the new asphalt than an empty van would. The van turned onto a dirt road that led into the thick foliage along the main highway. By watching the dust billow up into the air, I judged that it travelled into the wooded area for about one kilometer and stopped. The engine could still be heard, faintly. No other person in the work crew, not even the SS guards, had noticed that the truck turned from the main highway. Since they were not aware of the truck's location, they did not notice the slight murmur of the running engine.

"I thought the truck had stopped for a gate or some mechanical problem, but the engine idled too long for that. After about ten minutes of the sound of the idling blending with the other noises of the forest, it suddenly stopped. I decided to try to investigate this unusual business. I told the guards I had to relieve myself and went into the forest. I ran as quickly as I could to the area where the truck had stopped.

"It was not far from the place where we were working, about three hundred meters into the dense forest. Backed to a large ditch, the truck's double back doors were just being unlocked by the SS men. The guards swung the large doors open, creating a swooshing noise. The inside of the van faced the direction where I was hidden within the thick brush. I could clearly see the inside of the van. Tangled together in a web of arms, legs and torsos were all of the people that had been loaded into the van, dead. The entanglement of bodies covered the floor of the van, their arms and hands clutching at whatever was within reach, their faces grotesque masks. The inside walls were covered with marks where the desperate people had pounded and scratched as they tried to find a way out of the van.

"A hose ran from the exhaust into the only opening in the truck's interior. This was covered with a fine wire mesh and a piece of cloth dangled from it. In a last, hopeless effort, someone had tried to plug the hole with the cloth. The wire mesh prevented this. Dangling from one corner of the mesh, the cloth flapped with the sudden suction of the opening door. When it stopped moving, I noticed that it was someone's shirt with the yellow Star of David still on it.

"The SS men pulled, pushed and shoved the bodies into the open pit. They were all Jewish. The Stars of David tumbled into the man-made ditch in a rolling, falling milky way of stars. I could not look into their faces; instead I watched the yellow stars as they cascaded into the earth. Men, women and children of every age and size were transferred from the truck to the open hole.

"The doors of the van were closed and the SS men left the open pit in the van and other vehicles that were already there. I was the only one remaining. I had to see how large the pit was. I ran to the edge of the hole and looked down into it. The gaping hole was much larger and deeper than I had thought. Only some thirty people had been unloaded from the van. The short look into the pit revealed hundreds of bodies, not just the thirty or thirty-five I had seen being unloaded. There was still room in the burial hole for many more. I thought I saw movement among the corpses, twitching of limbs and grasping. Moans reached up from the ditch. I decided it had to be the winds singing a dirge through the trees. There was no life there in that place of death. Unable to endure what I saw in the deep ditch, I turned away and began to vomit.

"I managed to slip back to the road where we were working. I was crying and one of the guards asked me why. I told him I didn't know."

Franz told Van that what he had learned about the trucks enabled him to save the few who would believe him. With the prospect of relocation and perhaps something better, many of the prisoners were anxious to leave in the trucks.

"No more, please, no more, Franz," Van finally said to him. "The rumors I have heard must be true. Maybe I shouldn't say this, but I must. We have got to face the truth. We are going to die here and there is nothing we can do about it. And when it happens, no one in the world will care at all. What is the death of one pink triangle to the world? It is probably cause for celebration."

"I know, Van," Franz said. "I used not to care what anyone thought about me and the way I lived my life. Now I see that I was wrong. If no one cares about you and the way you live, then no one cares about your death, or the way you die."

Van, realizing how late it must be, said, "Franz, listen. There is no noise above us in the barrack. How long have we been out here?"

"I don't know. I believe about two hours."

"Two hours! Shit, we have probably been locked out. Come on. We better hurry and try to get back in."

They crawled from under the barrack into the deep snow and the bright camp lights.

"Keep in the shadows, Van. If anyone catches us out here, they'll kill us or worse."

They edged along the sides of the barrack, trying to be quiet and move quickly. Franz whispered to Van, "You must learn that, wearing that pink triangle, you can't go anywhere alone. Stay with a large group for protection."

The door was locked and they couldn't pry it open. Van tapped lightly, hoping to wake a friendly individual near the door, not the Kapo or guard. No one heard or, if they heard, would leave his sleeping spot to let them in. They were not sure what they expected a friend within to do. He could not have opened the door since the key was kept by the Kapo and the guards. No one answered their knock.

"We must hide, Van. We can't stay out here. It is too cold and we'll be caught and God knows what they'll do to us."

"I know, Franz. The only thing I know to do is get back under the barrack and try to slip into roll-call tomorrow morning. Let's go."

They retraced their steps back to the other side of the barrack. Franz crawled under first. Van bent down on his knees to follow him.

Someone grabbed him and pulled him backward, throwing him onto his back in the snow. A young man was standing over him, his back to the place where Franz had crawled under the barrack. The man began to unbutton his trousers.

"Just what I was looking for. If I can't find any women, you'll have to do. You know what I want, so do it or I'll kill you."

The knife he was holding reflected the light, sparkling with many slivers of piercing light. His trousers fell around his ankles in the snow.

Behind him, Franz came bounding from under the barrack and was on the man's back in one leap, his arms around him. They fell together in the snow and struggled for the glittering steel blade. Their struggle sent snow flying around them. Both men were grunting and breathing hard, both fighting for the weapon. Bunched around his ankles, the man's trousers impeded his efforts. Franz managed to wrench the knife from his grasp. The stranger was lying on his back with Franz astride him. The knife sparkled in Franz's hand, its downward thrust to the man's chest a vicious, gleaming movement. Again and again, Franz stabbed him. He stabbed and stabbed insanely, until, in exhaustion, he fell forward on the man.

Van had gotten up and managed to get to Franz, pulling him from the man's body. Franz was covered with the blood of the man he had just killed. He sobbed uncontrollably while Van used snow to clean the blood from his clothes and his face and hands. He cleaned the knife with snow and took Franz back under the barrack. His crying had subsided to quiet sobbing. Van crawled out again, knowing he had to get the man's body away from the area. Grabbing the dead man around his ankles, he dragged the body as far away as he could, without being seen. He tried to destroy the stains in the snow, hoping that more snow would fall during the night and cover the trail he had left when he dragged the body away and the signs of the stabbing and the struggle. All around the place where Franz had killed the man, the snow was pinkish red from the blood.

He crawled back under the barrack where he found Franz still crying.

"Franz, don't cry any more. There is nothing to cry about," Van whispered. Trying to get some response from Franz, Van continued, "He was a Jew, Franz. I saw the Star he was wearing."

"Van," Franz replied, gulping to catch his breath, "he was a man. I killed another human being. I might as well be wearing that damn swastika."

"Franz, that is ridiculous. You killed him to save me. He would have killed me when he finished with me. It was self-defense. Actually, the whole thing never would have happened if it weren't for the

Nazis. They put him here and they put you here. The Nazis have made desperate men out of you, me, all of us. It's *their* fault, for they brought us all here and created these hell-holes. They are the murderers, not you."

It was becoming much colder. The wind whipped under the barrack, bringing fits of snow with it. They lay there silently for some minutes. Van put his arm around Franz for warmth and to comfort him. His mind returned to Crystal Night. He moved closer to Franz and held him tighter. Wiping the melted snow from Franz's face with his shirt sleeve, Van found that he had gone to sleep, completely exhausted from the ordeal of the long, long day.

23

FOR DAYS THEY WERE BOTH concerned that the body of the man Franz had killed would be found and, in some mysterious way, be connected to them. They finally realized that Franz had merely killed another Jewish prisoner. No one cared.

The following day, some four hundred of the pink triangles were selected for transport to a brickworks plant seventy-five kilometers from Auschwitz. Franz declared it would be the worst kind of work. Another man chosen for the detail said that the brickworks was the work detail "of the damned". To his knowledge, the only people ever sent to the brickworks were the pink triangles.

When roll-call was over, all the men whose numbers had been called were led to five parked trucks. Only fifteen from Van and Franz's barrack were sent on the detail. They were led to the trucks by Kapo Fritz who left them there with the nearly four hundred others waiting to board the trucks. Franz strained to see if the trucks were enclosed vans, like the one he had seen in the forest at Oranienburg. If so, he thought, they are not sending us to the brickworks. That would be just a guise to get us in the vans for our final trip to another of those deep, deep ditches. He was finally able to see the waiting trucks: they were open, not enclosed.

The guards worked to divide the assembled crowd into five groups, one for each truck. They shouted and screamed their commands, punctuating them with their whips, popping them in the cold air above the inmates' heads. Some of the guards carried large sticks with which they beat and prodded any of the prisoners within their reach. The black sticks were being used with a vengeance, their blows were harsh and dangerous. There seemed to be a new fever pitch of insanity running through the group of guards supervising the loading of the trucks. Their smiles would broaden each time they inflicted a crushing blow on a pink triangle.

Van and Franz were in the middle of this activity and managed to avoid these waves of violent beatings that fell upon the outer fringes of the group. Men screamed their pain as the guards furiously beat the group into the five desired formations. When the five groups were finally arranged, each group consisting of some eighty men, bodies lay all around where they had fallen from the more fatal blows.

"We will load now," the ranking SS officer was announcing. "When I sound the whistle, each group will get onto the truck assigned to it. We are running late already, thanks to your laziness and uncooperativeness. Speed is important. We must make up the lost time." He blew the whistle, a shrill, high, piercing sound that made the ears echo the ring for minutes. Each group rushed to its truck. The guards pushed and shoved them into the trucks, still beating them unmercifully. Van and Franz were among the last ones to climb up into the back of the truck.

Van stepped up on the metal bar over the truck's rear bumper and grasped the railing above to pull himself up. He was still sore and aching from the ordeal of his beating. Straining to pull himself up, the pains shot through his body. He faltered and one of the guards raised his club high to strike Van across the back. Franz saw the approaching fatal blow and reach up with both hands to push Van into the truck. Propelled by Franz's violent push, he fell into the large group already in the truck. The guard lowered his weapon and stood there, watching the loading. Franz climbed into the truck as rapidly as he could.

The man behind Franz was getting ready to step up onto the metal bar when he dropped something. He bent down and retrieved a short cigarette butt. Earlier, after roll-call, he had watched one of the guards smoke his cigarette down to a short stub and throw the remaining butt to the ground. Along with four or five other prisoners, the man had fought for the butt and he had won. It was a prized object and he intended to smoke it on the truck. Just as he moved to step up, the guard with the club roared, "You god-damn slow son-of-a-bitch, I said hurry!" He jumped onto the railing, drew the club back and whacked the man on the back of his head as hard as he could, splitting his head and skull instantly.

The man, clasping the cigarette butt in his right hand and holding the support railing with his left, had been poised to jump into the truck. The force of the ferocious, crushing blow to the back of his head thrust him forward into the group of men in the truck. Out of

181

his peripheral vision, Franz had seen the man behind him and the guard raising his club to strike. He turned to help pull the man into the truck before the guard hit him. With both hands extended to pull him forward, Franz stood with open arms when the guard struck the man, thrusting him forward with a great force into Franz's arms.

Franz caught the poor man and held him a moment, not realizing that he was already dead from the blow. His head rested on Franz's chest and then, as Franz released him, slid limply down the front of Franz's body. As it slipped downward, it left a trail of blood, brains and other matter along its path from Franz's chest toward his feet. He stood there, in total shock, holding the dead man up by his smashed head. The front of Franz's body was covered with blood and whitish lumps of the man's brains. Finally, the guard grabbed the dead man by his two feet and pulled him out of Franz's grasp and from the truck. He threw the body to the side and slammed the back gate of the truck.

Franz remained standing in the same position, as though he were still holding the man. His mind was reeling, and a soul-shattering scream escaped his lips, reverberating against the canvas walls of the truck, stabbing the senses of all those within and echoing out the back opening. The scream melted into great sobs and retching. Franz fell forward and vomited out the opening of the truck, while Van held him. When nothing remained but dry heaves, Van pulled Franz to the floor and cleaned him as well as he could.

Franz continued to weep while the truck rumbled out of Auschwitz. Van tried to quiet him and bring him out of his shock. Eventually, Franz was able to talk. Still crying, he mumbled, "This is the end. I can't fight any more. I can't stand another day of this. I give up."

"No, Franz. You can't surrender. That is what they want us to do. That is what they expect of us because we are pink triangles."

"I don't care what they expect, Van. I don't care anything about them at all. To hell with them. I just can't stand any more. I want to die."

"Don't say that, Franz! It's a lie! Don't say it! We must live. This won't last forever. We're certain to get out of here soon."

"Oh, Van, you are still so naive. We'll never get out of this place. We're going to die here the same way that poor man just died. You said that yourself last night under the barrack. We're going to die in this place. And no one cares."

"Franz, I was wrong. Someone does care whether you live or die. I care."

Franz looked at Van and understood. He said, "Well, you are the *only* one that cares." He paused a long while and then added, "I suppose we will have to try to survive, to live for each other because no one else in the world seems to care."

Like a large troop of dark and dreary ants, they were forced into the bowels of the earth. Down, down the steeply slanting incline hewed out of the ground they descended; so steep was the pitch of the path that their descent quickly became a trot, then a run and finally a full stampede. Their speed was heightened even more by the lashes of the whips expertly aimed at the moving mass of humanity descending to the bottom of the immense open pit, dug to such a depth entirely by imprisoned men.

Franz and Van felt the rapier-like slashes and ran still faster, pushing those in front of them to greater speed or carrying them forward by their own evasive force. The pathway they followed ran along the west bank of the pit, the earthen side forming a wall along one side of the path while the sheer drop to the bottom of the pit served as an invisible wall on the other side. The push and speed of the movement of the large number of men thrust some from the path and they fell to their death in the mine's depths, their frail screams transformed into echoing shouts of dying desperation by the size and emptiness of the vast hole in the ground. Van pulled the weaker Franz along with him as he ran, wedging the two of them as far away from the drop-off as he could.

Around the base of the dirt runway, where the downward rush terminated, the prisoners were being beaten, the guards using both the whips and their club-like night sticks. Relentlessly, they whipped the exhausted men, forcing them into one tight circular group much the way wagons formed into a protective circle against the attacking Indians in the American West. Those on the outer edges of the growing orb received the bashings and lashes, forcing them to scratch and claw for the innermost protected pockets of the circle. It was a picture snatched from one of Lucifer's most horrid nightmares, a *mise en scène* of unimaginable human suffering and unbridled sadism.

When all of the prisoners had reached the lower level of the cavern, the guards stopped their pointless beatings and began to form the group into ranks. Franz glanced at the ground along the length of the base of the dirt trail leading to the top of the pit. He saw the broken and dead bodies of those who had fallen from the rout down into the brickwork pit, some few still alive, moaning and crying for the one thing they would never receive: help.

"This is the brickworks!" a guard at the front of the formation was shouting. "Here you will dig the clay for the making of bricks. You will fill those buckets you see there with the clay and then raise them to the top. The bricks are made above, on the ground level. You must work fast. Speed is important as the bricks are needed for the further construction of the glorious Third Reich."

He pointed to a large pile of buckets, each bucket big enough to hold forty or fifty liters of mud. Franz noticed that along the banks of the pit, situated about every thirty-five or forty meters, were apparatuses for raising the buckets to the top. These structures consisted of large wooden platforms, able to hold three or four buckets, with ropes tied to each corner and then gathered upward into one great rope that travelled to the top of the pit. At the top, on the lip of the cavern, were the pulleys which raised the wooden platforms with their buckets of clay out of the pit. All of this equipment was hand-operated no electrical motors or devices were needed or used; the slave labor was cheaper than electricity or petrol to run any machines.

"We have picks here," the guard continued, pointing to a stack of small picks. "If there are not enough picks, you will use your hands to fill the buckets!"

A group of about one hundred prisoners were taken inside and informed that they would go back up to ground level to do the brick-making. They slowly started up the incline, its steepness almost impossible to negotiate. Behind them the whips and clubs began again, but no increase in speed occurred. The slow climbing continued until they reached the top. They did not march in orderly ranks up the pathway, but struggled in higgledy-piggledly fashion trying to avoid the crushing impact of the clubs and the flesh-slicing bites of the whips.

Those remaining were taken to the area where the clay would be dug. Since there were more men than picks, many had to dig the earth with their hands. Van had managed to get a pick, but Franz had not. They all worked in one section at a time until they got the dirt down to a specific level. The work would then move to the adjacent section and dig it down to the same level. This continued until the entire pit had been dug to the same level. Then the group would start again and dig still deeper, section at a time, across the entire floor of the broad expanse of the brickwork open-pit mine.

Guards patrolled the perimeter of the men digging the clay, continually using their whips. They were the worst group of SS ever encountered by either man.

"We can't stay on the edges of the work," Franz whispered, as he dug the clay with Van's pick.

"Yes, I can see that. They'll beat us to death if we stay on the sides. We have got to try to slip into the middle so they can't reach us with those damn whips."

Van was on his knees, using his hands to fill one of the large buckets. The bitter February cold numbed him to the fact that his hands were already bleeding from the almost impossible digging. The clay was of a consistency that digging by hand was arduous and painful. It was, Van thought, already brick-like in nature. Not only was the ground naturally hard, it was also partially frozen by the long cold winter.

He started crawling through the other workers, worming his way into the middle of the detail. Franz followed his path, pushing and fighting off those who resisted. They finally worked their way into the middle, escaping the whips.

The filled buckets were carried to one of the wooden platforms which was hoisted to the top when four of them were placed on it. Often individual buckets would fall from the upward moving platform which had no sides. At other times a platform would lose its entire load and all the buckets would plummet to the pit below. Working under the area where one of the pulley lifts was located was fraught with danger. The platforms moved upward slowly, lurching along their hand-pulled path. If the men operating the pulley let it slip, as they often did, the buckets would tumble down and crush to death anyone who happened to be working where they fell.

The work always began at first light and continued until it was too dark to see. At night, they were housed in buildings that had never been built for human abode. They thought of the Auschwitz barracks as luxurious by comparison. The food served was heavily salted to increase their thirst. While working, they were given no water.

The stories about the work detail in the brickworks were true. It was Van's first exposure to total physical labor, with death always hovering over them. Men died all around him. The guards abused them as they pleased and killed merely to have something to do. Nearly every day at least one pink triangle hung himself or took his life in some way. None of the guards took notice of these suicides, and nothing was done to discourage or prevent the men from taking their own lives. It was as though, Van concluded after about a week at the brickworks, the objective was to kill as many of the workers as possible. The objective of the detail was not really to make bricks for the Third Reich. It was to rid the Third Reich of those sent on the detail.

They were at the brickworks a little more than a month. Approximately four hundred of them were sent in five large trucks. One truck was enough to bring the sixty-three survivors back to Auschwitz.

There was very little talking or other activity during the trip back to Auschwitz. With only sixty-three people in the truck, there was more room than there had been when they went to the brickworks. Franz and Van sat quietly on the floor of the truck. After a long time, Van spoke. "Franz, I think you were right. We are going to die here. And I no longer care. I'm ready to die. In fact, I want to die. I'm so tired. I can't go on much longer."

"Van, don't talk that way. You are the one that was right, not me. You must try to survive because I care. I don't want you to die. But there's another reason to get out of this place alive, a more important reason, perhaps."

"What's that, Franz?"

Franz looked around at the other men in the truck and then at Van. Then, in a louder voice so all could hear him, he said, "Some of us have got to get out of here alive so we can tell what is happening here. Maybe the world doesn't care, but we still must tell them."

During that year the course of events in the Nazi concentration camps changed drastically and dreadfully. Before the new policy was instituted, the camps had served as slave-labor and detention camps, medical experiment sites and as an unexpected source of SS amusement in sadism. An inmate's life was as worthless as yesterday's evaporated tears. Thousands died of typhus, malnutrition, starvation, heartbreak and a myriad of unknown and unnamed diseases.

Mid-1942 was the beginning of the official Nazi policy of planned, efficient extermination of selected classifications of people. From the sewers of the Nazi soul, the policy forever changed the meaning of the words prejudice, bigotry and racial purity. The crematorium became the crucible for the theory that to be different was to be evil.

Those few pink triangles that returned from the brickworks were amazingly relieved to be back in Auschwitz. When they arrived, Van knew something had changed. They had thought that Auschwitz could be no worse than it was, the ultimate in human degradation. They soon discovered that they had been wrong.

Franz and Van were sent with a group of pink triangles to a work detail in the far northwest corner of the camp area. They passed

Mengele processing a large group of people that had just arrived. He saw Van as they passed near his table staffed with those terribly efficient clerks. He called to the SS guard leading the group and they all stopped. Mengele walked briskly over to them.

"Queer-Van, I certainly could use your help. The work load is staggering. Of course, that is out of the question now. How is your new life as a pink triangle?"

Surely he need not ask that question, Van thought. Van's clothes were now draped on his frame the same as all the other inmates. His loss of weight, the sunken, dark look of his face and the terrible month in the brickworks made him resemble the paintings of the hooded figure of death.

"Life seems to go on, one way or another," Van replied to him.

"Maybe so," he said, smiling that same wicked smile. "Then again, maybe not. Are you aware of the new selection process that I have instituted?"

Van wanted to crawl into the nearest hole. He did not want anyone to know he knew Dr. Mengele, much less that he had worked with him.

"No, Sir. I have been away for the last month."

"Really! And where did you take your holiday, Queer-Van?" Mengele replied, loudly emphasizing the first half of Van's new name. The SS guards and the processing clerks laughed at his cleverness.

"About four hundred of us went away to the brickworks. Only sixty-three of us came back, Sir. Really a waste, don't you think, Dr. Mengele? Those who didn't return could have been of great value in your experiments."

"No matter. There is a tremendous number of your kind to serve my needs. I have been trying to decide on something special for you, Queer-Van."

Dr. Mengele went back to the waiting multitude and Van's detail continued on their trip. Dr. Mengele had done a rather curious thing while talking to Van. Taking a pen and pad from his pocket, he had noted Franz's tattooed number on the pad. Franz was beside Van during the conversation and it must have been evident to Mengele that Van and Franz were indeed friends as Van had told him, perhaps even more.

The work detail passed a newly arrived group of people preparing for delousing. The building was divided into two sections, one for males and the other for females. Inside the male section, they could see all the men removing their clothes and hanging them neatly on pegs along the wall. They placed their shoes in neat rows beneath their hanging clothes. The yellow Stars of David on the neatly hanging clothes announced that all were Jewish. They were of every age, from five or six, to old, rabinnical-appearing gentlemen approaching a hundred.

The leader of the work detail, the ranking SS guard, made them stop while he discussed something with the man in charge of the delousing. While they stood waiting, they watched the men and boys file from the dressing area into a larger room equipped with shower heads along the ceiling. Van shuddered at the word over the rooms for bathing: "baden." He thought of Baden-Baden and the beautiful baths there.

The people entering the baden rooms were orderly and quiet, embarrassed by their nudity. Some of the pink triangles enjoyed this sight and made comments. Franz and Van stood silent. Something about the activity was not right; they felt an odd foreboding about the situation.

The giant metal door of the shower room slammed shut and was locked. It had a small thick glass hole, through which the interior could be seen. Van assumed that the SS guards had installed the window to watch the women shower. How strange, he thought, that a shower area would have that strong metal door, with locks.

On the roof, an SS man, wearing a gas mask, opened small metal covers and dropped something into the openings. He quickly closed the covers. The SS guard in charge of Van's work detail peered through the glass hole for a long time. Eventually, he returned to the work detail and they started for the wooded area outside the general camp area.

Van looked back at the shower room when they had travelled several meters past the buiding. The doors on the opposite side from where the people had entered the building were open. Because of the distance, he could only faintly see the inside of the shower room. Trusty prisoners were carrying bodies from the room. In the center, there was a tall pile of something. He could not be certain, but it looked like people. He grabbed Franz's arm.

"Look at that shower room, quick!"

Franz turned and looked at the building.

"My God! Is that what I think it is?"

"I don't know. I think it is a pile of men, all those men we saw going to take a shower."

"Oh God! That truck I saw in the woods at Oranienburg! They

have improved their methods. They intend to kill us all!"

As they approached a large ditch with tongues of fire leaping toward the sky from the long trench, the SS men told them to stop talking. The stench in the air was almost unbearable, so thick they could hardly breathe. They passed close enough to the ditch that they could see into the fire. In the long, deep ditch, the Nazis were burning bodies.

One of the pink triangles fainted when his eyes beheld the deep trench of burning bodies. He lay where he fell, beside the ditch, while the detail kept moving. The SS man would not allow any of them to help him. They marched on, leaving him there, near that terrible fire.

"I don't believe it!" Franz whispered to Van. "Look back there! Hurry, look!"

He looked back and was sorry. Two of the trusties had lifted the man who had fainted and were carrying him toward the ditch. They threw him into the fires. His scream was barely heard over the roaring, crackling and hissing of the flames.

Van and Franz, speechless, continued their trek. They noticed large areas of fresh turned earth scattered all over the field in which they were walking. Each patch had a small stake with an emblem attached near its edge. As they passed one of the stakes, Van saw that the emblem was the Star of David with dates and numbers written on it.

They stopped at one of the large areas. The stake was obscured from Van's view by the men in front of him. The guards gave each of them a shovel. Van moved closer to the stake and was able to see that the emblem was a pink triangle with the numbers 3-20-42–481 written on it.

The SS guard spoke in a loud, clear voice.

"There are four hundred and eighty-one of your kind buried here. They have been here since March twentieth. That's about two weeks. You are to dig them up and dispose of their bodies properly, in the ditch back there. Get started! Get every one of them and put them over here. You can carry them to the ditch once you have recovered all of them."

The SS men put on gas masks and moved back from the area. As the men dug, they began to uncover the nude, decomposing bodies. All of them were crying from the sting of the odor and from the reality of what they were uncovering. They stacked the remains along the edge of the area. The SS forced them to continue until all were accounted for.

The detail then had to carry them to the ditch and throw them into the fire. The condition of the remains of the pink triangles made it difficult to move them intact. It was almost impossible to get close enough to the flaming pit because the heat was so great. Van and Franz both found it difficult not to plunge into the ditch themselves. Neither had ever felt so near death, so completely bound by Hell's terrible clutches before.

When they had finished, they were allowed to move away from the fire, and to rest. Franz and Van looked at one another speechless. The SS men were visibly disturbed. They chain-smoked their cigarettes about thirty minutes.

Van tried to think coherently. He could not. He looked at the sky, clear except for the smoke and the terrible odor, a sickeningly sweet odor that made him gag with each breath. In the midst of all the evil and death, Van considered his own God, the God he had killed because He had allowed these horrible things to happen. He understood at last that none of the responsibility was God's, it was man's. Van desperately needed his God alive. Franz, as good and decent as he was, was not enough. The evil was too great. He recognized that the only relief from so great an evil must come from the one, true good: the God of Abraham and God of Van.

Silently, in his heart, he prayed, "God! Oh, God! Where are You? Help me, I beg for Your help. I can't stand this much longer. Oh, God, deliver me from my enemies! Deliver me from all of mankind!"

24

Auschwitz, Poland—1942

T HE PINK TRIANGLES WERE FORCED to become grave robbers, a grisly Nazi attempt at concealment. Thousands of people had been gassed and buried in mass graves when Van and Franz returned from the brickworks. Nazi policy decreed that the dead must be burned, and in a macabre twist, bury the evidence became burn the evidence.

The open pit flames were fed from two sources. Straight from the showers, the dead were brought to the continuing blaze, while the decaying remains of those who had died in the gas chambers were unearthed and consumed by the fire.

An insane determination to keep the atrocities secret developed and ran like a thread through the fabric of Nazi barbarism. For miles around each camp, the smell of burning flesh lay over the land like a thick fog; a fog that was ignored and denied by the Nazi authorities and, in Germany, by the general population living near the camps.

Eventually the open pit method of burning the victims proved to be too slow and inefficient. Huge crematoria were specially designed and constructed, to more rapidly dispose of the increasing numbers of dead.

In silent desperation, the Nazis created the Sonderkommando Units for each crematorium, commonly called the kommandos. Each unit consisted of eight to nine hundred prisoners, usually men. Their primary duty was to insure the smooth operation of the crematorium. While they were kommandos, their food and quarters were better. They prepared people for delousing, removed the bodies from the shower room, removed gold from the teeth of the dead and collected all of the personal items left behind by those going to the showers. They also fed the fires of the crematorium.

After a time, the kommandos were gassed and burned and replaced with a new group of prisoners. This continuing process of killing and replacement was intended to insure secrecy.

Franz and Van remained on the work detail that dug up the bodies and fed them to the open fire. The work lasted for weeks that seemed an eternity. Sleep for them, when it would finally come, was a series of nightmares. Although the pitiful remains of the dead were consumed in fire, they still ranged through the dreams and nightmares of the men on the detail. Van and Franz slept next to each other but were never alone. The barrack was crowded beyond capacity with people who would have given anything for a moment of privacy.

Van's health was failing. He knew he looked terrible; he felt he would not survive the winter. Franz looked even worse. He never talked much any more, and when he did he expressed his revulsion against everyone except Van. After the night he killed the man to protect Van, he became full of bitterness.

The barrack Kapo was not a pink triangle; he wore a green triangle which meant that he was a criminal. He had been in prison or concentration camp all of his adult life. Fritz was very wise to all of the things that happened in places of confinement. After Van bribed him with some gold he managed to get, Kapo Fritz agreed to let them out of the barracks one night, after everyone had gone to sleep. Van was ashamed of the way he obtained the gold.

One of the kommandos had been watching him for many days. After the work of exhuming the bodies was finished, Van was assigned to the detail where he worked with the dead. He was not a kommando but he had the job of separating the human hair into types before shipment back to Germany. Human hair was valuable, and the Germans wasted nothing from their victims. Van was on this detail for a long time, seeing the kommando every day and knowing that the man was watching him.

The kommando was a young Jew from Dresden. He wore the Star of David but no pink triangle. He had only been in the concentration camp about two months and was still in relatively good health. He had desires, sexual desires, that had to be satisfied. Van was not interested in him at all and ignored him for some time, but the facts finally became clear. He would do anything the young man wanted for a price. He could then use whatever he was paid to get the key to be alone with Franz. Van knew Kapo Fritz would sell anything he had. Bribing their way out of the barrack could have been done every night, if they had had anything of value to use as a bribe.

The kommando had a place to go and was able to arrange for Van to meet him. He paid Van with gold fillings from the teeth of the victims. Van serviced him sexually. When it was over, Van felt that once again he was nothing more than a whore.

Kapo Fritz unlocked the door and Franz and Van slipped out. The door was closed and they heard the snap of the lock. They were on their own until roll-call the next morning. They could not go under the barrack, with its painful reminder of the man Franz had killed, so they quietly made their way to the crematorium. It was running at full capacity, belching smoke and fumes from its giant smoke stack. Van found the small storage room where he had met the kommando. It was unlocked. They entered and tried to adjust their eyes to the total darkness, but there was not even one small shaft of light.

The room was attached to the crematorium. They could hear the giant oven doors open and close each time they were fed. It upset Van, and Franz was near hysteria when he realized what they were hearing.

Van sat down on a pile of clothes on the floor, gas chamber victims' clothes, waiting for shipment back to Germany, and pulled Franz down beside him into his arms. He held him as if for the last time in their lives. At first tense and nervous, Franz finally relaxed a little and returned Van's embrace.

"Van, we're going to die here. This is the end. I feel death so near."

"Let's not talk about it."

"All right. I'm so tired. I wish we were back in Berlin in my apartment."

"Franz, we can pretend."

"Yes, we can, I suppose."

They were silent for a while. Then Franz spoke. "Van, you know I love you."

"Yes, I know, Franz. I love you too. I have since Crystal Night. I always will." Always isn't very long in this place, he thought.

"Hold me closer, Van."

Van held him closer, their bodies and spirits blending into one. They lay together all night right next to the death room of the ovens, the sounds of the opening and closing oven doors and the bodies being pushed into the fire drowning out any whispered words between them.

25

Auschwitz, Poland–1942

L IKE ALL THE OTHERS IMPRISONED IN AUSCHWITZ, Van lived with an ever-present sense of unalterable fatality, resulting from his existence with so little hope or no hope at all. His exact moment of death was no longer of much concern to him. Before Dachau, he had been consumed by his own personal malaise, concerned only with his own secret feelings and problems, seeing nothing else around him of great importance. This self-centered attitude of his youth, like so many other attitudes and beliefs, had changed in Dachau and Auschwitz.

His surroundings could not pass unnoticed as they had in those earlier years. Masses of humanity, huddled together in unending, repetitious, faceless copies, stared out at him from deep within individual souls. He tried never to forget that these were not simply thousands of Jews, homosexuals, Jehovah's Witnesses, Gypsies, beggars and political prisoners, but distinct individuals: men and women individually facing the horror of Auschwitz, struggling and dying individually, not as a group.

Coming to Dachau as he had, in the throng of Jews arrested on Crystal Night, Van had assumed that the camps were predominantly filled with Jews. Over the years in Dachau and Auschwitz, he found that he had been correct in this assumption. However, Christian inmates were more numerous than Van had at first thought. Jehovah's Witnesses, many of the political prisoners, a large number of the pink triangles and the few clergymen who dared to oppose the Nazis were Christians. When Germany occupied a country, many Christians who resisted were sent to the camps.

In Van's ordered German life, there had always been a distinct line between good and evil. At Auschwitz, he began to understand that all men do not fit into these two definite categories. All Christians were not bad, nor were all Jews good. The two forces, good and evil, merge in all men and struggle for control. Only in a few does one force win complete dominance. When the good wins, mankind benefits and marvels. When evil is totally triumphant, the world endures a Hitler, a Rudolf Hoess or some other horror.

In Auschwitz there were few complete saints or total devils. Almost all of them, guards and guarded alike, were a mixture of the good and evil of all mankind. The natural mix was not unique within them; the degree of control exercised by either good or evil was the distinguishing factor between the jailor and the jailed. The men in Van's barrack were not a homogeneous group. Binding them together as a unit were two commonly shared qualities: they were all men and they were all wearing the pink triangle.

The extreme crowding of the barracks had already forced the Nazis to place the long, rough-hewn, creosoted boards along the three tiers of the bunks, and six men shared the arrangement of the beds. Together with Franz and Van were two other Germans, a Christian and one who claimed no religion, and two Polish prisoners. Steuben, the German Christian, was a frail, scholarly, young man, perhaps twenty years of age, from Berlin. Usually quiet, seeming to automatically blend into almost every background, he was considered by the others to be a thinker. Steuben loved birds, the one subject on which he would talk incessantly. None of them were saintly, but Steuben came closer to the mark than most.

One evening, during the lengthy roll-call procedure, Steuben noticed a particularly rare species of bird sitting on the high barbed-wire fence near the barracks' area. Enthralled with the bird and oblivious to his surroundings, Steuben left the formation and silently approached it.

"Halt! Where are you going?" the SS man yelled at him.

Steuben continued walking toward the fence, rapidly nearing the neutral-zone, when two SS men grabbed him and carried him toward the guards' compound.

"Trying to escape in front of us all!" one of the guards yelled.

"No, I just wanted to take a closer look at that beautiful bird on the fence. Did you see it? I think it was a rare..." Slapping him across the face, the guard prevented any further explanation.

Noisily, the bird flew from its perch on the fence, leaving the camp area. They took Steuben into the guards' building and he did not return that night.

All through the night, the prisoners in Van's barrack could hear Steuben's screams of pain. As the night wore on, the agonized screams became more horrible. No one in the barrack slept that night. They knew the Nazis were killing him, but they truly did not want to know *how* it was being done. Some prayed for his quick death. Praying for his release and safe return to the barrack would have been a waste of time. The whispered, muffled prayers throughout the night were punctuated with Steuben's high-pitched screams. His empty sleeping spot remained unoccupied even though the barrack was overcrowded.

Toward the end of roll-call the following morning, a lifeless form was dragged from the guards' compound to the front of the formation. He was dropped in the muddy slush of the formation area. Lying there, face down in the mud, he appeared to be dead. Immediately the large rats began to crawl from their dark hiding places toward the lifeless form. The rats in the camp were huge and fat, and, over the years, they often attacked people.

"Here is one who thought he would escape! I don't think he will try it again," the SS man in charge of roll-call informed the massed pink triangles. Closer and closer the rats approached Steuben.

Continuing to talk, the guard watched the rats and the revulsion on the prisoners' faces. The Nazi sadists were going to keep them in formation while the rats did their feasting in front of them, Van thought. Steuben moaned and tried to get up. He fell back into the slime, unconscious again. The prisoners were surprised that he was alive, and panicked at the realization that the rats would be upon him shortly.

The diatribe continued, "We have fixed this loathsome queer so he can serve so much better. After we all had our sport with him last night, and he was a choice one, we decided he could better serve us if he had no teeth."

"I don't think I can stand much more of this," Franz whispered.

"Those teeth of his were too painful to us," the Nazi was saying. "We happened to have some pliers in our shack. So we removed his teeth, one by one. we could not find anything to deaden the pain. I suppose that makes us painful dentists instead of painless dentists. Ha!" He laughed at his intended joke, and the other guards roared their approval of his intended humorous remark. Crawling over Steuben, the rats were beginning their work. He began to moan and scream. His screaming, mixed with the guards' laughter, was beyond endurance. As an aroused giant, the formation of pink triangles broke and rushed the seven or eight Nazi guards around the formation. Van got his hands on the SS man who had spoken, wrapping his arms around him. Squeezing as hard as he could, venting all his years of rage and hatred, Van broke the guard's back, the crack of the break audible to him. He dropped him in the mud and ran to Steuben.

Steuben's face was a mass of blood and mud. Van lifted him from the mud and carried him into the barrack, placing him on the board they used for a bed. Franz soon joined them.

"We killed them all! All of those bastards are dead!"

Outside, the sirens sounded as the rebellion spread. Other groups in their roll-call formations, had rushed the guards and killed them in the most primitive ways. Arms and legs were ripped from bodies. Heads were crushed with any makeshift weapon that could be found. It was a ghastly scene, and yet it was heart-warming to most of the prisoners. Saints became devils as the prisoners used the same evil methods of the Nazis. The helpless scum of the earth, the homosexuals, had taken man's abuse too long. They rose up and proved, in actions that the Nazis could understand, that pink triangles were also men.

The staccato bark of the machine guns ended the mass insanity. Those who could escape the guns rushed back into the barracks. Everything became quiet, but some twenty from Van's barrack did not return. Franz and Van tried to wash Steuben's swollen mouth and clean his other wounds. They carefully washed his face, and the bites of the rats. The Nazis had abused him in other ways. The blood flowed like a river from his body. They could not stop the hemorrhage, and Steuben died soon after he had been carried into the barrack.

"They'll kill us all now," Franz said. "They won't let us get away with this."

"I agree we won't get away with it, but they won't kill all of us. They need us to work," Van replied.

Van was correct. The SS men burned seven pink triangle barracks. A few tried to escape; they were shot and their bodies thrown back into the fires. The rats ran from the buildings and were allowed to leave, while the pink triangles were burned alive. The screams were unendurable and no one could bear to watch.

No work details left their areas that day. Both sides needed the day to regroup. By late afternoon, the pink triangles ventured outside. They found that their friends' bodies had been removed. Except for the seven burned barracks and the strong, oppressive odor of burning flesh, the camp seemed to be back to normal.

Franz and Van walked to the edge of the neutral-zone, as near to the barbed wire fence as they were allowed. Standing in the mud, they looked past the fence to the trees on the outside. A lark flew to the fence and alighted on the top strand of wire. It looked at them and began to sing, a beautiful sound in the midst of that awful place.

"Look, Van! He's looking at you and me!"

"Yes, I noticed."

"Van, it's as if he is singing for poor Steuben."

"Perhaps he's singing a song of celebration that Steuben is now free, like itself."

The lark sang for a long time, watching them all the while. Then it flew away into its freedom.

26

T HE VOLUME OF PRISONERS BECAME TOO GREAT for the facilities. In Auschwitz, they built an entire sub-camp, Birkenau, to dispose of the unwanted peoples of Germany and occupied Europe. Birkenau, with its imposing entrance, the "gate of death", had four crematoria. They were forced to run day and night with two complete shifts of kommandos.

In January Van was brought to the office of the home town hero of his youth, Rudy Hoess, Commandant of Auschwitz and its satellite camps. When he was ushered into the opulent office, he was not at all impressed. He had seen it before and knew the origin of all of the fine furnishings: everything had been stolen from the victims of Nazi brutality. The guards that brought him did not enter the office but closed the door behind him. Rudy was not there. Van waited fifteen minutes and Rudy still had not arrived.

He walked over to a large, ornate china closet that Mama would have filled with dainty porcelain figurines, fine crystal and her best china. The elegant piece of furniture probably came from a wealthy Jewish family who were changed into smoke to pollute the air and ashes to be used in paving the roads.

Van was now as knowledgeable about the Nazis and the concentration camps as anyone in Europe. He had been in Dachau and Auschwitz for over four years—to remain until death, he assumed. He knew his enemy, having seen him at his worst. He knew him well.

The cabinet was filled with Nazi memorabilia, fine porcelain commemorative Nazi plates and porcelain pieces made near Dachau, perhaps some painted by Professor Neumann. There were autographed pictures of Hitler and other high ranking Nazis and Hoess family pictures. Van recognized some of the family from Baden-Baden. Rudy's father, who had wanted him to be a priest, smiled from an old picture. Van wondered how his son's occupation and reputation measured up to his father's saintly wishes for him. His musing was interrupted by the entrance of Major Rudolf Hoess.

Van had not seen him since that chance meeting in the open area of the selection process in Auschwitz, nearly a year ago. Rudy had aged twenty years. He looks as bad as I do, Van thought. The jailor suffers the torment of the jailed.

"Van, how are you? I haven't seen you in months. Are you managing all right?" Rudy seated himself on the large, plush divan.

"I'm still alive," was all Van could say.

"Do you need anything? Is there anything I can do for you?" he asked conversationally.

"Yes," Van replied, to his own amazement. "As Moses said, 'Let my people go'!"

Rudy laughed loudly, and with gusto. "Don't quote those old Jew-dog lies to me. None of that crap is true. It's all a bunch of Jewish fairy tales." As he became angry, his laughter diminished. "Why do you plead for that Jew trash anyway? What possible good have you known from being a Jew?"

"I was never given any choice as to whether I would be Jewish. But I wasn't only talking of the Jews when I said my people."

"Who in God's name were you talking about, the queers?" he asked with terrible sarcasm.

"Yes!"

Rudy shuddered, a look of disgust and contempt on his face. "Never!" he screamed so loudly that Van was startled by the sudden volume of his voice. "Those queers, all of them, including you, are going to die right here in Auschwitz and every other camp in Europe. We are going to rid the world of two of its worst miscarriages, Jews and queers. And you, Van Bertholds, fit both categories! You are dead! The only way possible to stay alive is by my intervention on your behalf."

Van could not believe Rudy's assertion of intervention. He had seen no evidence of any intervention on his behalf, by Rudy or any other person.

Rudy then came to the point. "My lovely wife is in Paris. She has been away for two weeks and I miss her and need her. Do you understand, Van?"

"I understand. But I have one question I'd like to ask."

"Certainly."

"You are demanding certain things of me, but in the next breath, you tell me how the Nazis are going to rid the world of all queers, since they are one of the most evil things on earth. How do these feelings of yours, your hatred of queers and your need for the services of one, coexist within the same man?"

"Don't start any of that stupid Jewish psychiatric shit with me. Get over here and do as you are told!"

Doing as he was told was, for him, the foulest act he had ever committed. During the ensuing sexual travesty, his mind dwelled on the digging up and burning of those pink triangles, Jews, Gypsies and others murdered on this man's orders. The sights, sounds and smells of that grave-robbing, body-burning experience enveloped him. He thought of the opening and shutting crematorium doors, the bales and bales of human hair, the wretched conditions of those that were still alive. He recalled the image of a man called Franz the night he had met him and the shadow of a man called Franz that he knew in Auschwitz.

Rudy was finished with him and sent him away. Death, where is thy sting? Van wanted only to die. There was no reason to live, except to try to help Franz live.

He passed the camp orchestra. Their rendition of Schubert's *Rosamunde* was ending. They started playing *The Blue Danube* as the throngs of newly arrived innocents marched to the delousing area. The music was lovely and soothed the inmates, thus serving its purpose.

When Van returned to the barrack, Franz was not there. "The guards have taken him to the hospital for some experiment by Dr. Mengele," the Kapo said.

Van ran from the barrack to the hospital. Rushing through the waiting area, filled with young Jewish women waiting for the x-rays that would sterilize them to put an end to David's seed, he burst into the experiment room and there stood Mengele, completely out of character, smiling. Franz lay unconscious on the operating table. He was covered with a sheet, only his head could be seen.

"Hello, Queer-Van." Mengele smiled at Van as he spoke.

"What have you done to him?" Van demanded.

"We have done nothing to him. We were examining him in preparation for a small experiment. The examination revealed a cancerous growth on one of his testicles. We did what we had to do to save his life."

Van stumbled backward and fell into a chair. His legs would not support him.

"What did you have to do—to save his life?" he managed to ask.

"The cancer was much deeper than it appeared. We had to remove both testicles."

"God—damn—bastards!"

"Please don't interrupt me. I'm not finished telling you what we had to do," he said, still smiling.

There could be no more unless Franz had died due to complications, Van thought.

"We had to remove something else to get all of the cancer," Mengele continued. "His penis was cancerous as well. We removed it also. We have attached a tube he will learn to use for urinary purposes."

Van lunged for Mengele, grasped him around the neck and began to choke him. "I'll kill you, you dirty, sadistic son-of-a-bitch!" Van shouted.

They fell to the floor. Van knew he had a death grip on the monster's throat. One of the guards struck Van on the back of the head with his rifle butt. He fell beside Mengele. The guard had to pry Van's hands loose from the doctor's throat.

Kapo Fritz dabbed Van's face with a cold, wet cloth, bringing him back to consciousness. They had sent for some pink triangles to carry him back to the barrack. Franz's usual place next to his was vacant. Van sat up on the edge of the bed, his head reeling. The pain was intense, even blinding.

"Where is Franz?" he asked when the pain had abated somewhat.

The Kapo looked at him with compassion, an emotion Van had not seen displayed in a long time. When he spoke, his tone of voice was new and foreign to the barrack. No one spoke kindly in those surroundings, not even the fellow prisoners.

"Franz is to remain in the hospital for some time so they can be sure he heals right. They said something about the danger of gangrene." He paused a moment and then said, "We are all sorry about what those butchers did to him."

Van could not believe what he was hearing. Had he suddenly been transferred to a place of kind words and humane treatment, he wondered. He shook his head and looked at the Kapo, almost speechless from the shock.

"What did you say . . . ." he asked the Kapo.

His head lowered, his eyes staring at the floor, the Kapo repeated, "We are all sorry about this. Pink triangle or not, it is wrong to do that to a man."

One of the group gathered around Van spoke, "He had no cancer. I'll never believe that! They came looking for him by number. They knew exactly who they wanted. They had some reason for doing that to him and it wasn't cancer."

"They did it because he was one of us. Now he's asexual, a eunuch. And they are keeping him in the hospital because they want to make certain he recovers to live a life of no sex, until they decide to kill him," another member of the group said.

Still another voice from the group was heard to say, "What do they think we are? Animals?"

Kapo Fritz quieted them. He wanted to say something, something difficult for him to express. They watched and waited for the order that would send them all to some terrible task. He had never shown any feeling for the pink triangles, any acknowledgement that they were human.

"I have been your Kapo since you came here. You all know and hate me. You should. I have always despised queers and have done my share of beating and killing.

"Somehow I feel different now. I don't understand you and your ways any more today than I ever did. But I don't hate you. I'm not an educated man. All I know, I've learned in the streets and in the prisons. So, I'll say what I feel in my own words. Auschwitz is the hate, full grown, we've all had for you, the Jews and all the others. It's like a pot of rice. By the time all of us put in our little bit of rice and the whole thing is cooked, it is much more than expected. All of the small portions, added together in one great pot, have created a kettle of rice that is tremendous in volume, its size much larger than anyone would have expected."

The barrack was silent, the disbelief among them was almost a material thing. The Kapo was the resident symbol of the Nazis, their surrogate Nazi. From one who had never shown a single moment of human decency, the disclosure of commiseration was impossible to believe.

"Fritz, what kind of trick are you playing on us this time?" Van asked.

"I know it's hard for you to believe me, but I'm serious. I must continue to keep you in line or I'll be fed to the ovens, but I'll also help you all I can. You'll see that I'm serious."

None of them truly believed him. Although he sounded sincere, they simply did not believe he would be any different.

Franz was held in the camp hospital more than a week. Van heard that he had to be strapped to his bed for two or three days when he discovered what they had done to him. He also learned that Mengele was injecting him each day with some drug that made him passive and docile. Van tried to prepare himself for Franz's death, a prospect he could not face.

Franz returned to the barrack during the day, when no one was there. Late that night, after a full day of sorting and baling human hair, the exacerbation of roll-call and the wasted time in the soup line, Van returned to the barrack. He had not seen Franz since the day of his surgery. He rushed to the bed where Franz was lying, where most of the other men were gathered. Sitting on the side of the bed, Van placed Franz's hand in his and held it tightly.

"Franz, I'm so glad to see you back! I've missed you so much!"

Franz did not speak. His eyes were a glazed set of glass orbs, dead and cold, with no spark within them. Van waved a hand before Franz's eyes. He did not blink or appear to see the moving hand. The Kapo brought a wet rag and some vodka, something Van had not seen for years. They lifted Franz into a sitting position and washed his face with the rag. Franz made no response, staring straight ahead, as though his eyes were focused beyond space. Van poured the vodka into his mouth. He swallowed none of it, the vodka trickling down the corners of his mouth and onto his shirt.

"Shock," the Kapo said.

"Shock, hell! He's drugged!" Van raged.

Time proved both of them wrong. Franz had withdrawn from the mass lunacy of the concentration camp into his private world of insanity or of escape and defense. He never spoke or made a movement on his own, from the day he returned from Mengele's "hospital." Van led him everywhere, fed him and tried to serve his every need, but he was even unable to use the toilet. Van cleaned the unpredictable messes each day. Terrible sores appeared on Franz's body when it became impossible to keep him clean. The Nazis did not send him to the ovens to torture him, Van reasoned. It was almost unbearable to see that shuffling skeleton, with those terrible blank eyes, following Van every hour of every day.

Several days later, as he walked from the crematorium with Franz following behind him, holding his jacket tails, and not even looking where he was walking, Van came face to face with Major Rudolf Hoess and some of his staff. Van turned to avoid them but Hoess called to him. Van stopped and faced him, staring at the ground.

"So, we meet again," he sneered. "Who is that behind you?"

When Van did not reply, he shouted the question in a voice that could be heard all over the camp. He was upset about something else and Van was not helping.

"A friend," Van answered.

"Is he also a queer?" Rudy asked.

Van looked up for the first time. He stared into Rudy's eyes with loathing and said clearly, emphasizing each word, "He is a man, a good man. The nature of his sex life is a matter known only to him . . . and God."

27

T HERE IS, PURPORTEDLY, A RIVER CALLED LETHE that flows through the lower regions of Hades. Those wretched, thirsting souls who drink its waters lose all recollection of the past. Remembering the tale of this mythical river, Van fantasized that Franz had drunk from its waters, which undoubtedly flowed somewhere through Auschwitz. Franz noticed nothing around him, including the mounting toll of crematoria victims, and would have slept twenty-four hours a day if possible. Van did everything for two.

Kapo Fritz *did* change, to Van's amazement and surprise. In small ways, he helped all of the pink triangles in his barrack. The Nazis would have instantly sent him to the ovens if they had known of his change in attitude. Because of this, he had to be cautious and try to appear as vicious and inhuman as usual.

The work with the human hair was not Van's only duty. It became part of his work to help those who sorted and prepared for shipment the clothing and other personal belongings of all who were gassed and burned in Birkenau.

Most of the people shipped to Auschwitz thought they were being relocated by the Nazis. They brought trunks, suitcases, bags and packages with them. Upon their arrival in Birkenau, these items were taken from them when they went through the selection process. The strong and able were sent to work details until they were exhausted and then to the ovens, while those not fit for work moved from the selection process to the gassing rooms. The personal packages were part of Van's responsibility. Added to these items were clothing, eye glasses, false teeth; anything removed from them before the shower or after the shower.

These properties of the dead were desperately needed by war-weary Germany. Many prisoners worked on that detail during those last years in Auschwitz. Over fifty large barracks buildings were constructed to hold the growing volume of personal property destined for Germany. It was not long until all these barracks were full and they had to stack the goods outside and between the barracks. The stacks grew taller and taller until some were higher than the barracks buildings.

The orchestra played while the new arrivals went to their death; the gas pellets were poured into the vents while the screaming, dying, naked prisoners scratched and clawed for freedom. The ovens blazed and polluted the air of Europe with the foul smoke and repulsive odor of buring flesh while the kommandos rushed to keep pace with the hectic activity; and Van separated and grouped the personal belongings of the countless victims with Franz vegetating at his side.

The men in Van's barrack had been there almost a year. When they arrived, they were chosen for work because they were relatively healthy and strong. The year had transformed all of them into thin, sick shadows, incapable of most physical exertion.

When Van returned to the barrack one night in July, he found there was no one there but the Kapo. Franz followed behind Van, holding to his shirt, as Van asked the Kapo where everyone was. Kapo Fritz was sitting on the side of the bed crying.

"Fritz, where is everyone? What are you crying about?" Van asked. The sight of Fritz crying was an amazing sight.

"They're gone, all of them, gone!"

"Yes, I can see that. Where have they gone?"

"To the crematorium! All of them are dead," he sobbed louder in real anguish.

Van looked at him mutely.

"They took them all this morning. I watched as the long line marched to Birkenau, through the 'gate of death', down the 'street to heaven' and into the shower area. They were forced to strip and led into the shower room, two thousand at a time. All day they gassed them and I watched. I knew it was happening every day here, but I had never seen it.

"The SS men let me look through that glass in the door and watch the dance of death. Oh, it was awful," he sobbed. "I have seen into the pits of hell.

"I never realized there were so many pink triangles in this area of the camp. When they were all together at the showers, the size of the crowd was amazing. There must have been at least a hundred thousand of them. The SS ran the gassing room so many times I lost count and there were at least two thousand in there each time they slammed those big metal doors.

"How can I describe it? Seeing them die was the most horrible thing I have seen in my life. So many, oh God, so many of them. But worse than that, Van, they knew. From the minute their line of march started toward Birkenau, they knew they were going to their death. Some of them had to wait a long time, those that were not gassed in the first few groups, and that waiting was the worst.

"Can you even imagine what it must have been like? Standing there for as much as three or four hours, waiting your turn to enter the shower room, knowing that there was no hope of reprieve, no possibility of being saved at the last minute?

"Oh God," he wept uncontrollably, "this place has been with me too long, too much!"

Van placed his hand on Kapo Fritz's shoulder and tried to comfort him, tears flowing from his eyes also. He whispered age old expressions of compassion and consolation, of hope and faith, expressions rooted deeply in Jewish history and tradition.

Once again the shattering reality of the horrors of the camp touched Van personally. For almost six years he had lived in the constant presence of man's immeasurable cruelty to man. Only at those times when it touched him personally did he completely realize its full measure of evil and sorrow. The horror became his, embracing him like a giant, clinging spider web. At the time of Papa's and Mama's deaths; at the death of Professor Neumann, when he was beaten for trying to help the old man; at his finding Franz at Auschwitz so changed and full of hate; at the murder of his cubicle mate, Steuben; when Mengele performed his sadistic surgery on Franz; and now, with the extermination of all those who had lived in the same barracks with him for so long. It was no nightmare; it was real and it was happening to him and to those he loved. People were not dying and being murdered by the thousands; they were dying and being murdered individually, one at a time, with a personal eternal finality. The thought was almost too much for Van to endure.

He glanced at Kapo Fritz and felt as one with him, understanding the source of his tears. He again tried unsuccessfully to console the Kapo.

"Fritz," he said, "here in this place of death, we have to expect it and not be surprised when it happens. I must tell you, though, that you did more for those that are now gone than anyone else in this place. No one in this camp was ever decent to the pink triangles. At least you tried to help us after Mengele did that awful thing to Franz."

Franz and Van remained alone in the large section reserved for pink triangles, but others arrived the following day. The healthy reported for slave-labor, but the majority went straight to the gas chambers. The new residents did not stay long; in less than a month, they were also gassed.

For those in Germany's concentration camps, there was rarely any authentic news concerning the progress of the war. Almost every day they heard a new story about the status of the war. "Germany is winning." "Germany is losing." "The Russians are advancing toward Poland." "England has fallen." Never able to separate rumor from fact, most of them considered all talk as rumor.

The best gauge was the behavior of the Nazis that ran the camps. About the middle of the year, it became evident that Germany was not winning many battles and was, hopefully, losing the war. Van had long ago resigned himself to getting out of Auschwitz in one of two ways. Death was so much with him that he expected it each day. The only other way out lay in Germany's defeat and liberation of the camp before the Nazis could kill them all.

Van knew that escape from Auschwitz was almost impossible, especially for pink triangles. A successful attempt at escape required help from someone in authority within the camp or assistance from outside the camp. There may have been a large group of Germans who did not condone what the Nazis were doing to the Jews, the Gypsies or the other groups. Few Germans, however, would help a pink triangle escape, since most of them agreed with the Nazi policy of annihilation of all homosexuals. Therefore, Van never seriously considered trying to escape.

Extermination was noticeably accelerated about the middle of the year. The crematoria belched forth their smoke in heavier, more constant surges. Due to the frantic pace at which they were forced to work, the Sonderkommandos revolted and were quickly dealt with. The fake delousing in the disguised gas chambers was conducted at such a speedy pace that many were sent to the crematorium still alive, having spent only enough time in the gas to be dazed.

The trains were more frequent and carried more people. The selection process was all but abandoned. Entire train loads were immediately dispatched to the "showers". Mengele, the father of the gas method of mass extermination, was cheated of his experimental subjects by the volume during the final months of Auschwitz. Sorting the personal effects of the victims became a never-ending job. All the storage buildings were filled. The articles were stacked in the open to an unbelievable height. There were no trains available to ship the sorted articles to Germany where they were so badly needed; instead they were employed to transport the enemies of the Third Reich to a quick and sure death. Still the flood of prisoners continued.

This whirlwind activity, and the maddened dedication to the killing of as many undesirables as possible, suggested a revised Nazi policy: the greater the number killed the lesser the crime. Van wondered why they increased the mass murders of the prisoners in those final months of the war when they knew the war was lost. Again, Van thought of these victims not as large numbers of people. He remembered that within those numbers were unique and individual human beings. Therein lay the true horror of the madness called the Third Reich.

During this hectic pace, he had little time to consider the implications of what he was witnessing. He avoided contact with the people marching down the "street to heaven", to the strains of "The Blue Danube", as much as he could. Handling their personal effects was reminder enough.

Franz, or Franz's pitiful human shell, was still Van's shadow; always with him. Van could not look at him without wondering where the real Franz was. He talked to Franz about things of great importance and things of absolutely no importance. Franz's expression, or lack of expression, never changed. Van often felt that he was truly dead and that the near skeleton attached to him, like a limb grafted to a tree, was merely an extension of his own physical body. There was nothing left of the Franz he once knew and loved.

Another mystery was how and why he and Franz had survived in Auschwitz for so long. All around them, people were being rushed at breakneck speed to their deaths. Yet they were allowed, even sentenced, to survive. Someone, either Mengele or Rudy, had decided it was far worse to live in the hell of Auschwitz than to die in the gas chambers. They were right.

Franz had, for self-protection, withdrawn to a safer place within himself. Many times Van considered the idea of putting Franz's body out of its torment by sending him to the delousing himself. He finally recognized that he was actually trying to end his own torment, not that of Franz.

"Well, how did it go today for you and your shadow?" Kapo Fritz asked as Van returned from endless hours of sorting the last wordly possessions of innumerable victims.

"Fritz, I am too tired to even think. My shadow, as you call him, is the same as always."

"He is so sad, Van. Don't you think it would be better if he were dead? I think I can arrange to slip his body out of the camp and have him buried instead of being sent to the ovens. Wouldn't it be better than this?"

"Never! I am not God. If I play God and do that, I am no better than the Nazis. Besides, Fritz, I don't really believe he suffers. He sees no evil and has no pain that I can tell. If I have learned nothing else in here, I have learned that a human life is precious, the most precious gift we have. No human ever has the right to end another's life, except perhaps in self-defense. Any other death should be in God's Hands, not mine."

Kapo Fritz looked at Van and then at Franz. He looked away, staring off into the distance. In deep thought, he appeared to be seeing something a thousand kilometers away.

After a while, he spoke, "I once said I did not understand you pink triangles at all, and I still don't think I ever will. But I have a better understanding of love than I did then. It's not that you love more or better than other people. I think it's that you love when everything in the world is against you. For a man to love a woman or a woman to love a man, that's easy. I mean the world says, 'fine, great, our blessings'. But for a man to love a man or for a woman to love a woman, it's doomed from the first sigh."

"Fritz, you're right about that. But I personally don't believe it is doomed in the eyes of God. I know what organized religion says, but I don't think they are speaking for God. Do you?"

"I don't know. What I remember of church, and it has been a long time since I went to church, they always taught that it was evil in God's eyes. It's hard to unlearn something you've heard since you were a child."

"Well, Fritz, if God does view me as evil, an abomination, then I suppose I will spend eternity in Hell. All I can say is these last few years have prepared me well for that prospect."

Fritz laughed at that idea. Then he said, "I just can't imagine God, a loving, forgiving God, sending anyone to Hell after having lived for as long as you have in Dachau and Auschwitz."

The Nazis continued to eradicate as many as possible, as well as to dismantle Auschwitz. By November, the camp was in a state of confusion and turmoil. The elimination of people vied for priority with the destruction of all evidence that Auschwitz ever existed.

Rumors of the Russian troops approaching from the east became more numerous. The haste with which the camp was being destroyed by the Nazis indicated that these rumors were based on an element of truth. With December ending, Auschwitz was left with only one crematorium, the others having been destroyed. The remaining crematorium was worked beyond its intended capacity, unable to handle all of the bodies coming from the gas chambers. The remaining bodies were loaded into trains to be transported to Germany, for final disposition in camps that were farther from the advancing Russian troops.

On a midmorning in late December, Van passed a gathering of some two hundred people near the railroad tracks. Franz, of course, walked behind him, clutching Van's jacket tail, while they made their way through the chaos. They had worked through the previous night and were fatigued and sleepy.

The small crowd was listening to a man speak, a man whom Van recognized immediately as a priest from Leipzig. From the beginning of the Nazi reign, he had been one of the few German Christian leaders to speak out against the Nazis and their methods. The German government had ignored his voice until it became too loud and truthful. When he demanded the immediate release of all Jews in the concentration camps, he was arrested and imprisoned. He had been moved from one camp to another until he arrived in Auschwitz some six or seven months earlier.

Like a number of people in his audience, he wore a red triangle, identifying him as a political prisoner. All the symbols were represented in the attentive crowd: pink triangles, Stars of David, Gypsies, Polish citizens and many others. Van wondered about the Jews, his curiosity aroused by their presence in the priest's gathering. Tired as he was, he paused on the edge of the crowd to listen. The man was not dressed in the usual attire of a priest; however there seemed to be an aura about him, an aura that confirmed his pious nature.

Everyone gave the speaker their complete attention; the gathering was an oasis of calm and attentiveness in a desert of clamor and confusion. The SS men ignored the entire proceeding, hurrying about the camp to hasten's the camp's destruction or to rush the crowds into the shower rooms. The priest quoted from the Bible. Van did not recognize the quotation and assumed it must have come from the New Testament.

*And I looked, and beheld a pale horse: and his name that
sat on him was Death, and Hell followed with him. And
Power was given unto them over the fourth part of the
earth, to kill with sword, and with hunger, and with
death, and with the beasts of the earth.*

"Thus spoke Saint John the Divine in the book of the Apocalypse.
People of Germany and of other countries of Europe, do you realize
what Saint John's vision of the future was?"

He paused for his audience to consider the question. No one vol-
unteered an answer. Van certainly did not know. His knowledge of
the Christian Bible was sorely limited. The priest continued, "The
beloved Saint had a vision of future evil in the world. 'Death' is
indeed running unfettered in our world today. It rode into our lives
on a pale horse and has been among us since. And what was that pale
horse that carried this horror into modern history? Think about it
for a moment. How did those in power gain their power? What was
the vehicle that transported them and their racial purity theories to a
position of command? You remember, those of you who are old
enough, on what emotions and feelings this monster fed and grew fat
and waxed strong. How were they able to secure power in Germany
and then spread their sickness throughout Europe? Behold the pale
horse on which Death was riding: prejudice and bigotry.

"The Nazis thrived and grew in numbers and strength where preju-
dice was widespread. For centuries, these seeds have been planted
and fertilized in our fatherland. We were taught to hate the Jews, the
Gypsies, the homosexuals and those others you see among us. Don't
cringe at my inclusion of the pink triangles because I am telling the
truth. We all have been taught to hate and despise the homosexuals
all of our lives. The prejudices and bigotry against all of the people
that were different was among us, just waiting for the right leader-
ship. It found that leadership in the Nazis. They rode in on our
feelings of hatred for our fellow man and the horseman that led their
entry was 'Death'.

"Let all of the future generations read the words of Saint John and
look at the pages of history that will record the events that are
occurring in these camps all over Europe. The lesson is obvious. If
future generations allow prejudice and bigotry to flourish, then they
must be prepared for the consequences."

No one in the crowd said a word. The only sound was that made
by a train passing close to the group, heading toward Germany. Its

open cars were loaded with the bodies of the victims of the Third Reich, going to the crematoria deep within Germany. The priest looked at the train, loaded with corpses. His congregation was also watching the grisly sight. He spoke in a loud, resonant voice, pointing to the train, "Behold a pale horse and his name that sat on him was Death."

28

Auschwitz, Poland—January 1945

A USCHWITZ WAS RAPIDLY BEING ABANDONED. The retreating
German military units had confirmed the rumors of the ap-
proaching Russians. Fear gripped the Nazis, their SS and all of the
people who for years had been the source of so much fear for so
many. The prisoners watched them change from the masters of fear
to the slaves of that terrible emotion as the news became more fright-
ful to them and more encouraging to the prisoners. While they
looked to the east for deliverance from the Nazi monsters, the Nazis
looked to the east with fear and anxious forebodings.

Where there had been five crematoria capable of disposing of the
remains of over 4800 individuals a day, only one remained, handling
fourteen to fifteen hundred a day.

They burned approximately forty-three of the large buildings used
to store the personal possessions of the deceased. Van had spent
nearly a year of his life sorting the contents of the buildings. The
Russians, when they did arrive, would find only six buildings re-
maining. Seeing his work go up in flames caused mixed feelings with
Van. A year of difficult work was destroyed, but he was elated that
this hell, run by Rudolf Hoess, was actually being destroyed.

Kapo Fritz was busy getting his pink triangles ready for the trip
westward.

"All of you that can walk will be ready to leave in two hours. We
are being transferred to Gross-Rosen. A lot of the others are going to
Mauthausen."

"There are no trains to carry us," Van said. "Are they going to use
trucks?"

"Every possible type of transportation is filled with retreating
soldiers and the bounty they have stolen," Kapo Fritz explained.
"You don't think they are going to transport us when the military
needs the vehicles? They don't even have any way to move the dead

that are now piled around the railhead and the crematorium. There are train cars loaded with bodies that are just sitting there with no engine to pull them and no prospect of an engine. It's a mass retreat."

One of the others in the group asked the obvious question, "You mean that we're going to walk?"

"I'm afraid that's what I mean. Those unable to walk will remain here at Auschwitz. God knows what will happen to them."

The members of Van's barrack wondered how, with walking to the soup line a supreme effort, they would ever be able to walk to Gross-Rosen? They did not know how far it was, but one kilometer was too far.

"Walk all the way to Gross-Rosen. How far is it?" another asked.

"I'm not sure but I think it's about 270 kilometers."

Van knew he would never make it to Gross-Rosen and Franz would have less chance than he. It was mid-January and the snow and bitter cold would make the long trip impossible. None had sufficient clothing and their food had been so meager for such a long time that they had little strength. Most of the prisoners were sick. Had they only had some small amount of hope, the trip would have at least been possible. Without hope, it was to be a trip of torture and death.

"Van," the Kapo said suddenly, "where is your shadow?"

Van had been unaware of Franz's absence from his side. This was the first time since he came from Mengele's experiment that he had been out of Van's sight.

"I don't know. I didn't even realize he was gone. He has never done that before. Help me find him." They were starting to search when Franz walked in the barrack door, with the same unseeing, unknowing expression.

"Where have you been, Franz?" Van asked, hurrying to him.

Franz did not reply or register any emotion whatsoever. He grasped Van's jacket tail as he had always done, as though he had never left Van's side.

The Kapo whispered, "Now what could he have been doing outside the barrack?"

"I don't have any idea. How long was he gone? I thought that he was behind me, holding my shirt tail like he always does."

"I didn't see him leave so I don't know how long he was gone," Kapo Fritz said.

None of the prisoners had to carry luggage, packages or personal belongings. Most had what was on their bodies and that was all.

They gathered in the large assembly area, where Mengele had originally made his selections. He had later moved the selection process inside the walls of Birkenau, to be nearer the incoming masses. When the pink triangles arrived at the assembly area, the other prisoners moved away from them with their traditional remarks of derision. For a short time, they were kept away from the others, but the crowd grew so large that the space between them vanished. They merged with the Stars of David; the murderers, rapists, thieves and other criminals; with the Jehovah's Witnesses, the political prisoners and all the rejected of Germany and Europe.

Franz was at Van's side, holding Van's light coat tail, symbolically holding his lifeline. He began to growl, a skin crawling, deep-throated sound, like a snarl of rage made by a large animal. His grip on the jacket tightened and then suddenly fell away. He released Van's coat and began making a horrible, guttural sound of misery and hate. That was the first sound Van had heard from him since the day he was taken to the hospital and Mengele's experiment room. Franz walked away from Van, or rather stalked away, like a zombie drawn to some perverse thing. Quickly grabbing Franz with both hands, Van stopped him. He struggled to escape his grasp but Van held firmly. Groaning, snarling and struggling to get free, Franz exhibited the first emotion since Mengele had "saved him from cancer".

Franz had seen Mengele coming from the hospital. He appeared as frantic as the other Nazis. The files with the records of his experiments in human suffering and degradation were being loaded into a truck; the prisoners would walk while the records of horror would ride.

As the truck with Mengele moved away, Franz returned to his withdrawn condition, clutching Van's coat for direction and support. Van then understood that Franz was not dead or insane, only hiding to avoid any additional pain. How good that he could do this, Van thought. If only I could escape reality until this horror is over, one way or another.

The march started through the falling snow. Groups of four to five hundred people were started on the road, in the falling snow. A contingent of SS men guarded them. The members of each group were wearing the same badge. Even in the retreat from Auschwitz, the Nazis were still keeping them segregated by crime. So many groups had already departed before Van's group that he was unable to estimate the number of people involved.

More than fifty thousand prisoners were marched out of Auschwitz before the onrush of the Russian Army. These departures continued for about a week. Only the extremely ill and those who could not walk were left in Auschwitz. Nearly five thousand remained in Auschwitz when the Russians reached the camp to free them.

The pink triangles departed in groups numbering about five hundred. Van's group was close to the end of the long line.

Approaching the main gate, Van saw Major Hoess sitting in a car watching the parade of misfits leave his domain. He looked as if he had been cheated of something. When he saw the pink triangles, his interest grew. Looking closely at the faces as they passed, he eventually saw Van. The SS men guarding Van's group were told to halt and one of them was sent to bring Van to Hoess's car.

Van was led, with Franz trailing after him, to Rudolf Hoess. There was a scowl of fury on his aged, tired face. Nothing about him was reminiscent of those almost forgotten days in Baden-Baden. Peering into his eyes, Van searched for a hint of the Rudy he had known. It was not there.

Sending all of the SS men out of hearing range, Rudy spoke to him in a low voice.

"So, we have come to this day, Van. You see, I didn't forget your help that night in Baden-Baden. All this time in Auschwitz, you and your friend have avoided the ovens because I willed it to be that way. Yes, I made certain you were never sent to the delousing and the flames because I felt I owed that to you. I suppose we are now even."

Van looked deep into his eyes and, with as much deliberation as he could summon, told him, "No, Rudy, we are not even. We could never be even, not in a million years. I am still ahead of you and always will be."

Rudy, glancing downward at the ground, would not look at Van. Motioning Van back to his group, he turned and faced the opposite direction. His SS men were called back and, in a few minutes, he was driven away from the departing thousands.

They were moving again. As they passed through the main gate, Van looked back at the Nazi slogan about work making one free. Behind him, many were following them toward the gate. Ahead of him, as far as he could see, was a line of humanity, knotted into groups that were flanked by SS guards, struggling for miles and becoming tiny specks that disappeared over the distant horizon.

Had Van been familiar with the term "Death March", he would have used it to describe that trip from Auschwitz to those other camps inside Germany. Their survival during the march was not important to the SS men who guarded them. Anyone who fell back or fainted from exhaustion was shot. Those who became too ill to continue were also killed. The number of SS guards was too small for the large movement of people, and some of the SS men no longer cared. The word spread through the columns that the guards were allowing prisoners to escape. This may have been true in the other groups but not for the pink triangles. Some tried to walk away from the moving columns, but they were shot and left where they fell.

Snow fell the entire time they were on the road. The endless black line moved through the newly covered white landscape at a plodding pace. All along the route, black dots lay where the sick, tired and attempted escapees were killed and left to be enveloped in the snowy blanket. Peace had finally come to them in the comfort of the snow-covered road between Auschwitz and Van's homeland, Germany.

Their path led through Legnica, Poland and across a river. The next village was Zgorzelec, the last Polish town. Gorlitz, Germany was but a few kilometers from Zgorzelec. They came to another small German town, Bautzen, where they crossed the Spree River and stopped for the night.

No food was prepared or served that night. Each prisoner had been given a small amount of hard bread before they left Auschwitz. Additional bread was stolen, whenever possible, from the prisoners killed along the way.

The guards built fires to warm their food and themselves. The prisoners slept on the ground in the snow, huddled together for warmth. Franz and Van burrowed a place out in the snow and both were asleep almost instantly.

Sometime in the deep of the night, Van was awakened by Franz shaking him. Van sat up and Franz, pointing with his finger, swept the entire area around them. Van had no idea what he was trying to tell him, and could see nothing in the dark.

Franz spoke, his voice a cracking whisper, "Everyone is asleep, even those damned SS guards. We can escape. Come on!"

His long silence was broken. The shock of hearing Franz speak brought Van completely awake. Franz moved toward the trees Van had noticed when they stopped beside the river. Franz led, while Van followed.

They crawled quietly into the trees. When they were well into the forest, far enough from the camped prisoners and guards that they would not be heard, they stood up and started running. They were running as fast as possible, through the trees and other obstacles, when Franz stopped suddenly, causing Van to run into him.

"Shh! Listen! Someone is behind us!" he whispered.

They stood perfectly still and listened intently. Someone was approaching from the general direction of the night camp. Through the trees, they saw a beacon of light drawing nearer to them. Approaching the spot where they had stopped at a rapid pace, the light suddenly flashed into their faces and a voice shouted, "Halt! You're not going anywhere!" The SS guard had followed them from the camp and was pointing his Luger at them. He was going to kill them for they were nothing to him.

Franz stood between Van and the SS man. Van caught a glint of light shine or reflect from something in Franz's right hand, as Franz held his hand along his leg. It was the knife he had used to kill the man in Auschwitz. Franz had seen Van hide it under the barrack that night. That was where he was when Kapo Fritz missed him, just before they left Auschwitz.

With a brutal thrust, Franz brought the knife up and plunged it into the chest of the SS man. As the Nazi's pistol discharged, they both fell to the snow-covered ground. Van rushed to them, turned Franz over and pulled him off the dead guard. Sitting in the snow, against a large tree, he held him. The guard's light was beside him, still shining its beacon light into the dense forest. Van picked it up and, shining it on Franz, examined him. He was covered with blood, gushing from a hole in his stomach. Van placed the flashlight in the branch of a small tree nearby.

Franz's breath was labored and faltering. Van knew that he was dying and he could do nothing to save him. The bullet hole was large, the blood spurting from the wound. Franz had saved Van twice during their confinement and, perhaps in Berlin, on Crystal Night.

"Van, did I kill him?"

"Yes, Franz, he's dead. You saved me again. He shot you but you're going to be all right."

"No, I'm dying. I can tell I'm dying."

"Oh, Franz, don't leave me! Not now! We are so close to freedom! Don't leave me!"

"I'll never really leave you, Van. You are the only one I've ever loved."

"Franz, I love you more than life. I have loved you since that first night in Berlin, and I always will. I want to be with you, that's all, just to be with you."

Franz did not speak. Van brushed the snow from Franz's face and tried to warm him. Franz was cold, so cold.

"Franz, I want to go with you. If you die, I want to die also."

He bent and reached for the Nazi's pistol, wrenching it from the dead man's hand. Franz opened his eyes and saw the pistol in Van's hand.

"No!" he said strongly. "Life is too precious. Too many of us have died. Life, Van, life, that is the most prized of all gifts."

Franz coughed weakly, his frail body shook violently. Blood trickled from the corner of his mouth and down his chin. He managed to speak again. "Van, you have to survive." He struggled for breath and then said, "Someone has to live and tell what they did to us. You tell them, Van, you tell them."

Van dropped the pistol and put his arms around Franz, pulling him to him and crying.

As he breathed out, Franz weakly said, "I love you, Van."

"I love you, Franz."

Franz did not hear Van's declaration. He died in Van's arms, his blood soaking Van's clothes. Holding him long after death, Van wondered why it had to be that way. What harm had their love for each other done to the world?

Beside him lay the slashed body of the dead Nazi, while in his arms lay the emaciated remains of another man, a bullet hole in his body. Van's tears fell upon Franz's face and he heard the priest's voice, ringing clear and strong,

"And I looked, and beheld a pale horse: and his name that sat on him was Death."

ABOUT THE AUTHOR

Lannon D. Reed currently lives in Dallas, Texas, where he is employed in the computer field. This is his first novel. Included in the research for *Behold A Pale Horse* was a stay in Germany and England.

Published in paperback
There is also a special edition of ten numbered copies,
handbound in boards and signed by the author.